THE CONTEMPORARY GARDEN

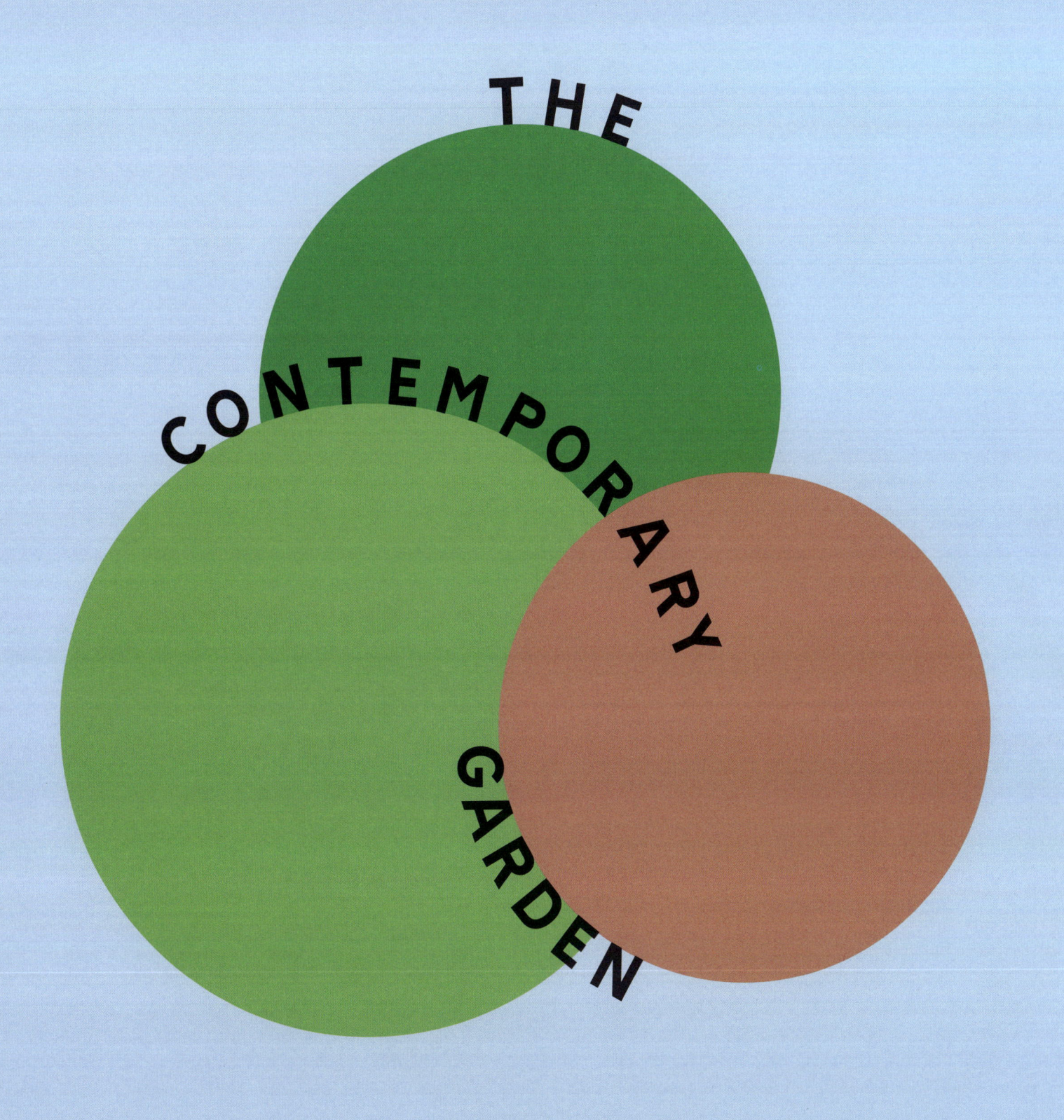

THE CONTEMPORARY GARDEN

PREFACE

The human desire to cultivate a domesticated landscape has endured over millennia, a dynamic endeavour that melds culture, art, vision, practicality, multifaceted research, collaboration, nurturing and curiosity. We are now a quarter of the way through the 21st century, and although trends in garden design seem to evolve slowly, the gardens and landscapes we see around us do indeed reflect the sensibilities and understandings of our times. Where historically a garden was largely the preserve of the rich and powerful, with a focus on ornament, many of today's gardens and landscapes are more all-encompassing, with a layering of purpose and intent.

This book aims to consider humans' relationship with gardens and green spaces and the ways in which we curate them for our pleasure and use. Current concerns play heavily in the design of gardens today. Foremost, perhaps, is the climate and biodiversity crisis, but we also grapple with worries about health and well-being, the impact of technology on our working lives and our relationship with the world around us, and a widespread disconnection with nature.

Contemporary gardens and green spaces are facing this changing context head on – and rising to the challenge. Plant experts are prioritizing the idea of 'right plant, right place' with renewed urgency, for resilience to extremes of climate and weather. This concept extends to garden and landscape design, encompassing water-management systems, using innovative materials and creating diverse habitats for wildlife. Research into soil health and rhizosphere interactions, mutually beneficial plant combinations, rewilding, alternative substrates and underused species is driving horticultural practice. The rapid exchange of ideas through social media and, most pertinently, AI-powered analysis accelerates this evolution, reaching a diverse audience.

Against this background, *The Contemporary Garden* is a comprehensive review of 300 gardens created between the mid-1990s and the present, showcasing the momentum of these trends. Organized alphabetically by designer's surname or studio name, the book follows the precedent of Phaidon's *The Art Book* series in prompting new connections and juxtapositions beyond a chronological framing or geographical segmenting. This international selection, created by leading designers, horticulturists and impassioned owner–makers, defines contemporary garden and landscape design, and celebrates horticultural creativity across a wide spectrum, from the smallest pocket park (a term now regularly used in the horticultural lexicon), such as the Toronto Music Garden by Julie Moir Messervy (see p.152), to thought-provoking gardens created against a background of conflict, such as Victoria Manoylo's garden in Ukraine (see p.176).

Iconic public spaces, such as New York's High Line and the Mei Garden in Jinhua City, China, demonstrate the transformative power of urban greening, repurposing disused infrastructure into vibrant public parks. This trend extends globally, with post-industrial landscapes offering vital new spaces to the benefit of urban dwellers. Similarly, India's Rao Jodha Desert Rock Park exemplifies ecological restoration, where painstaking reclaiming of native flora is fostering cultural connection for its visitors.

Alongside groundbreaking public projects is a rich vein of private gardens, including some designed by their inspired owners. For example, the renowned garden at Federal Twist in the United States, created by self-taught gardener James Golden, showcases a unique approach to naturalistic planting, while his thoughtful writing and his willingness to experiment have made him an influential and respected figure in the profession. Private gardens are key to much of the work of professional practitioners, and this book illustrates creative responses to diverse climates and client needs, as well as exciting architectural collaborations.

There is much to explore, and the varied entries presented here offer insight into the proactive role green spaces play in addressing contemporary challenges. The selection does not claim to be a definitive list of gardens and their creators, but it highlights the positivity and hope that arise from a creative, considered interaction with the natural world. It celebrates the work of more than 200 leading designers around the world to demonstrate the power of gardens to shape a more sustainable and fulfilling future.

Victoria Clarke, Sorrel Everton and Rosie Pickles
Editors

INTRODUCTION 8

THE GARDENS 12

INDEX 326

FURTHER READING 333

GARDEN DIRECTORY 332

INTRODUCTION

When I started to think about writing this introduction, it dawned on me that the timespan of this book, covering the past thirty years or so, reflects my own years spent studying, designing and teaching garden design. This gave me the perfect opportunity to reflect on the gardens of this period and, at the same time, consider my own journey through the world of contemporary landscape and garden design.

Back in the early 1990s I had just embarked upon my new career as a garden designer. The books that inspired me were John Brookes' *Garden Design Book* (1991), which is in my opinion still one of the best books written on the process of design. Also on my shelves was *Bold Romantic Gardens* (1990) by James van Sweden and Wolfgang Oehme, a book that launched a completely new style of designing with plants; who knew romantic planting didn't have to be airy and pretty? And then, a book that every aspiring designer had close to their drawing board, *The Essential Garden Book* (1998) by Terence Conran and Dan Pearson. This stunning, large-format tome written by an illustrious pair of designers – Conran at the very top of his game and Pearson just rising – begins thus: 'Gardens have never been as important in our lives as they are today. In our stressful world, the garden has become a sanctuary.' It is a truth evident through time and a comment often referenced by today's garden designers and garden critics, ensuring our abiding connections with these curated spaces. I mention these books because they captured the zeitgeist. Now, with this book, we are treating the 1990s as the jumping-off point to a new millennium and examining what the first quarter of the 21st century has brought in the world of garden design.

First, it's worth considering what a garden is. I have always been struck by the definition in the title of Elisabeth Beazley's classic landscape architecture book *Design and Detail of the Space between Buildings* (1960). This seems relevant to our increasingly urban society, yet we shouldn't lose sight of the importance of more expansive landscapes, too. This brings us to the question of when a garden becomes a landscape. Is it to do with size, location or use? I prefer to blur the boundaries between these definitions, to avoid limiting how we think about and approach the design of outside spaces. We should also consider what defines a 'contemporary' garden. Surely it means 'a garden of the moment', created now – but how long does that 'now' extend? The Dutch landscape architect Mien Ruys's garden in Dedemsvaart, the Netherlands, was created in the 1920s, but after a hundred years there are areas of it that to me still feel remarkably fresh and contemporary. Unlike a piece of art, architecture or fashion, gardens continue to grow and evolve over time, but unlike interiors they are subject to the outside elements and face the challenge of an unpredictable and changing climate. This is what makes garden design such a remarkable art form, and why designing and creating gardens can be so challenging. And why I love it.

To understand the past three decades of garden design, we must first acknowledge the pivotal period from the late 1970s to the early 1980s. This marked a horticultural renaissance, if you like, and I believe the restyling of that time established a legacy of innovation that continues to shape modern practice.

Perhaps the most visible change of direction emerging at that time was the New Perennial movement. This naturalistic approach, which foregrounds plants, mimicking or taking inspiration from nature, originated with a group of professional plant-growers, thinkers and plant specialists in the Netherlands (it is sometimes referred to as the Dutch Wave). It gathered momentum in the 1980s with, perhaps most visibly, the work of Piet and Anja Oudolf, who were at the core of the collective and who owned a nursery in the eastern-central part of the country. This dynamic group also included Henk Gerritsen, Coen Jansen, Rob Leopold and Ton ter Linden. Piet Oudolf later described them as an 'international hub' of new thinking, and they really did shake things up. Gone were the traditional height-graded borders, a legacy of the work of influential garden writer and designer Gertrude Jekyll (1843–1932), with taller plants and shrubs at the rear and lower plants and groundcover at the front. The New Perennialists used a greater number of perennials and grasses in more flowing, immersive combinations.

In Germany a change was also taking place, primarily in public planting, since the post-war Gartenschau movement of large garden shows left behind legacy parks in many major cities. The design and planting in these parks were generally relaxed, using predominantly perennials and grasses. Ecology was foremost, with a much greater emphasis on grouping plants that would naturally thrive together, and sustainability was essential given that these parks were intended to thrive for many years and require little maintenance. In 1999 German professor and planting designer Cassian Schmidt took over the running of Hermannshof (see p.258) in Weinheim, southern Germany. This forward-thinking research and trials garden earned a place as one of the most significant gardens in recent history. Schmidt (who left the garden in 2023) worked with a complex blend of ecology and design in which consideration of aesthetic appeal was as important as botanical knowledge.

In the United States, meanwhile, Wolfgang Oehme and James van Sweden were changing the world of American garden design. In both private and public spaces, their naturalistic style was a departure from the traditional, manicured lawns of suburban America. They worked on a grand scale in a style that could be described as 'stylized naturalism', rather than ecological, using massed planting composed largely of herbaceous perennials and grasses. But there were others in the United States who were already practising a much more ecology-based approach to garden and landscape design, including Ian McHarg and Darrel Morrison. The work of these pioneers opened the pathway for many US designers, including Dan Hinkley, Larry Weaner and Roy Diblik (see pp.131, 163 and 83).

Prominent garden designers and plantspeople in the United Kingdom at the time included Beth Chatto at her garden in Essex, Christopher Lloyd at Great Dixter and Derek Jarman at Dungeness. All were skilfully pushing planting boundaries and creating gardens of lasting importance.

From this backstory, a gradual change in garden and landscape design began to gather pace, and within the past thirty years the profession has become more formalized, more widely debated and recognized by a wider audience. Within these decades, too, the complementary discipline of planting design has come to be considered as a valid and much-needed skill.

It is at this point that *The Contemporary Garden* takes up the narrative. While it is not easy to isolate how trends have moved forwards, we might start by noting how societal and economic changes have influenced both the public and private spheres. A good example is the redefining of abandoned post-industrial landscapes into public spaces. One of the earliest was the Landschaftspark Duisberg-Nord (see p.164) in Germany, a derelict ironworks turned into a 180-hectare (445-acre) leisure park by Latz + Partners in the early 1990s. It was extraordinary; the skeletons of the industrial buildings were left intact and a bold, beautiful landscape created to surround them. Built on a grand scale, it certainly had an impact on designs for similar contaminated sites across Europe and North America. Later that decade, landscape designers Gilles Clément and Alain Provost worked with architects Patrick Berger, Jean-François Jodry and Jean-Paul Viguier to transform the site of the old Citroën factory in Paris into Parc André Citroën. This 14-hectare (35-acre) landscape set the scene for many more city-centre parks.

New York's High Line is a prime example of how the movement of reimagining post-industrial sites can play out (see p.101). Involving creative collaboration from the very start, it is one of the best examples of the transformational power of landscape. Observe how people move on the bustling streets of Manhattan, with minimal interaction. When they venture up on to the High Line, one can immediately detect a change in pace and body language; people slow down, linger and interact with one another. Design is a powerful thing.

This movement of regenerative gardening on post-industrial or brownfield sites is beginning to filter into private gardens and more opportunistic spaces, such as car parks and bus-shelter roofs. One of the leading lights in this context in the United Kingdom today is John Little, who uses his garden in Essex, east of London, as a living laboratory (see p.169). His plantings thrive in soils devised from substrates including sand and waste ceramics, creating varied habitats that promote both plant resilience and enriched biodiversity, while also advocating for a 'zero-waste' approach to gardening.

Moving beyond the foundational expertise of garden practitioners, who in previous times might more usually have been working in isolation or within tight circles of knowledge, we cannot miss how the pace of evolution in garden design has been increasing alongside the proliferation of media sources, particularly those with strong visual content. In the late 1990s television makeover programmes brought garden design to a wider audience, popularizing such features as decking and promoting gardens as recreational spaces. Print media, exemplified by such magazines as *Garden Design* (founded 1982) in the United States and the United Kingdom's *Gardens Illustrated* (launched in 1993), provided designers with a vital platform to showcase innovative work and share stylistic inspiration through high-quality photography and informed yet approachable commentary. Today, social media and other online activity have further accelerated this trend, offering a direct and rapid channel for designers themselves to reach a savvy global audience, thus dramatically increasing awareness, expectation and understanding of what can be achieved through good design.

Margarida Maia in Portugal (see p.174), for instance, largely came to public awareness through her Instagram posts of her dreamily planted perennials garden photographed at first light. Designer Ann-Marie Powell forged a supportive gardening community through her daily Instagram Live chats during the COVID-19 lockdowns in the United Kingdom in 2020, bringing comfort and shared expertise when people felt isolated. She has now developed her outreach to the newsletter platform Substack, where (as do several successful designers) she shares, pretty much in real time, the development of ongoing projects, giving subscribers behind-the-scenes insight into the process of designing and planting a garden. In the United States, planting expert Kelly D. Norris has set out his own approach to wild plant communities and landscape ecology in his New Naturalism Academy, a virtual school that opens up learning from his Three Oaks Garden in Iowa (see p.204) to enthusiastic gardeners and designers everywhere.

Among such media successes will be the gardening names of the future, but only those grounded in horticultural knowledge and with a consistently authentic voice will endure. Even after thirty years of practice, Piet Oudolf remains arguably the best-known international planting designer. His early work, such as that for the Lurie Garden at Chicago's Millennium Park in 2004, brought a new planting aesthetic to public schemes, emphasizing more naturalistic planting with structural interest through the year and a freer arrangement of plants based on compatible communities – an approach not generally seen at the time. Through his numerous projects, from RHS Garden Wisley in southern England, Toronto's Botanical Garden and the Vitra Campus in Germany (see p.216), to one of his most recent projects, at South Korea's Taehwagang National Garden, Oudolf continues these themes but embeds a deeper understanding particularly of ecological aspects, public interaction and the longevity of plant communities. He is open to working collaboratively, and many are following in his footsteps.

In the United Kingdom, Dan Pearson and Tom Stuart-Smith have been consistently creating remarkable public and private landscapes for many years, while in the United States such designers as Martha Schwartz and Steve Martino have forged impactful portfolios. Topher Delaney's conceptual approach in the early years of this century both marked out the influence of talented women within what can sometimes seem like a very male-dominated profession, and demonstrated how alternative ideas are as valid an expression of garden design as the more conventional plant-filled approach.

I mentioned earlier the rise of the planting designer, and these are skilled horticulturists, as opposed to trained garden designers or landscape architects. Dare I say, some of the most innovative gardens have been created by gardeners and horticulturists who are, perhaps, less constrained by career parameters. We have been so fortunate in the United Kingdom as to have the Sheffield School of Planting from Sheffield University in northern England, the driving force being James Hitchmough and Nigel Dunnett, who have worked together and separately on extraordinary projects all over the world. Of course, coming from an academic background, both are fully committed to sharing their huge wealth of knowledge through teaching and writing.

Stories of experimentation and necessity abound in this book, too. In Western Australia, it was the very real threat of bushfire that led garden owners Bill and Diane Mitchell to surround their house with fire-retardant, xerophytic planting – naming their garden Fire and Beauty – and educating people to an alternative, more resilient planting palette. In the South of France, nurseryman Olivier Filippi has become the go-to resource, admired for challenging the conventional approach to Mediterranean planting, and instead observing and mimicking nature. His researched approach, which eschews highly irrigated, high-maintenance traditions, has gained traction with a generation of dry-climate plantspeople who are now adding their own experiences in the face of climate uncertainty.

When drawing up the contents list of this book about contemporary gardens, the inclusion of historic examples was hotly debated. Yet it would be a mistake to overlook their role. I've noted that gardens never really stand still, and it is that layering of time and the accumulated creativity of great gardeners that gives some of our best-loved gardens ongoing relevance. As such, we have included some long-cherished examples. Great Dixter House and Garden (see p.106) in southeastern England is an obvious example, where the early 20th-century Old Rose Garden was transformed into an exotic garden, initially by Christopher Lloyd in 1993 and latterly by head gardener Fergus Garrett. The estate as a whole continues to develop and change in an exemplary spirit of education and experimentation.

Longwood in the US state of Pennsylvania began its formal garden history in 1906, when industrialist and passionate garden-lover Pierre du Pont bought the neglected estate and set about creating his great garden. Today, it is open to the public and acknowledged as one of the country's most important gardens. In remaining true to its significance over the decades, Longwood Reimagined, a new programme of development, will ensure its relevance for decades to come (see p.312).

And so we come to the future of gardens and their design. Current trends and areas of interest include soil health and the role of mycelium, a re-examining of what we consider to be garden pests and even garden weeds, the rejection of chemicals, a sharing of space with wildlife, the desire to grow our own produce and the idea of food forests, a more naturalistic aesthetic that looks to the surrounding landscape and even the rewilding of our spaces to a messier, less intentioned look, more conscious water management (or SuDS) and sustainable design practices. Many of these are already reflected in the projects included here.

Hand in hand with gardens and green spaces as the battlegrounds for the health of our future planet comes the idea of gardens as therapeutic places for humans themselves. Back in 1996 in Scotland, Maggie Keswick Jencks used her own experience of having cancer to create the first of many Maggie's Centres. There are now twenty-four such gardens in the United Kingdom and four overseas, each created by a notable designer and linked to a cancer treatment centre (see p.165). Here is a moment of release for those living with cancer, and for their families. The measurable impact on people's well-being when they have access to green spaces has driven many such extraordinary projects, and giving moments like this to our children, too, has become increasingly important for their own sense of calm and connection to the natural world. We include here examples of school gardens that are part of a movement towards designing green spaces for active learning. For example, Cristina Mazzuccelli's design for nursery school Clorofilla in urban Milan (see p.184) is a joyful addition of exuberant planting to an otherwise bare terrace, creating a restful green space for engaged play and learning. What more positive way to look to the health of our future generations?

It's interesting for me to ask myself how my own work has developed over the span of time we've been analysing, and what changes I have embraced. I began my career living in the city and designing small urban spaces, concentrating on the art and materials, supported by planting. But since 2001 I have lived in a rural location and my focus has changed significantly. I now try to work out how little I can remove from a garden in terms of materials and mature plants. Seasonality, sustainability and planting that supports wildlife are foremost, and I make a concerted effort to use more of the 'forgotten' planting choices and shrubs that have been left by the wayside. A looser, more relaxed approach to garden design has permeated my work and that of my peers, along with a sense of working more collaboratively with nature.

Having come full circle, I want to return to those words of Dan Pearson and Terence Conran I cited at the start. Most definitely, the garden is a sanctuary, as they say. But that it should be also a place of healing, combined with respect for the future of the Earth, is where we seem to be heading. There may still be some resistance to the rewilding movement, but that is possibly caused by a misinterpretation of the term itself (a huge debate all of its own). For those with gardens, I maintain that the idea of rewilding can embrace a huge range of possibilities, styles and outcomes, from simply letting the lawn grow a little longer to mimicking how wild goats would 'prune' the shrubs or focusing more on native planting. Over the next thirty years I believe gardens will become much more relaxed in style, reflecting the way we want to live and to respect nature. It is indeed as Pearson and Conran wrote: 'Gardens have never been as important in our lives as they are today.'

Annie Guilfoyle
Garden designer and international lecturer

AGENCE APS WITH OLIVIER FILIPPI AND VÉRONIQUE MURE

JARDIN DES MIGRATIONS
MuCEM, Marseille, France, 2013

In 2013 the 17th-century Fort Saint-Jean on Marseille's harbour was transformed into MuCEM – the Museum of Civilizations of Europe and the Mediterranean. An adjoining 6,500 square metres (70,000 square feet) of 'garden promenade' were entrusted to Agence APS, notably Jean-Louis Knidel and Hubert Guichard. Each part of the new Garden of Migrations echoes some aspect of the city's heritage. The best craftspeople working in stone, wood and Corten steel created easy changes of level and direction with crisscrossing perspectives, while Mediterranean plantsman Olivier Filippi and ethnobotanist Véronique Mure undertook the planting according to the museum's cultural mandate. Some parts illustrate plant migrations (the Ailanthus garden, for example), others the site's own history (as in the myrtle and wild salad gardens). Whole biotopes are reproduced in miniature: olive groves, fig and pomegranate plantations, a threshing floor, a Mediterranean potager. Each planting makes the most of its orientation, exposure and microclimate – the wind garden (mainly tall grasses) faces the northern Mistral directly, for instance – and the results are varied, balanced and delightful. The gardens also offer a rare public example of the summer-dry methods perfected by Olivier and Clara Filippi. Almost all the plants are grown in gravel 6–15 centimetres (2½–6 inches) deep, watered only in their first year after planting, and kept free of organic matter, such as fallen leaves, that would enrich the soil too much. APS took pains to find gardeners who would understand the gardens' unique approach and could also communicate with the public.

JAMES ALEXANDER-SINCLAIR

HAILSTONE BARN
Cherington, Gloucestershire, England, 2015

Set in the open, stony and, in winter, rather bleak landscape of the Cotswolds in southwest England, the garden at Hailstone Barn does what Cotswold gardens traditionally did not do: opens itself to its surroundings rather than sheltering behind hedges. This 1,200-square-metre (12,900-square-foot) garden responds to the harsh conditions of a former cattle yard with tough, resilient planting that thrives with minimal intervention. Garden presenter, writer and designer, James Alexander-Sinclair has embraced the contemporary movement in perennial planting and eschewed traditional detailed planting plans in favour of scattering plants at random, ensuring a meadowy look. A number of Mediterranean perennials, among them *Cynara cardunculus* (globe artichoke) and *Euphorbia characias* (Mediterranean spurge), not only flourish in the shallow calcareous soil but also look their best in the winter and very early spring — an important consideration in a scheme dominated by herbaceous plants that die away over the winter. Somewhat surprisingly, damp-loving *Valeriana officinalis* (valerian) is a standout performer, adding a delicate floral haze that links the garden to the surrounding countryside, where many of the most common wildflowers have a similar appearance. There are few grasses, however; indeed, in parts the garden looks as though a goodly selection of meadow perennials have escaped their normal grassy companions and set up on their own.

AMAZON HORTICULTURE WITH NBBJ AND SITE WORKSHOP

THE SPHERES
Seattle, Washington, United States, 2018

Designed by architect NBBJ and interior landscape architect Site Workshop as part of the headquarters campus of the giant online retailer Amazon, and occupying half a downtown city block, three intersecting spherical domes ranging in height from 24 to 29 metres (79 to 95 feet) collectively enclose an area of 6,040 square metres (65,000 square feet). With terraces, waterfalls and river features, and a four-storey living wall covering 316 square metres (3,400 square feet) and planted with more than 40,000 plants from 400 taxa native to the cloud-forest regions of over 30 countries – the internal environment is cool and humid – The Spheres are also a botanical institution in their own right, with an emphasis on conservation. To pursue this aim, Amazon Horticulture (a horticultural team) was recruited at the outset to curate the plant collection. They worked closely with various botanical partners, including the University of Washington Biology Department; Ron Determann of Atlanta Botanical Garden; Chad Husby of Fairchild Tropical Botanic Garden; Dylan Hannon of the Huntington Art Museum, Library and Botanical Gardens; and Martin Grantham of San Francisco State University. The project pushed the boundaries of contemporary glass-dome design, but its inspiration was the great Victorian conservatories filled with rare treasures resulting from pioneering botanical exploration. The mix of historic and innovative, the blend of verdant interior landscape and the variety of event and informal gathering spaces (including a treehouse conference area) are intended to create an immersive, nature-rich, restorative workplace that relieves stress, invites curiosity and sparks creativity.

AMELD

PRIVATE GARDEN
Devon, England, 2017–

It was a simple request for a lookout reading room that led designer Duncan Nuttall to rework the whole of this 0.3-hectare (¾-acre) garden to be more sympathetic to its rugged surroundings. The sloping site is exposed to wind, rain and stormy seas, as well as to onlookers from the coast path, so setting the garden within the landscape would afford it more privacy. Nuttall removed a dominating driveway to create new borders, using the extracted stones to build a series of curving drystone retaining walls that lead down the slope and form an amphitheatre deck with swimming pool. Salt-tolerant plants were formative, but as time has gone on, the shrubs have matured and the *Pittosporum tobira* (Japanese pittosporum) have grown tall enough to create different microclimates that allow for softer additions. These include *Thymbra capitata* (conehead thyme) and the annual *Staphisagria requienii* (syn. *Delphinium requienii*) for scent and colour, and *Watsonia* for structure and textural evergreen foliage. Working with gardener Will Cumberlidge, the gentle editing of plants continues, and some forms are clipped, while others are left to grow more naturally. Below the deck, the site drops to the water's edge. Here, Nuttall has created paths and steps that nestle into the rocks, while *Armeria maritima* (thrift) and *Crambe maritima* (sea kale) peek from crevices, set off by the bright orange lichen *Caloplaca marina*. The name of the design studio Nuttall runs with co-designer Conrad Batten, AMELD, stands for Artistically Made Ecological Landscape Design and speaks perfectly of the approach taken here.

TADAO ANDO

HILL OF THE BUDDHA
Makomanai Takino Cemetery, Sapporo, Japan, 2015

This deeply thoughtful and evocative sculptural intervention began life in 2002 as the unrestful composition of a 13.5-metre-tall (44-foot) Buddha alone in a field. When the Japanese architect Tadao Ando was commissioned some years later to create a serene, contemplative atmosphere by bringing the sculpture and the generally flat Hokkaido landscape into closer harmony, his interest in the qualities of mystery and ambiguity in architectural space was aroused. He asked himself how a statue becomes a more solemn, attractive figure, and his bold and unorthodox answer, based in part on his belief that 'our imagination is piqued by what we cannot see', was to submerge the statue to head height beneath a gently sloping hill. That hill is clothed in 150,000 lavender plants set in grass and arranged in concentric circles that surround the statue at their centre. What Ando called the 'head-out Buddha' (the statue is now titled *Atama Daibutsu*, Buddha's Head) forms a balance between architecture and nature. But one does not experience it by climbing the hill. Inspired by Ando's experience of visiting caves in India and China and looking up at Buddha statues bathed in faint sunlight, the visitor navigates around the rectangular pool garden at the foot of the hill (a boundary between secular and sacred) before encountering a hidden, dark tunnel 40 metres (130 feet) long that leads to the centre of the artificial hill. There, from a tranquil shrine and prayer hall, one looks up at the Buddha against the ever-changing sky.

ANNA ANDREYEVA

PRIVATE GARDEN
near St Petersburg, Russia, 2021

This 1-hectare (2½-acre) garden for a contemporary house in forested surroundings allowed Anna Andreyeva (with the help of UK colleague Morag French) to evoke both Russian natural habitats and dacha gardens of the Soviet era, something for which both client and designer have a certain nostalgia. Andreyeva is known for introducing New Perennial-style plantings into public spaces in Russia, particularly in Moscow, where her studio, Alphabet City Landscape, undertook a range of innovative projects. This private garden is subdivided into named sections. The Babushka Garden includes familiar Soviet era plants, such as lilac, spiraea and, for late summer, *Rudbeckia laciniata* 'Goldquelle' (the only rudbeckia available in Soviet times). Within it a meadow evokes the shallow, very alkaline habitats known as alvars that are found over limestone, typical of the old limestone quarries that supplied material for the building of St Petersburg. A matrix of meadow grasses creates a backdrop for wild perennials. The Meadow Garden (illustrated) is based on the varied habitats of meadow steppe grassland; the seeds of some species were collected by Andreyeva herself and grown on in a nursery near Moscow. The Forest Garden, which makes the most of the site's surviving spruce forest, is planted with native species. Andreyeva's own description of the garden can be taken as a lyrical guide not only to this wonderfully atmospheric space, but also to the spirit of much contemporary naturalistic design: 'The planting is cosmopolitan, combining native and non-native species chosen for their ornamental character, making for a joyful interaction.' In 2020 Andreyeva founded Planting Strategies, a UK-based landscape practice.

AREAL LANDSCAPE ARCHITECTURE

JARDINS DE LUXEMBOURG
Luxembourg City, Luxembourg, 2020

These are the 'other' Jardins de Luxembourg, not the renowned formal 17th-century gardens in Paris but a series of open spaces, paths and steps surrounded by trees and varied planting that define the new residential district in the west of Luxembourg city, the capital of the tiny landlocked European country of the same name. With the completion of new homes on the site of a former dairy, Areal's brief was to create 7 hectares (17 acres) of private and public spaces to provide a welcoming environment that not only allowed people to move easily around the area, but also would appear established from the outset, hide the underground areas of parking and include plenty of seating to allow people to socialize. To this end, the planting needed to be quite intensive and so combined matured trees alongside shrubs and varied perennials. Areal ensured that plant choices were resilient but also offered a combination of points of interest – be that for winter interest, autumn colour, flower, scent or ecological benefit. Nearby, Place Joseph Thorn, which is notable for its magnificent, shade-providing plane trees, was replanted to connect the new neighbourhood to existing infrastructure, its beds filled with various low-growing flowering shrubs and hardy perennials. Opposite the square, a new public park was created as a place for residents to meet and relax. The poured concrete used for the benches and flower beds provides a textural contrast with the stone mosaic paths, and the predominantly white planting palette creates calm in the midst of the city.

ARTERRA LANDSCAPE ARCHITECTS

PRIVATE GARDEN
Tiburon, California, United States, 2012

Damage caused to the foundations of the house by stormwater run-off prompted the design of this garden. It is a fine example of the work of Arterra, a practice founded in 2003 by Kate Stickley that specializes in the design of contemporary, sustainable landscapes. The design for this 2,500-square-metre (27,000-square-foot) site is underpinned by two key features: a sinuous swale (storm drain) to divert water away from the property and a slope that has been regraded into undulating landforms. Both features intertwine with a winding pathway, with steps that link the house to the pool below. The path's meandering route through the garden is interrupted by a small landing that offers a quiet place to sit and enjoy the view to the San Francisco Bay. Stickley founded Arterra on her return to the United States after several years of living and working in Provence, in southeast France, during which time she became increasingly interested in and knowledgeable about Mediterranean plants and water-wise planting. A palette of fiery shades was requested for this garden, to shine through the fog that is common at certain times in the San Francisco Bay Area. Emphatic foliage and brushstrokes of red and yellow kangaroo paws (*Anigozanthos*) punctuate more softly textured planting. Fire resistance is also essential in an area where wildfires are becoming increasingly unpredictable and fierce, so the herbaceous planting is kept low and irrigated sparingly to ensure resilience. In the landscape beyond, oaks have their canopies raised to reduce 'fire ladders' that can aid the spread of wildfire flames. In this garden Stickley shows that functional design and sustainable planting can produce beautiful results.

ASSEMBLE

GRANBY WINTER GARDEN
Granby, Liverpool, England, 2019

In 2010 the future was not rosy for Granby, one of Liverpool's oldest neighbourhoods. The residents had done their best, painting murals on derelict walls and otherwise trying to put an upbeat spin on the downturn, but the real catalyst came when they began planting roadside containers. In 2015, as part of a wider regeneration project, an idea was hatched and facilitated by the Granby Four Streets Community Land Trust, which comprises equal parts residents of the Granby Four Streets area, Liverpool residents or workers, and representatives of organizations with a stake in the area. Although gardening was bringing the community together, 'the neighbourhood had few public meeting sites,' explains architect Anthony Engi Meacock of London-based Assemble, which designs and makes buildings, artworks, gardens, furniture and events, aspiring to preserve industrial space while defending public and cultural space. The idea to transform two of the saddest buildings into a 150-square-metre (1,600-square-foot) glass-topped 'winter garden' turned the neighbourhood around. Fundraising ensued, generosity flowed, and Assemble stripped out the remnants, leaving the brick skeleton intact. After four years, with fortifying steel beams (painted a strident blue evocative of Victorian palm houses), a double-glazed roof, in-ground planting beds, workspace, a potting shed, drainage lines, insulated meeting rooms and ventilation, the result has become a community hub. Although no formal design was drawn up for the planting, donated trees and tree ferns flourish, tended by community gardener Andrea Ku. Says Engi Meacock, 'This is what happens when you respect and preserve.'

STEFANO ASSOGNA

PODERE CASANUOVA DI SICELLE
Barberino Tavarnelle, Florence, Italy, 2023

Trained at the prestigious Scuola Agraria del Parco di Monza in northeastern Milan, and following time honing his plantsman skills as a head gardener, Stefano Assogna returned to his alma mater as a lecturer in garden design and planting design with an emphasis on the Mediterranean. His ethos is to create gardens with a natural character, the result of a combination of careful site analysis and artful reinterpretation of natural ecosystems, but always foregrounding sustainability and the wise use of natural resources. This resilient, water-wise garden graces a mid-15th-century Florentine villa-fortress built to protect its inhabitants against Sienese marauders. To mitigate erosion and the need for irrigation on this dry site, swathes of gravel laid over biodegradable mulching sheets are planted with drought-resistant plant choices. The style is what Assogna calls 'Mediterranean Mixed Planting', which nods to northern European matrix planting (also known as wildscaping, modular planting and New Perennial or New American style), with a southern European twist. With each plant having a role to play (groundcover, seasonal interest, structural form and so on), the effect is naturalistic. But Assogna reveals that 'the different taxa . . . symbolize the numerous transition zones of our Mediterranean environment, often populated simultaneously by different biological forms. This is how the mixing of woody plants, light and foamy herbs, and surprising geophytes creates an environment with obvious references to the natural one, but expertly designed and with a single purpose: to evolve to become the best possible version of itself.'

AUTONOMOUS PROVINCE OF BOLZANO/BOZEN – SOUTH TYROL

THE GARDENS OF TRAUTTMANSDORFF CASTLE
Merano, South Tyrol, Italy, 2001

Held in the natural amphitheatre of the snow-capped Gruppo di Tessa mountains and enjoying a surprisingly mild climate, the 16th-century Trauttmansdorff Castle was initially renovated in 1850. In 1977 the regional government took ownership but it wasn't until 1988 that local civil engineer and passionate botanist Manfred Ebner, together with partners from the Autonomous Province of Bolzano/Bozen – South Tyrol, began talking of a botanic garden on the steeply sloping 12-hectare (30-acre) site. The gardens opened in 2001. Within this fusion of nature, culture and art, more than eighty botanic habitats are collected into four 'worlds' that explore the connections between climate, location, natural vegetation and human interaction, with plants grouped by geographic origin and arranged to reflect natural plant communities. On the sunny slope beneath the castle, enjoying spectacular views, the Sun Gardens are characterized by Mediterranean flair with fragrant shrubs and herbs, an olive grove and vineyard, citrus, cypresses and succulents. In the Forests of the World, mini forests from North America and East Asia rub shoulders with a fern glen, more than 300 types of rhododendron, ornamental cherries, and artificial landscapes of rice paddies. Inspired by the beauty and culture of northern Italy, the Landscapes of South Tyrol flank a newly created mountain stream lined by alluvial forest, and incorporate a cottage garden and meadow orchard with heirloom varieties that pay homage to the region's traditional cultivated landscapes. In contrast the Water and Terraced Gardens (shown) are inspired by formal historical European styles, such as Italian Renaissance and English perennial gardens.

ALISTAIR W. BALDWIN

THE ROSE GARDEN AT WYNYARD HALL
Stockton-on-Tees, County Durham, England, 2015

One of the most magnificent rose gardens in the United Kingdom is that at Wynyard Hall, home to more than 3,000 David Austin roses of 135 different cultivars. Originally developed in 1822 as the Londonderry family's residence, the property was purchased in 1987 by Sir John Hall, who had long dreamed of opening a fine rose garden to the public. He hired internationally renowned landscape architect Alistair W. Baldwin to transform 1 hectare (2½ acres) of the historic yet badly neglected estate into a rose garden. Opened in 2015, it is now a floriferous haven, maintained by head gardener Mark Birtle. Together with rosarian Michael Marriott of David Austin Roses, a collection of shrub, wild, climbing, rambling, floribunda and old English roses of every form and colour was chosen and arranged chromatically, creating a gradation of hues. The result is an astonishing variety of roses that bloom from spring through to autumn. The garden also includes swathes of densely planted perennials and grasses from around the world, forming a fragrant floral display. Spring bulbs, *Verbascum* (mullein), *Aquilegia* (columbine), *Salvia* (ornamental sage), *Echinacea* (coneflower), *Helenium* (sneezeweed), various succulents and *Calamagrostis* × *acutiflora* 'Karl Foerster' (feather reed grass), among other plants, extend the season and lend an air of informality. Inspired by Persian garden design, a geometric grid is formed by rills and gravel paths, while raised galvanized-steel beds provide an update on the traditional English kitchen garden. Cedar pillars lend height and evoke the medieval *hortus conclusus*, or enclosed garden.

BALJON

GRONINGEN CITY GARDEN
Groningen, The Netherlands, 2013

Groningen's City Garden presents a new vision for urban green space with bold perennial-dominated planting. The landscape architecture studio, founded in 2001 by Lodewijk Baljon, worked to enliven this public space surrounding the Kempkensberg building, combining carefully crafted planting with functional infrastructure. Across the 1.1 hectares (2¾ acres), a vibrant mix of perennials, grasses and woody plants transitions seamlessly into the meadows and woodland of the adjacent 18th-century Sterrebos park, forging a link between the city, its history and a more natural environment. Consequently, the garden should function as a wildlife corridor rather more effectively than the low-diversity planting and mown grass that in the past would have been almost inevitable for this location. The central part of the garden, built over an underground car park, is effectively the same as a roof garden, containing trees and a rich array of perennials in a shallow substrate. Multi-stemmed trees chosen for their modest height and scale echo coppiced woodland, while yew hedges and innovative ivy screens provide structure, evoking the 'garden rooms' of classic English gardens, as well as breaking the force of the downdraughts that are the curse of the surroundings of tall buildings. 'We have repeated a similar combination of plants throughout the area to encourage a sense of movement,' explains Annemieke Langendoen, Baljon's planting design specialist, 'which complements the curves of the paths.' A rich visual experience is the result for the many people who pass through every day.

PAUL BANGAY

STONEFIELDS
Denver, Victoria, Australia, 2004–

Nestled in Victoria's Central Highlands, Stonefields was designed as a residential retreat for its designer. By this point Paul Bangay had been running a successful garden-design consultancy in Melbourne for two decades, the early stages of a prolific career. Although the climate is temperate, searing summer heat and wind can be counterpointed by a light dusting of winter snow. Bangay's response to a 20-hecture (50-acre) paddock with generous views was to create a formal core of hedges around the house, painterly dots of specimen trees, and a rich array of seasonal flowering shrubs and bedding. While the plan amplifies the main axis of the residence, this is not slavish symmetry. Stonefields has not leapt straight from a Tuscan hillside (although Bangay's style nods to the great formal gardens of Italy, France and Spain), but rather is softened by the Englishness of William Robinson's Gravetye Manor (see p.71), Vita Sackville-West's garden at Sissinghurst in Kent, and Christopher Lloyd's Great Dixter (see p.106). Bangay acknowledges that after two decades the 1.5-hectare (4-acre) garden has become much less formal than he intended. He credits 20th-century British designers Russell Page and David Hicks as major influences on his planting style, and remains inspired by early experience working at Marnanie for Kevin O'Neill, doyen of Australian florists. This floral inspiration is best seen in eye-catching displays of tulips, *Allium* 'Purple Rain' and billowing wisterias, while the hedged compartments offer playful nods to the Arts and Crafts movement with a small tower, ancient copper planters and whimsical topiary.

JULIAN AND ISABEL BANNERMAN

THE COLLECTOR EARL'S GARDEN
Arundel Castle, Arundel, West Sussex, England, 2008

Julian and Isabel Bannerman are renowned for designs that reflect the legacy of a site and combine a strong sense of history with a romantic, theatrical atmosphere. The results are contemporary gardens rather than historic recreations, as this garden aptly demonstrates. Named after Thomas Howard, 14th Earl of Arundel, the garden stands in a walled area that was formerly a visitors' car park. While historic connection was central to the brief, this is an evocation of the fine 17th-century garden that Howard created for himself and his wife, Alethea, at Arundel House, the London home of the earls of Arundel next to Somerset House (a royal residence at the time). Howard was an aesthete, an important collector of English art and a patron of Peter Paul Rubens, Anthony van Dyck and Inigo Jones. His garden reflected the arts and cultural thinking of the time, and some described it as the first museum or theatre garden. Arundel House and garden were later dispersed, and Howard's collection formed the foundation of the Ashmolean Museum in Oxford. The Bannermans were inspired by details in 17th-century paintings, including a portrait of Howard that shows the antique statuary he collected during trips to Rome, and drawings by Inigo Jones for the stage set of Ben Jonson's masque *Oberon, The Fairy Prince*. Armorial motifs are reflected on features throughout, and massive lengths of oak were given contemporary lines by craft experts using traditional tools. The strong sense of theatre throughout is another nod to the earlier lost garden.

STUART BARFOOT

LA PELLEGRINA
Viterbo, Lazio, Italy, 2013–

An 'enchanted, magical, chemical-free garden and grounds' were the exact words of the brief given to landscape designer and gardener Stuart Barfoot when he was asked to design this family garden of about 1 hectare (2½ acres). It is set within a spectacular, undulating Umbrian estate of 10 hectares (nearly 25 acres), dissected by an oak-fringed drive 200 metres (656 feet) long, all on fertile, volcanic soil overlaying tufa rock. The project was not without its challenges. The winters can be cold, sometimes as low as -5°C (23°F), with occasional snow, while the summers have long periods of extreme heat, reaching 30°C (86°F), along with hot, drying winds; in addition, with an estate of such scale it would be critical to blend the family garden into the surrounding agricultural landscape, which includes ancient woodland and meadows. 'The harmony between wild and garden was very important here,' Barfoot explains. 'I've used soft planting that blends with wild meadow and drifts into the wilder estate, but also clean lines to delineate and create a picture frame to contain more chaotic planting, that can be let go but still appear deliberate and looked after.' Before embarking on the design, he walked the land, observing the light and shade. Space and enclosure were also important factors, so he tried to imagine how people would feel as they walked through the garden. Although this is an ongoing project, he is confident that the garden already feels both protected and protective.

BART & PIETER

THE PANORAMIC GARDEN
Antwerp, Belgium, 2019

For more than twenty years Belgian garden architects Bart Haverkamp and Pieter Croes have been greening challenging urban spaces, including roof terraces, balconies and community gardens, as a calm contrast to the hurried pace of city life. This 60-square-metre (645-square-foot) terrace garden on the top floor of a city-centre apartment building exemplifies these transformations. The challenges included the garden's partially shaded aspect, weight restrictions and the owners' request for evergreen planting that would not obscure the breathtaking view, through floor-to-ceiling windows, across the river. Drawing on their experience of rooftop planting, Haverkamp and Croes chose a palette of plants that would cope with the shallow soil and shady conditions. A mix of low-growing ferns, *Carex* grasses, strappy *Liriope* (lilyturf) and compact *Ophiopogon japonicus* 'Minor' frame the garden, while ground-hugging *Soleirolia soleirolii* (mind-your-own-business) and *Galium odoratum* (sweet woodruff) are allowed to creep over the gravelly substrate, a mix of volcanic materials that the designers first encountered in Tenerife's botanic garden. At the margins of the garden, where the soil is just 6 centimetres (2¼ inches) deep, a selection of sedum species form a living carpet in vibrant contrast to the beige rug beneath the original sofa. The soil around the base of the central pillar was mounded to provide enough depth for multi-stemmed *Rhus typhina* (sumac) and sprawling *Fatsia japonica* to thrive, adding a swirl of architectural foliage that anchors the dining table. The pillar itself is clad with fragrant *Trachelospermum jasminoides* (star jasmine) and *Parthenocissus quinquefolia* (Virginia creeper) that turns fiery in autumn.

JAMES BASSON

PRIVATE GARDEN
Saint-Rémy-de-Provence, France, 2020

This courtyard garden in Saint-Rémy-de-Provence is not typical of the naturalistic style of James Basson, a British designer based in the South of France. Basson's studio, Scape Design, has garnered acclaim for its distinctly rural Provençal gardens that are rich in floral diversity and often feel like subtle extensions of their surroundings. In this strikingly modern design created for an open-minded client, however, there is no direct, visual connection to the landscape, and the planting exists in monocultural blocks edged with Corten steel. Raised channels connecting large, open water tanks punctuate the 500-square-metre (5,380-square-foot) space, forming a network that echoes the historical canal system of the local area. The simplicity of the materials speaks to the land's agricultural heritage while providing a contemporary contrast to the traditional walls of local stone. The water in the channels and tanks of this abstracted canal system bring light and movement to the solidity of the hard landscaping. The play of light is enhanced by the dappled shade of multi-stemmed almond trees, which repeat and rise above a compartmentalized meadow that is primarily made up of *Achnatherum calamagrostis* (syn. *Stipa calamagrostis*; needle grass). The texture of this grass, especially when it is in flower, softens the stone and steel and brings added movement. The simplicity of the design and the use of other familiar native plants, such as *Salvia rosmarinus* (rosemary) and clipped *Pistacia lentiscus* (mastic) ground this explicitly modern design, affirming its sense of place.

LOUIS BENECH AND JEAN-MICHEL OTHONIEL

WATER THEATRE GROVE
Château de Versailles, Versailles, France, 2015

The first new garden at the Château de Versailles since the 18th century, the reimagined Water Theatre Grove (Bosquet du Théâtre d'Eau), by landscape artist Louis Benech, is a tribute to the historic designs by André Le Nôtre. Originally built between 1671 and 1674, this was one of the most elaborate groves within the palace gardens, which were in turn among the world's most extravagant. A favourite of Louis XIV, the water grove was originally used for outdoor theatre and water spectacles, but it fell into disrepair after years of neglect and successive storms. The long-dormant bosquet, a leafy 1.6-hectare (4-acre) garden within the 810-hectare (2,000-acre) forest park, has been revitalized. After winning an international competition for the monumental project, Benech gave it a new, contemporary look, while honouring the park and its past. Like Le Nôtre, he wanted to collaborate with artists to bring another dimension to the design, and he chose sculptor Jean-Michel Othoniel. For his permanent, site-specific installation, *Les Belles Danses* (The Beautiful Dances), Othoniel created three fountain sculptures inspired by the work of choreographer Raoul-Auger Feuillet, dance teacher to the Sun King. The playful piece recreates Feuillet's balletic notations with gilded glass beads. Using the lines of the original square, Benech's composition has a symmetrical effect, while embracing asymmetry. Circular pools, islands and walkways echo Le Nôtre's recurring use of multiples of three. Rows of dark evergreens sequester the garden and provide contrast for the glowing glass beads, while highlighting an existing lone yew, prominent on one of the islands.

BILL BENSLEY

BAAN BOTANICA
Bangkok, Thailand, 1997–

Anyone fortunate enough to have stayed in a luxury hotel or boutique retreat in Southeast Asia may well have encountered the work of Bill Bensley. One of the world's best-known hotel designers, Bensley has worked on more than 200 luxury properties across more than thirty countries. Having trained as a landscape architect at California State University Pomona, then in urban design at Harvard, he established a design studio in Bangkok in 1989 and in Bali in 1990, and has a reputation for creating escapist hotels with lush tropical landscapes and maximalist interiors. He shares Baan Botanica, his home and garden in Bangkok, with his partner, horticulturist Jirachai Rengthong. The property, which covers 3,000 square metres (34,400 square feet), is a riotous confection of themed rooms, inside and out, and operates partly as a creative laboratory for new ideas. The name Baan Botanica (Botanic Garden) derives from the 1,500 different plant species it contains, including orchids and variations on *Plumeria* (frangipani), bromeliads and *Aglaonema* (Chinese evergreens), many bred by Rengthong. A series of 'pocket gardens' around the house range in style from elegant courtyards to water gardens and party lawns. For all the immersive, hedonistic spirit of his work, Bensley embraces low-impact conservationist principles that aim to benefit local communities. In 2009 he established Shinta Mani, his hotel brand and foundation, which trains impoverished teenagers for roles in hospitality and conservation, and in 2020 he shared the key principles of his conservationist outlook in his manifesto 'Sensible Sustainable Solutions', aimed at the hospitality industry.

PETER BERG

PRIVATE GARDEN
Sinzig-Westum, Germany, 1989–

For more than thirty-five years, designer Peter Berg has worked relentlessly to bring the spirit of the mountains to his own garden overlooking Sinzig and the Rhine Valley. On the site of a former vineyard, Berg has built a steeply terraced garden, climbing up seven levels through drystone walls, massive boulder formations, characterful trees (such as *Pinus nigra*, the black pine), a rock-studded waterfall and more. The 0.3-hectare (¾-acre) garden invites exploration via natural stone steps, slabs and stairs, and each level has its own theme. The epic scale of the stonework is softened by tall, linear hedges and intermingled drifts of perennials, including *Echinacea* 'Green Jewel', *Salvia*, *Aster* and *Miscanthus*, that seem to grow straight from the rock. Known in Germany as the guru of stone, Berg trained with masters in Japan and Europe and employs natural materials in innovative ways. His own garden is also the experimental base camp for the design-build landscape practice he runs with his business partner, Susanne Förster, but it was not built alone. Berg's son Daniel helped to configure the stack of boulders in the waterfall; the modern minimalist structures at various levels were designed by his daughter Mirjam Schuth, an architect; and many of the lichen-encrusted walls were made by enthusiastic participants in drystone workshops (Berg's expert crew brings machinery to do the heavy lifting). This hillside garden continues to evolve upwards, ultimately proving what is possible when you set out not simply to climb the mountain, but to build it.

BERGER PARTNERSHIP

PRIVATE GARDEN
Whidbey Island, Washington, United States, 2013–18

If visitors can't discern the parameters of the landscape that Jonathan Morley (principal at Berger Partnership), along with associate Shannon Leslie, designed for his client, Morley figures he has succeeded. Rather than designing a 'garden', Morley and his clients strove to 'amplify the ecotone of the forest and meadow' when merging the newly constructed house into the scenery. Brought aboard early, Morley worked with architect Miller Hull to design a small-footprint, sunken-elevation house on this 32-hectare (80-acre) private site located on an island in Puget Sound. They pulled the steel-clad house back from the waterfront in order to minimize its impact, nestling it into the existing Douglas fir forest. To encourage interaction, parking is sufficiently distant to require strolling through nature to the front door. But the roof treatments really set the project apart. Irregularly shaped extensions jut from the front, forming a guest room and media room. Above them, 'vegetative roofs' host columbines, trilliums, alliums, phlox, alpine anemone and yarrow, augmenting the base of creeping sedum. The bulkier rooftop perennials can be seen indoors through round skylights, while scuppers channel excess green-roof water away from the foundations. On the far side of the house, a stone outdoor fireplace and dining patio offer further open-air opportunities, while the primary bedroom features the potential for the bed to be rolled outdoors on to its own terrace to create a 'camping out' experience. Further afield, a tiny bunker-like guest cottage is barely perceptible, sunken in a grassy mound. Here, minimal impact feels absolutely right.

ANIKET BHAGWAT

UDAAN
Vadodara, Gujarat, India, 2018

Set on two hillocks connected by a steel bridge, Udaan transforms a once barren landscape into a lush blend of nature and design. The 3-hectare (7½-acre) garden was designed by Aniket Bhagwat, principal of India's foremost landscape-design company, which was established by his father, Prabhakar Bhagwat, in 1973. The house, which was built in 2011, is 'a house to live by,' explains the designer, 'more than to live in; it is a stage from which to view nature'. Central to the concept, the bridge offers panoramic views of contrasting terrain: the garden and wild lowlands near a flood-prone stream, as well as fields. A pool lies near the lower house, echoing a nearby lake, and the garden also incorporates an amphitheatre for musical performances. From one end of the bridge steps lead down into woodland, offering a transition from the tamed to the untamed. The preparation of the site involved growing green-manure crops to add organic matter and nutrients to the very poor soil, and using local species of grass to stabilize the banks. The plants that are arranged in very ordered ways – such as grid-grown species of *Agave*, *Yucca* and *Furcraea*, and *Volkameria inermis* (syn. *Clerodendrum inerme*) in round, sculptural blocks – augment and enhance the feeling of wildness that is found in the small forested area. Such use of wild vegetation is a real novelty in India, and the contrast is crucial to the spirit of the garden and its spirit of place.

JIMI BLAKE

HUNTING BROOK GARDENS
Wicklow Mountains, Republic of Ireland, 2001–

Plantsman Jimi Blake gardened from a young age, earning money by selling the plants he propagated. He went on to study horticulture at the National Botanic Gardens, Glasnevin, Dublin, and was the driving force behind the successful restoration of the public Airfield Gardens in the city. But it is in his own garden at Hunting Brook in the hills of County Wicklow – begun in 2001 from an 8-hectare (20-acre) site that was little more than a field at the time – that he has allowed his passion for plants to flourish. Areas range from large, immersive herbaceous beds to shady woodland with meandering paths. Blake is constantly developing the garden, and his approach, as he claims himself, is creative and unconventional: always evolving, curated but naturalistic in style, and with an exuberant leaning towards strong colours – huge displays of salvias and dahlias are a favourite – and striking shapes, forms and textures. Worldwide travel, particularly in China, Australia, South Africa, India and the United States, has informed his plant choices with a current focus on woodland plants. 'I live in a woodland, so it's the most obvious way for me to go – I'm trying to do woodland gardening in a more contemporary way.' He has amassed large collections of snowdrops, epimediums and corydalis, while also featuring woodland exotics such as scheffleras. Another recent development is the Sand Garden, begun in 2020 and planted with a quirky mix of conifers, succulents and alpines. Hunting Brook is beautifully secluded, yet very much a garden for sharing, and Blake runs regular courses, workshops and open days, as well as lecturing and leading garden tours that allow him to share his dynamic outlook on plants.

JUNE BLAKE

PRIVATE GARDEN
Tinode, Co. Wicklow, Republic of Ireland, 2002–

A sloping 1.2-hectare (3-acre) field surrounding a handsome granite farmhouse and outbuildings dating from the 1860s has become one of Ireland's most innovative contemporary gardens. It is continually edited by owner and creator June Blake (sister of Jimi Blake, see opposite), who found her passion for growing unusual plants from seed and for garden making after earlier careers designing jewellery and farming sheep. This is a garden where every plant has to earn its keep, where spring comes late and summers are generally cool. The planting in the inner garden is immersive; perennials and grasses are woven through ten rectangular borders in loose combinations of stems, striking foliage and flower heads that climax in late summer. Each border has its own identity, but cohesion is provided by the repetition of key plants, such as scented *Actaea simplex* 'Brunette' and multi-stemmed *Aralia echinocaulis*. The crimsons and oranges of *Crocosmia*, tall *Alstroemeria*, seed-grown dahlias, and tiger and martagon lilies ripple through three of the beds. By contrast, an original drystone wall is crowned with a simple line of *Celtica gigantea* (syn. *Stipa gigantea;* giant feather grass) dancing above a rectangular pool that is painted black to intensify reflections. The mood changes in the outer garden, first to a grassy mount that reveals the geometry of the formal garden below, through a meadow embroidered in spring with *Tulipa turkestanica* and camassias, followed by *Knautia arvensis* (field scabious) and *K. macedonica*, down a grassy bank to a woodland walk and a leafy, contemplative enclosure ringed with mossy boulders and ferns.

PATRICK BLANC

CAIXAFORUM VERTICAL GARDEN
Madrid, Spain, 2007

French tropical botanist and modern innovator of the green wall Patrick Blanc is inspired by nature and the vertical habitats he observes during research trips, and his ideas have revolutionized urban architecture. The vertical garden at the CaixaForum museum in the heart of Madrid's cultural district uses his soilless hydroponic Mur Végétal (Plant Wall) system, patented in 1988, which is being continually developed. For this design, which covers 600 square metres (6,500 square feet), Blanc chose about 300 species that would tolerate Madrid's climate, which is extremely hot in the summer and cold in the winter. Replacements and changes over the years mean the exact number of plants within the living wall is unknown, but it is estimated to be around 15,000–17,000. Blanc's extensive experiments and encyclopaedic knowledge of plants and ecosystems enable him to select species that thrive in the habitats found at different points on the wall. The urban environment reflects some of the niches found in a rainforest, although plants from a range of habitats are used. This garden contains highly resilient species, including heat- and drought-tolerant *Yucca filamentosa* (Adam's needle and thread), *Cistus × purpureus* (rock rose) and the unusual succulent *Sedum alpestre*, with species of *Begonia* and *Bergenia* in the shade. All are carefully selected to require minimal or no pruning. Blanc's planting plans, usually conceived in a wavy design from top right to bottom left, reflect the formations he has observed on outcrops, cliffs and scree in the wild, where plants spread along water channels.

PIET BLANCKAERT

PRIVATE GARDEN
Condroz, Wallonia, Belgium, 1995

There is musicality in the dramatic interactions of light, colour and verdant structures that comprise Piet Blanckaert's design for a 16th-century *château-ferme* (fortified farmhouse) in southern Belgium. For Blanckaert, whose four-decade practice reflects an international scope of influence from Dutch, French, Italian and English gardens, the site offered a blank canvas upon which to re-envision areas that had reverted to grass, bereft of historical evidence. Today, crossing a stone bridge over a moat, visitors come upon a courtyard and a parterre of low box hedges that enclose exuberant drifts of perennials and roses. An English garden is invoked by inventively clipped yew topiary, *Ceanothus* 'Italian Skies', and roses – among them 'Francis E. Lester' and 'Sander's White Rambler' – climbing the walls of an old chapel. The remains of an orchard and expansive lawn open on to a row of yew beehives (nicknamed the Twelve Apostles) overlooking a ha-ha, a cleverly disguised sunken wall that permits a view of the distant forest. A passageway formed by two undulating beech hedges leads to an existing rustic pond, a pleached beech tree underplanted with wildflowers, and a meadow that glows on summer evenings with *Borago officinalis* (borage) and *Glebionis segetum* (corn marigold). History reasserted itself when, during the construction of a circular stone terrace, workers unearthed the footings and foundations of the old tower. For Blanckaert, who was the proprietor of an ethnographic art gallery before he turned to designing gardens from the Baltic to the Mediterranean, this was the perfect denouement.

JINNY BLOM

ARIJIJU
Laikipia, Kenya, 2015

Equatorial Laikipia County, a vast expanse of prairie grass, acacia and black olive trees, is home to key African wildlife, including the endangered black rhino. Blom, a multidisciplinary designer and expert plantswoman whose approach to each project is unique, was asked to create the garden for a guest lodge on a private conservation reserve, so the project needed a careful approach. The answer was to bury the house partially by mounding up the surrounding landscape to a high outer wall – to act as an elephant-proof ha-ha – and planting the slopes with native grasses so that it does not impact visually on the landscape. The house opens to a 25 × 18-metre (82 × 60-foot) courtyard, combining elements of French monastery and Moorish paradise gardens, formally landscaped and informally planted. Two small seating terraces are reached by formal crisscrossing paths of pale stepping stones accessorized by clay pots filled with white waterlilies and surrounded by choice plants. Palest blue *Westringia fruticosa* (coastal rosemary) and sky-blue *Plumbago auriculata* (Cape leadwort) shine against muted grasses; fragrance comes from *Carissa macrocarpa* (Natal plum), with its star-shaped flowers, and citrus. Climbers on the cloister walls include white *Petrea volubilis* 'Albiflora', and the natural sculpture of a dead cedar tree echoes the surrounding landscape. Only local materials and labour were used for the project, with a team of men tirelessly digging out the planting holes and filling them with soil dug and transported to the site by local women.

BLUEGREEN

MAGOON SCULPTURE GARDEN
Aspen, Colorado, United States, 2010

Displaying everything from a massive bronze toy dinosaur entitled *Made in China* by Sui Jianguo to the polished stainless-steel *Circle Dance* by Tom Friedman, the Magoon Sculpture Garden's world-class private collection of outdoor art is eclectic and whimsical. But Sheri Sanzone, principal of Bluegreen Studio, saw a missed opportunity. Her goal was to show Nancy and Bob Magoon the potential for a unifying landscape running through their collection of thirty or more artworks over nearly 0.8 hectares (2 acres). The project manager, Ryan Vugteveen (formerly of Bluegreen and now branched out into his own Lift Studio), recalls that although the scene had a wildflower bed (which remains), 'it was primarily lawn; nothing tied it together.' An invitation for interaction was also absent. 'There was no path through the garden, the sculpture was viewed from the house,' Sanzone observes. Bluegreen proposed overlaying the scene with beds and pathways while keeping most of the sculpture in place. Serpentine flower strips anchor and accent but do not upstage the works. To minimize visual competition, Vugteveen focused on purples, incorporating *Nepeta × faassenii* 'Walker's Low', *Salvia × sylvestris* 'May Night' and *Allium* 'Purple Sensation', among others. Sections of lawn were replanted with ornamental grasses *Calamagrostis × acutiflora* 'Karl Foerster', *Deschampsia cespitosa* (tufted hairgrass) and *Helictotrichon sempervirens* (blue oat grass) to weave the scene together while creating movement and crafting a 'conceal and reveal' pageant through the existing aspen trees. Nature now frames art, and the design has proved so successful that additional sculptures have been added.

GAËL BOËDEC WITH JEAN AND JACQUELINE SCHALIT

LE GRAND LAUNAY
Lanrivain, Brittany, France, 1997

A vision of Eden, it is the Verger des Tentations (Orchard of Temptations) that symbolizes the spirit of this garden with its large snakes of boxwood twining around twelve trunks, as if to anchor them better in the earth. This unusual plant tableau is the signature feature of Le Grand Launay in Brittany. The owners, Jean and Jacqueline Schalit, designed the 2-hectare (5-acre) garden in consultation with landscaper Gaël Boëdec, who had the idea of trimming the box like lace to dress the orchard trees. The appropriation of the spaces has been carried out little by little over thirty years. After the large courtyard was redefined, the garden expanded behind the manor house. It is surrounded by a secret path traced through the large clumps of rhododendrons and hydrangeas, which allow you to walk around it unseen. The garden as a whole is dominated by greenery and cloud-pruned or closely trimmed shrubs; flowers, although not neglected, remain secondary to the design. It was while clearing a further section of the garden that Jean Schalit discovered a hollow complete with a spring and an old washhouse, which he rebuilt in the shape of a tiny amphitheatre. Plantations of green and yellow foliage have taken over this shaded structure. Clearing the wild part further, Schalit and Boëdec have extended the garden with an artfully conceived area inspired by the gardens of the East, including a grass-lined gravel path and a tea house.

ARJAN BOEKEL

ROOFTOP GARDEN
Rotterdam, The Netherlands, 2016

Nine storeys up, amid Rotterdam's sophisticated architectural landscape, designer Arjan Boekel has created a naturalistic garden of ethereal delicacy. Intending a refuge for a business's employees, he experimented within a tight deadline, planting without a formal design into only 10–20 centimetres (4–8 inches) of low-nutrition compost over 330 square metres (3,550 square feet). Dependable ingredients – those likely to survive the climatic and environmental conditions – were grouped densely, forming the bulk of the garden. As a precaution against immediate calamity, Boekel simultaneously sowed seed, then visited regularly to observe and tend, watering by hand only where death looked imminent. An absence of regular irrigation initially made many plants summer-dormant, but they rewarded later in the year with an overwhelming and season-defying 'multi-coloured carpet'. Others delivered eccentric surprises, such as the euphorbias (*E.* × *martini*, *E.* Redwing and *E. amygdaloides* 'Purpurea'), which responded to stress with airy, delectable tints of orange and pink. Almost nothing died, and Boekel gained confidence in the resilience of plants. Sunken seating shelters in the form of timber 'cocoons' offer immersion and a distinctive structure among the soft planting, as does a wide boardwalk. The effect is invigorating, undemanding and perpetually surprising. The designer doted on plants from his first steps, and went on to find like-minded inspiration in the work of Piet Oudolf (see p.101 and p.216), Henk Gerritsen and Ton ter Linden (see p.168). Since setting up his own practice, Boekel Tuin & Landschap, in 2009, he has become recognized for his intuitive creation of intricately layered gardens.

BOERI STUDIO

BOSCO VERTICALE
Porta Nuova, Milan, Italy, 2014

Milanese by birth and architectural training, Stefano Boeri is a professor of urban planning in his home city and founded his studio in 1993 (now named Stefano Boeri Architetti). He considers vegetation to be an essential element of architecture, and explains that his objective with the multi-award-winning Bosco Verticale (Vertical Forest) is to contribute to combating climate change by increasing the number of urban trees. This remarkable development is the prototype high-rise residential building to be greened in this way, and in preparation models were tested in a wind tunnel to ensure the trees would not topple from the balconies in high winds. The complex consists of two structures: one standing 112 metres (367 feet) tall and the other 80 metres (262 feet). Boeri describes it as 'a house for trees inhabited by humans', and with more than 800 trees and 15,000 perennials (including groundcover plants) and 5,000 shrubs, it is a model of urban forestation. Steel-reinforced terraces form practical outdoor living spaces that are planted with, in the largest instances, more than a dozen trees 3–9 metres (10–30 feet) tall, as well as a rich diversity of shrubs and flowering plants. The impact is significant. The taller building alone contributes the equivalent of 3 hectares (7½ acres) of linear, ground-level woodland on a site of a few hundred square metres, and has added to urban biodiversity by attracting birds and insects. Together with sister developments in Switzerland, the Netherlands and China, Vertical Forest is part of Boeri's push towards the environmental survival of contemporary cities.

MARIAN BOSWALL

PRIVATE GARDEN
Sussex, England, 2019

This evocative meadow labyrinth is based on the medieval example at Chartres in France, still used today for meditation and prayer. Part of a larger garden of 12 acres (nearly 5 hectares) commissioned from designer Marian Boswall by a client who holds meditation retreats, this contemporary maze is a wilder complement to the more formal 'rooms' elsewhere. The position was key, on an identified land energy point, where the labyrinth could also help to heal the land from any historic trauma. Boswall, who is known for her sensitive, sustainable approach to garden design, created the 500-square-metre (5,300-square-foot) labyrinth using bricks laid four across in a staggered bond, with wildflower-meadow seed sown in between. A meandering path runs through four classical labyrinth quadrants that represent the four seasons and face north, south, east and west. It takes six minutes to walk to the centre, requiring a certain concentration and allowing time to focus on the close view of such plants as *Leucanthemum vulgare* (ox-eye daisy), *Vicia cracca* (tufted vetch) and *Silene flos-cuculi* (ragged robin), along with the butterflies and bees they attract. The centre point is the perfect place to sit and gaze at the sunrise and the long view across the deer park and the forest beyond, immersed in a meadow but with a large prospect beyond, echoing internal and external mindfulness practices. The simple intervention of a labyrinth, although fairly demanding to build, was intended to regenerate the land, promote the health of the people who live there, and support the local fauna.

BOTANICA

PRIVATE GARDEN
Riley Park, Vancouver, Canada, 2016

In a leafy, traditional residential neighbourhood in central Vancouver, the shock of the new is grounded in nature. A sharply minimalist home of metal and glass, by Evoke International Design, is brought down to earth by the curated wildness of its intimate 110-square-metre (1,180-square-foot) front garden. Planting that softens the hard edges spills out into the boulevard with a luminous hedge of *Deschampsia* grass lining the pavement for passers-by. The entry sequence shown here threads together all elements of a now signature look by Botanica, a Vancouver design-and-build company that teams up with architects to bring residential landscapes to life. The entry proper starts with wide blocks of concrete forming the crisp geometry of the walkway and front wall, and the gate and further sections of wall are of wood stained black. Flanking the walk, the formality breaks down into what Botanica hardscape specialist Otto Schaffner calls 'soft connections' with organic flagstone paths, scattered boulders, and a formal slab patio in lieu of lawn. Botanica founder and planting designer Karin Hers-Schaffner weaves the plant layers with four-season fascination in mind, starting here with the peeling bark of *Stewartia pseudocamellia* and the autumn vibrancy of *Acer palmatum* 'Osakazuki'. Inspired by West Coast landscapes and such naturalistic designers as Nigel Dunnett (see p.91), she appeals to the senses with fragrant, textured drifts of perennials. The planting meshes into the hardscape with creepers filling the crevices between stones. By cultivating relationships with both plants and architects, Botanica is creating believers in the heart of Vancouver, running wild by design where least expected.

CHRISTOPHER BRADLEY-HOLE

BURY COURT
Farnham, Surrey, England, 2003

This relatively small garden on a former farmyard is one of Christopher Bradley-Hole's best-known designs, created for plantsman John Coke. Known for his minimalist compositions and classic styling, architect-turned-landscape designer Bradley-Hole created a modernist grass garden that defies tradition, yet was simultaneously inspired by antiquity. Known as the Front Garden — to distinguish it from the rear courtyard, which was designed by Piet Oudolf — it abounds in formal simplicity. Twenty planted squares edged in rusted Corten steel are laid out in a grid. Loose plantings soften the linear formality somewhat, and the plant selections connect the garden to the Hampshire landscape beyond. Crisscrossed with straight paths, the garden includes a tranquil, angular reflecting pool with a large open-framed oak pergola at its centre. The limited plant palette of about eighty species is dominated by tall grasses, mixed with a few meadow perennials, so the garden is about texture and movement, rather than flowers. A feathery band of *Calamagrostis* × *acutiflora* 'Karl Foerster' mingles with *Celtica gigantea* (syn. *Stipa gigantea*; giant feather grass) and species of *Miscanthus*, *Molinia*, *Hakonechloa* and *Panicum*, along with structural plants that have distinctive forms, such as *Sanguisorba*, *Eryngium*, *Agastache*, *Datisca cannabina* (false hemp) and *Helianthus salicifolius* (willow-leaved sunflower). With a planting scheme that is primarily green, the garden is unified by its simplicity and the repetition of shapes. It is open to abstract interpretation, a contemporary study in the contrast between geometric austerity and naturalistic planting, its proportions informed by architecture.

RALPH BRISTOW

BARWITIAN GARDEN
Barwite, Victoria, Australia, 2019–

Many garden designs aspire to artistic status, but few are created organically by artists as a painting might be. Sole practitioner Ralph Bristow, who studied fine art, horticulture and landscape architecture, has brought his long experience of designing and rejuvenating gardens to his own plot. The Barwitian Garden is set amid farmland and bush in the foothills of the Victorian Alps; 1.2 hectares (3 acres) is intensively gardened, while a further, similarly sized area is earmarked for indigenous planting and a cool burning regime recognizing traditional cultural management on Taungurung Country, whereby controlled fires clear the undergrowth. It was established in 2019, with considerable planting carried out in 2023–4, and all preparations and plantings have been undertaken by the owner. There is no formal design, and instead Bristow approaches the ground the way he paints: making a mark and letting conversations between colours, textures and canvas dictate physical structure and emotional cues. Vibrant perennial plants predominate, while trees and other woody plants provide anchors. He calls his work an experimental wild garden, one that heaves with each season, engaging the gardener in an ongoing dialogue, yielding subtle editing and serendipitous expansion. The garden contains around 20,000 plants to date, and is being expanded using exclusively drought-tolerant species, via an organic design process that Bristow likens to a new limb growing from a torso. The Barwitian Garden pays homage to the New Perennial movement, yet its embrace of native plants alongside exotic favourites and its respect for local environments produce a distinctively Australian response to this international phenomenon.

JANE BROCKBANK

THE CHAPEL
London, England, 2017

This small city garden was something of a departure for London-based designer Jane Brockbank, who is known for her flowing, naturalistic schemes and use of reclaimed materials. Here, the geometric layout, designed by Craftworks, required her to create discrete planting zones that would allow the triangular volumes – which mirror the faceted architecture of the building's interior – to be legible. She wanted to give the owners of this converted chapel a range of plant experiences and seasonal changes – a challenge in the 35 × 13-metre (115 × 43-foot) plot, which narrows to just 7 metres (23 feet) in front of the lower-ground bedrooms. Gravel studded with low-growing perennials, such as *Armeria maritima* (thrift), *Ajuga reptans* 'Catlin's Giant' and *Bistorta affinis* (syn. *Persicaria affinis*) 'Darjeeling Red', is both an access path and a strip where the plants can be seen close up from inside. Behind is a taller zone of intermingling species, mainly in shades of pink, alongside a vibrant block of *Sesleria autumnalis* (autumn moor grass) punctuated by white *Astrantia*. The gravel zone leads to a terrace of Corten steel triangles, where the crisp metal edging contains a mix of clumping perennials backed by feature shrubs, such as *Viburnum opulus* (guelder rose) and *Philadelphus* 'Belle Étoile' (mock orange). This abuts a sloping, flowering lawn edged with a joyful band of *Celtica gigantea* (syn. *Stipa gigantea*; giant feather grass) and studded with bulbs in spring. A line of tall screening trees provides shade for woodland-edge plants. Flow is created by repeating key plants, such as *Salvia nemorosa* 'Amethyst' and *Silene coronaria* (rose campion), and in time Brockbank expects the zones to blur together.

FIONA BROCKHOFF

KARKALLA
Mornington Peninsula, Victoria, Australia, 1996

In its early days Karkalla, the home and 0.8-hectare (2-acre) garden of Australian landscape designer Fiona Brockhoff and her partner David Swann, radically changed many Australian gardeners' attitudes to pruning native plants, and sparked new approaches to designing with local flora. Brockhoff's seemingly relaxed yet disciplined gravel garden represents a studied response and connection to its place on the traditional lands of the Boonwurrung people of Mornington Peninsula, the limestone plateau that divides the ocean and bay south of Melbourne.

At Karkalla (the name relates to *Carpobrotus rossii* – a local native succulent) *Allocasuarina verticillata* (drooping sheok) was radically pruned into sculptural forms. The windswept local *Alyxia buxifolia* (sea box) and *Melaleuca lanceolata* (moonah) were trimmed into domes that anchor the design among mass planting of groundcover and grasses, such as *Austrostipa stipoides* (prickly spear-grass) and *Lomandra longifolia* (basket grass). Stands of *Leptospermum laevigatum* (coastal tea tree) and *Banksia integrifolia* (coast banksia) form the upper canopy. Although Karkalla is consciously gardened, the species choice connects it to the broader landscape and the ocean beyond, a quality honed by Brockhoff's deep observation and understanding of the local landscape. Limestone-clad walls unite the house with the landscape and form courtyards for wind protection. Olives, *Echium candicans* (pride of Madeira), succulents, *Phormium tenax* (New Zealand flax) and other architectural species combine with *Westringia fruticosa* (coastal rosemary) in striking groups that contrast with the strongly horizontal walls.

BROOKLYN GRANGE

BROOKLYN NAVY YARD FARM
Brooklyn, New York, United States, 2012–

Founded in 2010, Brooklyn Grange is one of the world's leading rooftop farming and green-roofing businesses. After building its first rooftop farm in the Queens neighbourhood of Long Island City, which it no longer maintains, Brooklyn Grange – with cofounders Ben Flanner and Anastasia Cole Plakias and current CEO Sam Murray – now operates two such farms in Brooklyn, growing more than 31,500 kilogrammes (70,000 lbs) of organic produce annually. Their produce is sold through farmers' markets, Community Supported Agriculture (CSA) shares, and distributed to community-based organizations at reduced or no cost. The Brooklyn Navy Yard farm, managed by Gareth Stacke, was built in 2012. It is a rooftop farm of 6,000 square metres (64,600 square feet) with views of the Manhattan skyline. Food crops and a lush lawn are sur-rounded by a flower habitat for pollinators. The second Brooklyn farm, managed by Connor Cushman, was established in 2019, and is located atop Liberty View Industrial Plaza in the Sunset Park neighbourhood. With views of New York Harbor, the farm has an agricultural space of more than 5,100 square metres (55,000 square feet). Leading the farm-to-table movement, Brooklyn Grange farms also include greenhouses, kitchens, event spaces, and even has chickens and beehives at the Navy Yard location. In Manhattan, the organization manages The Farm at the Javits Center, which comprises a rooftop farm, fruit orchard and a greenhouse, producing 9,070 kilogrammes (20,000 lbs) of harvest each year at what is one of the city's largest rooftop green spaces. As Brooklyn Grange expands and grows, the Navy Yard location continues to operate as its headquarters.

MIRANDA BROOKS

PRIVATE GARDEN
Mastic, New York, United States, late 1990s–

Reflecting on her longtime bond with landscape designer Miranda Brooks, British-American media executive Anna Wintour once said: 'My friendship with Miranda is one of the great joys of my life. She has given me and my family a very special world.' Wintour commissioned Brooks in the late 1990s to design her country-house garden. Underscoring their shared love for the abundantly flowering English cottage garden, juxtaposed with wild, naturalistic areas, Brooks's design also respects the indigenous character of the coastal salt marsh and scrub-shrub habitat. A pebble and dirt road bordered by wild cherry trees leads to a small, vintage wooden door set into a brick wall covered with 'Cécile Brünner' roses. The flat site and absence of dramatic views inspired Brooks to create drama via pathways through woods, swathes of uncut grass, narrow lanes of mowed lawn, and meadows planted with bulbs, such as *Camassia* and *Narcissus*. Mature, cloud-pruned box, clipped holly and pleached linden allées offer formal structure near the two houses, framing untamed areas beyond. Rustic gates made of twigs lead to a hidden pool, tennis courts and a crab-apple meadow. A haven for butterflies, the perennial garden spills over with peonies, *Baptisia*, *Geranium wallichianum* 'Buxton's Variety' and 'Tuscany Superb' roses enclosed in four square beds. Pictured, a box parterre that comes alive in spring with *Narcissus poeticus* (pheasant's eye) and *Malus* 'John Downie' in flower. In summer *Nicotiana mutabilis* softens the voids and brings a magical looseness. The effortlessness and simplicity throughout a varied ensemble of plantings still requires ongoing, expert labour – a hallmark of Brooks's artistry and her cultivation of enchantment.

BULLA

YPF SERVICE STATION
Buenos Aires, Argentina, 2019–23

Bulla is a pioneering urban planning and landscape architecture studio in Argentina led by Ana García Ricci, Ignacio Fleurquin and Lucía Ardissone. They have revolutionized urban design by reinterpreting it as the creation of self-contained ecosystems. Their groundbreaking approach is exemplified by the YPF project, a visionary reimagining of a service station by architects RDR and Estudio Emmer on a key block in Buenos Aires. Next to public parks along the Río de la Plata, the YPF project integrates urban flows and natural systems. Its ground floor seamlessly connects pedestrians, cyclists and vehicles, while its 0.3-hectare (just under 1-acre) green roof links local wildlife – including birds, insects and small vertebrates – with nearby parks and the river ecosystem. The design features two distinct plant systems. The ground-level landscape complements the city's huge Tres de Febrero park, by including some of the park's historically introduced European tree species, thus bringing an element of visual continuity to the scene. A mix of shrubs and herbaceous plants provide privacy and intimacy, enriching the surrounding public space. The green roof reintroduces native plant communities formerly displaced by 19th-century landscaping trends, drawing inspiration from the pampas and talar (the strip between the river and the pampa) biomes. Aligning each plant species with a depth of soil that suits it best ensures a robust ecosystem across the various layers: trees, shrubs and herbaceous plants. This innovative design not only bridges urban and natural landscapes, but also establishes a vital ecosystem hub, enhancing biodiversity and improving the liveability of the city.

MACARENA CALVO AND CRISTÓBAL ELGUETA

PALMAR DE PANQUEHUE
Aconcagua Valley, Chile, 2016

Macarena Calvo and Cristóbal Elgueta are undoubtedly game-changers in Chilean landscape design. Elgueta developed the term 'Ecosystemic Landscape Design' from an early point in his garden design career, at a time when few people understood its meaning, and he has been working on projects with landscaper and naturalist Calvo since 2012. Together, their commitment to designing sustainable gardens drives them to venture into the wild to identify plant species with ornamental potential, to understand how natural ecosystems function, and to reinterpret these dynamics in beautiful creations. The commission for this private garden arose from the need to rescue specimens of the endemic *Jubaea chilensis* (Chilean palm) – the world's southernmost palm and currently classified as vulnerable – from an abandoned park in the country's Valparaíso Region. There were some extraordinary *Phoenix canariensis* also worth saving. This initiative inspired the creation of a 1.6-hectare (4-acre) conservation garden. The surrounding hills serve as a dramatic backdrop, becoming protagonists through carefully crafted visual axes, materiality, and the symbolism of sculptures. A lagoon with biofilters acts as a refuge for wildlife, using water diverted from the irrigation canal of the adjoining field. Insects, birds and small mammals have transformed the garden into a biodiversity hub that integrates seamlessly into the ecological corridor of the Aconcagua River. Native plants that stand out include the grass *Amelichloa caudata* (syn. *Jarava caudata*), shrubs *Baccharis linearis* and *B. concava*, *Alstroemeria*, the cactus *Leucostele chiloensis* (syn. *Echinopsis chiloensis*) and broadleaf evergreen *Quillaja saponaria* (soapbark tree).

HELDER CANCELA AND JOÃO PAULO GOMES

QUINTA DO LAMEIRO LONGO
Oliveira do Hospital, Coimbra, Portugal, 2004

Twin brothers fell in love with the idea of the garden, inspired by historic Portuguese and Spanish gardens, with their Moorish influences, as well as the classical formality of France. After buying a small farm in central Portugal together, they built adjacent houses for their families and started to make a garden of bold ambition, which works exceptionally well on all scales. The 3-hectare (7½-acre) garden is in a bowl with slopes covered in the local wild scrub, much of which has been subtly manipulated by the removal of some species, enabling others, such as *Lavandula stoechas* (French lavender), to thrive and spread. *Pinus pinea* (stone pines) on the slopes are an important part of this wider zone of the garden. Hedges of *Buxus sempervirens* (box) and *Olea europaea* subsp. *europaea* (wild olive, known locally as *zambujeiro*) outline areas of grass or wildflowers, or are developed into strongly sculptural forms. The brothers' observations of the Portuguese landscape have led to real innovation, such as this use of *zambujeiro* as hedging. There is amazing botanical diversity within this framework, however. 'It always seemed to us,' says Helder Cancela, 'that in southern Europe, but in a mountainous region, we can mix different vocabularies and species, exotic and native.' Palms, small trees and shrubs create sheltered, shaded microclimates for a wide variety of smaller woody plants, roses, succulents and perennials, reflecting many years of plant-collecting and experimentation, and ensuring that the visitor's journey through the garden is one of continual discovery.

ANDY CAO AND XAVIER PERROT

GARDEN OF THE GIANT
Swarovski Kristallwelten, Wattens, Tyrol, Austria, 2015

Swarovski Crystal Worlds (Swarovski Kristallwelten) is a 7.5-hectare (18½-acre) theme park in the Austrian Alps, created by artist André Heller (see p.130) for the crystal glass manufacturer to mark the company's centenary in 1995. The entrance, a huge green earth mound shaped like the head of a mythical giant, leads to the underground Chambers of Wonder, a kind of cabinet of curiosities. Exhibits feature work by internationally renowned artists, designers and architects who have interpreted the sparkling, gem-like crystals in various creative ways. The surrounding landscape of small grassy mounds and real birch trees, by artist team Andy Cao and Xavier Perrot of Cao Perrot, is known as 'The Garden of the Giant' in honour of the iconic landform. At the centre of the garden is *The Crystal Cloud*, a monumental installation of 1,400 square metres (15,000 square feet). Inspired by trees and clouds, the glittery dreamscape is formed by a forest of columns holding up a cloud-like wire structure laden with about 800,000 hand-mounted Swarovski crystals. The installation drifts along a descending path into a black mirror pool, creating a dazzling display of light and colour. The crystals and their reflections shimmer like bright stars, even in daylight, resulting in an enchanting garden in which to marvel at the brilliance of the glass pieces. Inspired by the natural world, Cao and Perrot incorporate such elements as leaves, flowers, sky and light into every project, and clouds are a recurring motif. Their blend of landscape design, site-specific art and horticulture creates an otherworldly experience.

FERNANDO CARUNCHO

PRIVATE GARDEN
Estudio Caruncho, Madrid, Spain, 2002

Landscape designer Fernando Caruncho explains his design philosophy thus: 'to let the place speak to me and to listen to it through its light. That light is revealed within me and my connection with the place is expressed through the hand with the sketches.' Trained as a philosopher and gardener, Caruncho is renowned for his profound gardens that combine arresting simplicity with singular sophistication, striking geometry with classical and religious allusion, striving for 'a space that invites reflection and inquiry by allowing the light to delineate geometries, perspectives and symmetries'. This garden surrounds his studio with an austere, peaceful simplicity, its form and layout essential Caruncho but with nods to minimalism, the Baroque and the Japanese *karesansui* (dry garden). A key element is the entrance courtyard. In this introductory space, a scalloped box hedge encloses an expanse of raked gravel set with a circular pool, its jet creating perfectly circular ripples; this horizontal plane and the vertical of the building wall are 'slashed' by a dramatic open stairway. Above it, the small pavilion where the design team meet frames views across agricultural land to the mountains north of Madrid. With a reflecting pool alluding to Caruncho's interest in ancient irrigation systems, the garden oozes order and balance, restraint and culture, forging a connection with and interpretation of the place and space. Or, in Caruncho's words, 'the spatial–temporal feeling you get in a garden when you walk through it; it is an inspiration that has a poetic sense and tries to express that feeling of a forgotten memory'.

CHANTICLEER GARDENERS

THE RUIN GARDEN AT CHANTICLEER
Wayne, Pennsylvania, United States, 1999–2000

This 14-hectare (35-acre) 'pleasure garden' and former early 20th-century country retreat in suburban Philadelphia opened to the public in 1993 and is considered one of the world's most imaginative gardens, thanks to the vision of the Rosengarten family and their talented horticultural staff. A hallmark of Chanticleer, under the current leadership of executive director Bill Thomas, is allowing each gardener to creatively design and oversee their section. One distinct area, known as 'The Ruin', was built on the footprint of an old farmhouse and was developed by Chanticleer's first executive director, Christopher Woods, and landscape architect Mara Baird. It was created as a garden of follies resembling an abandoned, crumbling house, with the illusion of being overgrown, evoking a gothic sense of mystery. In reality, it is a meticulously designed, planted and maintained garden of three walled 'rooms': a great hall, a library and a pool room. The rooms are unified by a silvery-green plant palette and artfully framed views, with roofless stone walls covered in vines and espaliered trees. Each is whimsically furnished in stone and marble by sculptor Marcia Donahue. The hall's water feature is a reflecting table shaped like a sarcophagus resting on a tiled 'rug'. Stone books are scattered throughout the library, and a fireplace has a succulent-covered mantel. The pool room surprises with marble faces floating below the surface of a fountain. Inspired by such great gardens as Sissinghurst and Bodnant in the UK, Chanticleer is a gardener's garden, and the atmospheric Ruin is a favourite among visitors.

DALE CHIHULY WITH RICHARD HARTLAGE

CHIHULY GARDEN & GLASS
Seattle, Washington, United States, 2012

With a style that is best described as theatrical, Richard Hartlage of Land Morphology (which he founded in 2013) is known for daring displays, and the Chihuly Garden & Glass takes the drama many steps further, into the realm of the surreal. When Chihuly Studio teamed up with the Seattle Space Needle to convert an asphalt parking lot with remaining carnival rides into a glass sculpture garden, Land Morphology was the obvious partner. Whether in a private garden or a public space, sculpture often plays a pivotal role for this Seattle-based landscape design firm. Given just over half a hectare (1½ acres) in the shadow of the iconic 1962 World's Fair Space Needle, the team was charged with framing and complementing Dale Chihuly's colourful, curvaceous, imaginative glass art with plants that would add to the performance, with sustainability and smart water use also being part of the equation. The colour palette is key, and Chihuly Studio requested plants in bright and/or contrasting colours to play off the rainbow hues in this largest permanent installation of its art. Meticulously and naturalistically placed to enhance and echo the glass sculpture while bringing the arts together, a total of 250 plant species play key roles, with an emphasis on perennials and trees. Hartlage's favourite pairing is *Pacific Sun*, a dramatic work with yellow and peach rays of curvaceous glass framed in a mound of 7,000 black mondo grass (*Ophiopogon planiscapus* 'Nigrescens') plugs. But that triumph is just one in thousands of ever-changing, heart-throbbing and botanically brave moments.

GILLES CLÉMENT

JARDIN DU TIERS-PAYSAGE
Saint-Nazaire, Brittany, France, 2011

The Jardin du Tiers-Paysage (Garden of the Third Landscape) was developed in 2009–11 by pre-eminent French landscape designer and ecologist Gilles Clément on the roof of an abandoned submarine base covering 2 hectares (5 acres). Working with contemporary landscape design company Coloco, Clément used the large concrete structure to form an open terrace between city and harbour, adopting ideas set out in his *Manifeste du Tiers Paysage* (2004), in which he recognizes plants' adaptive, opportunistic tendencies to colonize neglected places. He wove in concepts from his earlier work, too: the 'Garden in Movement', notably applied at Parc André Citroën, Paris, and his own garden La Vallée in central France, where natural dynamics such as selective self-seeding are preferred to strict maintenance plans; and the 'Planetary Garden', underpinned by sensitive human custodianship of gardens in the context of wider biosphere care. In Saint-Nazaire, he nurtured three distinct plant communities using locally suited species. In the Bois des Trembles (Aspen Wood), a grove of *Populus tremula* emerges through the old concrete beams, its canopy fluttering at the slightest breeze on this exposed site. In Jardin des Orpins (Sedum Garden), such self-seeders as *Nassella tenuissima* (syn. *Stipa tenuissima*) and *Valeriana ruber* (syn. *Centranthus ruber*; valerian) are left to colonize, although diversity is ensured by monitoring competition and selective pruning. Finally, the Jardin des Étiquettes (Labels Garden) has a thin layer of imported gravel in which plants seed spontaneously, delivered by wind, birds and passing feet, creating a dynamic local eco-system that, carefully recorded and labelled, becomes a mini botanic garden.

CMG LANDSCAPE ARCHITECTURE WITH FRANK GEHRY

META ROOFTOP
Menlo Park, California, United States, 2016

Positioned atop the Frank Gehry-designed headquarters of Mark Zuckerberg's Meta empire (the building is officially known as MPK20), this roof garden covers 3.7 hectares (9 acres) – the entire length of the building. The inspiration came from Gehry, who envisioned a place for employees to be outside, since there was no opportunity for landscaping around the building. CMG Landscape Architecture was responsible for coordinating the design, which includes a sinuous pathway 800 metres (½ mile) long that winds around the roof in something of an echo of the New York High Line (see p.101). The planting is 90 percent native flora and boasts 350 deciduous, evergreen and flowering trees, attracting populations of resident and migratory birds. Moving through the garden the visitor encounters lawns dotted with furniture, Gehry-designed tepees and art installations by Smith Allen, Jay Nelson and Evan Shively. Ornamental plantings are to be enjoyed close up, while also being set against a succession of prospects over the borrowed landscape of adjacent marshland and distant Bay Area hills. Illuminated for night use, the garden is intended both as a leisure space for Meta's 2,800 employees and as a functional space; walking meetings are part of the company's culture, and whiteboards positioned here and there encourage outdoor meetings. The campus has since expanded through further collaborations with Gehry, including the MPK21 building, which features another large roof garden as well as extensive tree-planting led by CMG.

COBE

THE OPERA PARK
Copenhagen, Denmark, 2023

Cobe (founded in 2006 by architect Dan Stubbergaard) has undertaken several major projects throughout Copenhagen and is known for its innovative, future-proof urbanism, landscapes and architecture that actively enhance everyday life. This 2.2-hectare (5⅓-acre) landscape project transformed what was once a lawn on a former industrial site adjacent to the Royal Danish Opera into an urban green island. Reflecting the layout of an operatic stage set, it is designed with a fore-, middle- and background interwoven with meandering paths, organically shaped flower beds and carefully placed viewpoints. It is composed of six gardens and wooded areas highlighting different floras, among them North American, Danish Oak and Nordic Forests, Oriental and English Gardens, and a Subtropical Garden, the last of which is housed inside the flower-shaped central greenhouse. The planting of 628 trees, 80,000 herbaceous perennials and bushes, and 40,000 bulbs from around the world references Denmark's historic maritime tradition, harking back to times past, when seeds arrived on ships returning to Copenhagen. The rich variety of species aims to increase biodiversity, while creating constant change through the seasons; spring blooms in a rich colour palette, summer brings various shades of green, autumn showcases red and yellow tones, and winter is dominated by evergreen pines and frozen ponds. Sustainability is at the heart of the park, which includes permeable gravel paths, green roofs and solar panels. Although it is a park for the people, with a reflecting pool where drops of water from a mast gently strike the water's surface in a soothing rhythm, the Opera Park is a place where nature comes first.

ANDREA COCHRAN

CALISTOGA RESIDENCE
Napa Valley, California, United States, 2017

Landscape architect Andrea Cochran established the award-winning firm that bears her name in 1998. The San Francisco-based practice is renowned for its considered, environmentally sensitive designs of various types and scales. Gardens are tailored to varying site conditions, using a restrained palette of carefully crafted, high-quality materials that make complex and detailed projects appear deceptively simple. One such project, the 1-hectare (2.5-acre) garden surrounding the Calistoga Residence in the natural oak woodlands above Napa Valley, is linked to its location by rough-textured walls of field stone, as naturally found in the surrounding landscape. The walls structure the space around the building, defining courtyards and terraces that transition through relaxed planting to the open landscape beyond. Cochran's work explores the relationship between architecture and the landscape around a site, and this garden showcases views through trees to hills and vineyards beyond. A sense of harmony is evoked by the restrained palette of materials and plants in neutral shades. Four ancient olive trees with sculptural, gnarled trunks give a grounded feel to the gravel entrance courtyard. Paths are delineated by large rectangular stepping stones set in gravel, while areas for gatherings have a restrained atmosphere and an infinity pool enjoys an expansive view of the landscape beyond. A sense of movement is added through the use of fulsomely planted *Muhlenbergia capillaris* (pink muhly grass) and pale-flowered gaura *Oenothera lindheimeri* (gaura) that catch the hillside breezes.

COLWELL SHELOR

GHOST WASH
Paradise Valley, Arizona, United States, 2017

Being based in Phoenix, Arizona, Michele Shelor of Colwell Shelor knows what and how to grow in the desert. So, even before construction began on a new contemporary desert home, she erased the oleander hedge – which was nearly 5 metres (16 feet) tall – around the periphery of the 1-hectare (2½-acre) private landscape. With that move, Camelback Mountain came into the picture, large and clear. Similarly, she removed non-native plant material. The rest of the garden project then waited for the house to be completed, including a state-of-the-art roof system for water collection and diversion. In an ultra-arid climate with scant rain that occurs primarily from July through to mid-September, the concept was to feed into a seasonal 'wash' (a temporary mini-river) to distribute stormwater and nourish an arid-plant meadow. When rains occur, the water is funnelled from the roof via the contrived (or 'ghost') wash, down to a central core strip of cacti adapted to the challenging climate. Cacti salvaged from the original planting and boulders harvested on site were elevated to art status. To remain faithful to the ecosystem, 'and feel like the site is part of the mountain', Shelor surveyed the nearby flora while construction was underway. For shade and privacy, she chose native *Olneya tesota* (desert ironwood) and *Parkinsonia microphylla* (foothill paloverde) trees. Brick is used for walls that echo the surrounding reddish soil. Throughout, cacti are celebrated for their beauty, especially outside the master bedroom, where a private walled panorama is planted with sculptural and colourful cacti against the brick.

TANIA COMPTON

ILIAS ESTATE
Peloponnese, Greece, 2018–

Formerly a magazine editor and now a respected garden designer known for her intensively planted yet ecologically minded approach, Tania Compton spent some formative years in the Mediterranean. When she was asked to create a new 0.5-hectare (1⅓-acre) garden on a 4-hectare (10-acre) estate in Greece, therefore, it felt like a kind of homecoming. On visiting the property, which has views across the Aegean Sea and towards the Taygetos mountains, the need to frame and enhance the setting – 'to channel the wilder landscape', as Compton puts it – became clear. Work started in 2018 with the removal of overgrown trees that cut off the house from its surroundings. A few mature trees, including a stately almond and characterful downy oaks, were left to anchor the design, which evolved to include five terraces, each offering a different yet equally dramatic prospect. Compton commissioned local craftspeople and builders to create a sympathetic network of hard landscape features, such as paths evocative of the traditional *kalderimia* (cobbled roads), walls and gravelled areas of local stone. Surrounding the terraces is a medley of cultivated and wild Mediterranean species, all adapted to the searing summer heat, which can reach 45°C (113°F). Most of the plants were sourced from the nursery of Olivier and Clara Filippi in the South of France, and while certain genera (among them *Euphorbia*, *Cistus*, *Lavandula* and *Salvia*) are repeated throughout, each terrace has its own palette of distinct cultivars. The result is unmistakably a garden, but one that harmonizes rather than competes with its uniquely beautiful setting.

**JASPER CONRAN
AND MADISON COX**

VILLA MABROUKA
Tangier, Morocco, early 1990s–2023

This beautiful modernist house built in the 1940s high on the cliffs of Tangier became the secluded sanctuary of fashion legends Yves Saint Laurent and Pierre Bergé in 1996. In 2019 British designer Jasper Conran bought the property and transformed it tastefully into a hotel. The lush 0.8-hectare (2-acre) garden – originally designed in 1997 by Madison Cox in collaboration with Saint Laurent and Bergé, and one of Tangier's largest and most enchanting – was laid across a series of gently tumbling terraces below the villa. The intention was to draw the eye over sweeping lawns and rich planting out towards the glittering sea and spectacular prospects north to the Strait of Gibraltar and over the North Atlantic. The garden was also part of the renovation project by Conran, who said that he wanted to be 'very respectful of the atmosphere Madison created for Pierre and Yves, while working to complement and extend it according to my own vision'. Beside the original 1930s' pool carved into the cliff stands one of two Moroccan pavilions added in the 1980s by American architect Stuart Church, when Villa Mabrouka was owned by a Kuwaiti sheikha. A new pool was also added. Old and new stone-flagged paths shaded by bamboo, glossy-leaved rubber trees (*Ficus elastica*) and palm trees wind around emerald lawns with juxtaposed borders and pots planted with a mix of architectonic structure (agave, banana, palm and papyrus), harmonious colour (bougainvillea, hibiscus, oleander and plumbago) and scent (citrus, jasmine, pelargonium and roses) to beguiling and sophisticated effect.

CLAUDE CORMIER

BLUE STICK GARDEN (LE JARDIN DE BÂTONS BLEUS)
Jardins de Métis/Reford Gardens, Métis-sur-Mer, Québec, Canada, 2000–09

Arguably the most influential landscape architect in Canada, the late Claude Cormier belonged to a generation of 'conceptualist' designers. Pioneered in the 1990s by Martha Schwartz (see p.259), conceptual gardens fuse garden and art installation, idea and narrative, with the belief that a garden is as much about experience as it is about plants. Cormier's breakthrough came in 2000 with this installation for the inaugural Métis Garden Festival in northern Quebec. It was inspired by two key elements of the Métis garden created by Elsie Reford in 1926–58: the Himalayan blue poppy (*Meconopsis* spp.), which thrives there, and the mixed border of the Long Walk created in the spirit of famed English plantswoman Gertrude Jekyll. A photograph of the poppy was scanned and fractalized, the blue pixels becoming sticks that were painted blue on three sides and orange on the fourth and 'planted' to form an abstract reproduction of the traditional Victorian mixed border. In the designer's words, the idea and narrative 'trace the evolution of our visual culture, from impressionist brushstrokes to digital outputs'. The experience of moving through the garden is one of shifting views and vistas: chromatic, engaging and surprising. The installation subsequently appeared temporarily at Canada Blooms (2002), Hestercombe Gardens in south-west England (2004), and the Old Port of Montréal (2006). To celebrate the tenth edition of the festival, it returned to Métis in 2009 as a permanent installation (raising the question of whether it has become a garden in its own right), and in 2013 it reappeared at the Cool Gardens design exhibition in Winnipeg. Following Cormier's death in 2023, the company name became CCxA.

KATE COULSON

LUBERON GARDEN
Provence, France, 2013–

Motivated to echo the formidable local landscape in both its appearance and demands, Kate Coulson has created an expansive dry garden of mellow, resolute grace. Having studied at The English Gardening School in London under Rosemary Campbell-Preston and established a more traditional garden at her home in Cumbria, northern England, Coulson underwent an epiphany in Kyoto, Japan, where wider domestic landscapes were crystallized into quiet, refined expressions of elemental year-round beauty. She knew this principle would be appropriate for her newly acquired 0.5-hectare (1-acre) property on an arid limestone ridge in the Luberon region of Provence and, initially aided by dry-garden authority Olivier Filippi (see p.12), set about establishing a self-sustaining 'curated landscape' of clipped shrubs, intensely drought-tolerant herbaceous plants, existing downy oak (*Quercus pubescens*) and stone pine (*Pinus pinea*), and flat-topped pillars of cypress. Rivers of *Iris pallida* – a 'weed' found at the roadside, of which the garden now hosts thousands – cast a chiffon delicacy through the muscular splendour of summer, while giant fennel and mulleins tower, eminent and vivid. 'I want to grow flowers in just blue and yellow, the colour of the sky and the sun,' says Coulson. Extraordinarily wild, cacophonous storms beset the property and arid summers can bring months of drought. Yet this is a dignified garden intimately wedded to its environment, a statement of dedication, humility and reverence, as Coulson declares: 'The water is running out, and I'm trying not to take anything from the land that I shouldn't.'

TOM COWARD (BEGUN BY WILLIAM ROBINSON)

GRAVETYE MANOR
East Grinstead, Sussex, England, 1885, 2010–

Gravetye Manor was marked in its day by horticultural innovation: an Arts and Crafts garden steeped in the progressive ideas of its pioneering creator, 19th-century gardener and writer William Robinson. At Gravetye, his home, 14 hectares (35 acres) of grounds were conceived in contrast to the prevailing Victorian taste for formality and artificial-style bedding with feral yet hardy plant species permitted to drift and swell as they might in the wild. *Muscari* (grape hyacinth) and *Narcissus poeticus* (poet's daffodil) ran through the long grass; *Leucojum* (summer snowflake) and lily through the woodland copse. Even bindweed had its place. With renewed purpose as a boutique hotel, the continuation and development of Gravetye's renowned garden have since 2010 been under the stewardship of esteemed head gardener Tom Coward. Trained at the Royal Botanic Gardens, Kew, and formerly deputy head gardener at Great Dixter in East Sussex (see p.106), Coward has great expertise as a 'flower gardener', and this has given Robinson's wild ethos a fresh lease of life under the guiding principles of diversity and abundance. Restoring and developing Gravetye's propagation infrastructure enabled Coward and his team to turn out volumes of impactful, successional, often newly introduced blooms, from early *Myosotis* (forget-me-nots) to *Hesperis*, lupins and dahlias, bringing unparalleled, extended profusion to the border displays. In addition to its revered kitchen garden, Gravetye is now celebrated as one of Britain's most intensive flower gardens. 'There's that saying about historic gardens,' says Coward: 'The approach should not be to copy the acts of great gardeners, but to continue seeking what they sought.'

SAM COX

WOODLEIGH SCHOOL SENIOR CAMPUS
Langwarrin South, Victoria, Australia, 2009–

In their Australian context – and particularly that of Victoria, where his practice is based – the gardens of Sam Cox are timeless. The school landscape he has designed and built on the traditional lands of the Bunurong people continues the bush-garden tradition initiated by landscape architect Edna Walling (1895–1973) with help from Ellis Stones (1895–1975), with whom Cox's mentor Gordon Ford worked in the early 1950s before striking out on his own. Cox established his practice after Ford's death in 1999. The quiet designs in this genre combine carefully placed rocks, earth-shaping and layered combinations of native plants that engage with the local environment, blurring the boundaries between garden and bush. They are a contrast to the latest trends in clipping and pruning to create an art form of a garden, and are arguably a more sustainable mode of gardening. At Woodleigh School, where the appreciation and conservation of the environment form part of the curriculum, the ongoing project on the 20-hectare (50-acre) site includes the development of an adjoining wildlife reserve. Around the school buildings, the careful positioning of granite boulders, asymmetric planting and informal gravel paths hint at a knowledge of the underlying principles of Japanese gardens, skilfully adapted to Australian conditions. Gravel paths bordered with carefully layered native plantings connect informal, multipurpose classrooms known as 'homesteads'. Sam Cox Landscape is also involved each year for a day when the school community replants areas of the school grounds, a tradition aptly called 'bush week'.

CPG CONSULTANTS

KHOO TECK PUAT HOSPITAL
Yishun, Singapore, 2010

From the start, the 795-bed Khoo Teck Puat Hospital was designed to be energy-efficient and enhance patient care. One way in which it has succeeded in the latter is to take full advantage of its 3.4-hectare (8½-acre) surroundings, particularly Yishun Pond, which is in fact a substantial lake. Thus CPG Consultants (which also worked on Gardens by the Bay; see p.113) developed the idea of 'hospital in a garden, garden in a hospital'. The pond and its attractive setting (home to 96 bird species, 70 plant species and more than 100 each of insect and fish species) became a central element around which the hospital complex of four relatively small blocks is arranged so that all open out to it. The soothing borrowed landscape is thereby drawn into the hospital, while the shoreline offers paths for exercise. The buildings themselves are greened with therapeutic garden spaces. The main entrance has a landscaped canopy, and three of the blocks overlook the heart of the hospital, a peaceful, shady, verdant courtyard – which also opens to Yishun Pond – dotted with seating areas and private nooks. Adjacent are eighty-one balconies (each with planter boxes), five levels of corridor planters and eight roof gardens. Some of these rooftop spaces cater to specific patient needs and have controlled access, while others are gardened by volunteers and produce organic fruit, herbs and vegetables for the hospital's patients. The ornamental planting throughout is low maintenance but lush and more than 70 per cent native, including many endangered species.

CRAIG REYNOLDS LANDSCAPE ARCHITECTS

PRIVATE GARDEN
Key West, Florida, United States, 2020

Craig Reynolds – principal of Craig Reynolds Landscape Architects, a practice that focuses solely on residential design – is at home with the tropics, describing this region as 'my speciality'. He was contacted when a hurricane sent a tree crashing down in Key West, demolishing one of several homes in a private compound. Rather than rebuild, the owners opted to tie together the remaining dwellings on their 1,000-square-metre (¼-acre) site using a courtyard garden. But, far from the typical approach, Reynolds created an instant macro-jungle complete with koi pond and pool. To achieve a feeling of history and a handshake with the locality, he used native oolite stone, a distinctive, naturally porous material that quickly ages into place. For the focal koi pond, he draped creeping groundcover tropicals, such as *Pilea glauca* (grey baby tears), *Hedera* (ivy) and *Phyllanthus myrtifolius* (mousetail plant), where they would hastily serve as cover-ups. 'In the tropics,' he explains, 'you install a plant and it grows instantly.' Meanwhile, the pond (which uses ultraviolet filtration) is now home to various aquatic flora. The next layer up is dominated by bromeliads, heliconias, philodendrons and similar tropicals with intriguing foliage, in characteristically impressive, large-footprint sweeps of each species that Reynolds refers to as 'tropical prairie'. The upper layer is home to various palms and *Ficus* installed as mature plants to create instant ambiance and shade. Several seating areas (including a hanging swing and a cabana/porch extending from one of the houses) give the opportunity to admire the ecosystem and commune with nature.

DANGAR BARIN SMITH

PRIVATE GARDEN
Bellevue Hill, Sydney, New South Wales, Australia, 2014

The gardens of William Dangar (who founded his firm, Dangar Barin Smith, in 1991) are synonymous with Sydney's eastern beach and harbourside suburbs. The city's gardeners have been enamoured with subtropical species since the early days of its botanic garden in the early 19th century, and the lush, architectural species Dangar uses are in this tradition. At Bellevue Hill on the traditional lands of the Gadigal and Birrabirragal people, Dangar has designed a suburban garden to complement the sensitive renovation of a distinctive modernist 1960s house. An enormous *Ficus microcarpa* var. *hillii* (Hill's fig) with imposing aerial roots was the pre-eminent aspect of the garden. Dangar chose to keep the surrounding planting simple, with *Trachelospermum jasminoides* (star jasmine) and *Philodendron*. Mass hedge planting of *Rhapis* palms shields the garden from the street, while to one side of the pool is a group of *Howea forsteriana* (Kentia palms), transplanted from within the garden. Elsewhere, statuesque yuccas rise from a sea of blue succulent *Senecio*. Dangar's clever use of architecturally striking succulents to contrast with the white modernist architecture of the house gives instant effect. A mass of the tough *Furcraea foetida*, a species common to early colonial Sydney gardens, planted between two walls is complemented by variegated *Dracaena trifasciata* (mother-in-law's tongue) in a planter at an upper level. Honed over a career of more than thirty years, Dangar's planting style is marked by a generosity of foliage, texture and architectural forms layered to provide depth.

ELEFTHERIOS DARIOTIS

THE GOAT GARDEN
Paiania, Athens, Greece, 2015–

Eleftherios Dariotis is an irrepressible, maverick plant fanatic with a background in plant science and horticulture. After studying in the United States and England, he returned to his Greek homeland to work as a licensed specialist bulb and seed supplier. He travels to Mediterranean- and desert-climate biodiversity hotspots, his mission to support the collections of botanic gardens and widen the choice of commercially available seeds through his own business. His design portfolio is limited to his own experimental Greek gardens and those of a few close associates, and he is foremost a plantsman – one in a strong position to diversify his own planting palette. The Goat Garden in Paiania, an eastern suburb of Athens, is a naturalistic, drought-tolerant town garden of 300 square metres (3,230 square feet), wrapping around Dariotis's uncle's summer villa. This compact, unique 'front garden' is home to a mind-blowing 500 plant species. Inspired by natural ecosystems, unwatered and pruned only in the winter, it functions as both a living seed bank and a planting test ground. Dariotis has created a garden for close observation, where Cypriot salvias grow alongside the lofty spirals of *Echium onosmifolium* collected in Gran Canaria. The slender trunks and light canopy of Sicilian *Genista aetnensis* (Mount Etna broom) and Iberian *Retama sphaerocarpa* (yellow broom) provide structure and some shade, and the understorey is a scattering of tough, silver-leaved *Phlomis*, *Cistus* and *Teucrium* alongside an evolving kaleidoscope of a plant-collector's resilient, rare gems.

DDS PROJECTS

ENDEMIC SCHOOL GROUNDS
Green School, Paarl, South Africa, 2024

Founded in 2011 by landscaper and plantsman Danie Steenkamp, DDS Projects is drawn to work that has an integral environmental or cultural context. This magical landscape, with its endangered flora and inspiring views, is the perfect setting for a 'green' school that focuses on creative education, sustainability and environmental awareness while tapping in to natural curiosity and youthful wonder. What was once flat, overgrazed pastureland has been sculpted into 7 hectares (17 acres) of excitement and adventure. It is interwoven with paths – some covered by arbours constructed from poles of invasive *Acacia* (black wattle) – and organically shaped berms, and an edible garden links the site from kindergarten to senior school. All construction materials were locally sourced, including woodchips, bricks and laterite (a decomposed granite). Raised beds of homemade compost are perfect for learning to grow vegetables, while orchards of apples, pears, mangoes and more than ten varieties of citrus are underplanted with native and exotic herbs for pest control and biodiversity. The surrounding flora has also been welcomed into the grounds so that the pupils learn to appreciate its value and the importance of conservation. Critically endangered Renosterveld, a unique element of the fynbos biome, is home to shrubs predominantly from the Asteraceae family, as well as grasses, annuals and a diverse bulbous flora that creates a mass of colour in the spring. The whole garden is a thriving ecosystem in which education is enriched through children engaging with nature, so that it becomes part of their daily lives.

DEBORAH NEVINS & ASSOCIATES

STAVROS NIARCHOS FOUNDATION CULTURAL CENTER
Athens, Greece, 2016

'My goal is always to create a design in which architecture, ecology, programme and landscape respond to each other,' says Deborah Nevins of her approach. Commissioned to collaborate with architectural firm Renzo Piano Building Workshop on a landscape for the 16-hectare (40-acre) Stavros Niarchos Foundation Cultural Center in Athens, her New York-based landscape-architecture practice Deborah Nevins & Associates worked together with local landscape architect Helli Pangalou, to craft a design that would 'speak Greek'. To realize that vision botanically, they began the project in 2008 by approaching several nurseries specializing in Mediterranean natives to supply 'mother' plants that furnished cuttings for propagation. Grasses that now carpet green roofs on the opera house, library and garage were propagated from seeds collected from the hills of Attica. The total number of plants installed is staggering: 164,000 grass plugs, and 128,000 perennials and shrubs. The firm selected a textural broadloom of endemic plants adapted to the Mediterranean climate, with intriguing leaves and stems as well as flowers. Olive, fig, pomegranate, carob and almond trees also play their part. These drought-tolerant choices form textural blocks in geometric beds transected by numerous walkways that run not only straight but also diagonally, with a gradual grade for accessible access. Sensitive, sustainable solutions prevail throughout the landscape, including irrigation using a process of reverse osmosis, and strategies to collect water and prevent flooding. In this celebration of the locality in all senses, nothing is lost in translation.

TOPHER DELANEY AND CALVIN CHIN

IN THE LINE OF FIRE
San Francisco, California, United States, 2007

A small rectangular courtyard in San Francisco is the setting for an evocative installation by Topher Delaney, a student of cultural anthropology and philosophy whose design ethos is underpinned by phenomenology (the philosophy of experience). Her belief is similar to the early 18th-century concept of philosopher Anthony Ashley Cooper, 3rd Earl of Shaftesbury, that landscapes have a spirit – the *genius loci* – that interacts with the human mind to foster emotion. Understanding that a garden imparts a narrative to the viewer, Delaney believes her work 'reflects the collaboration between the narrator (the person who's asked me to do the garden) and [me as] the interpreter. It's a little reversed from what this profession is about.' She sees her designer's role as being to reveal the garden's message through a mixture of the client's requirements and personality, the site, art, and (innovative) materials, so that exposure to – and involvement with – the garden will generate a personal, interconnected conception, context and perception of it. Here, the focus of the garden is the towering, shade-giving *Magnolia grandiflora*; its gnarled, informal deep green sculpture contrasting with the clean lines, cool grey tones and perpendicular linearity of uplit walls and steps. The minimalist manicured horizontality of the gravel surface has echoes of the Japanese *karesansui* (dry garden), and the notion of the 'presence of absence'. But here, rather than from moss-encrusted boulders, verticality comes in the form of dramatic flames that frame the tree trunk in front and behind, introducing hot colours and dynamism into the otherwise tranquil scene.

DOMINIQUE AND BENOÎT DELOMEZ

JARDIN INTÉRIEUR À CIEL OUVERT
Athis-de-l'Orne, Normandy, France, 2000–11

In their transformation of a wetland into a 0.3-hectare (¾-acre) contemporary garden, visual artists Dominique and Benoît Delomez have created a multidimensional vision. They developed it piece by piece, building different universes of shape, level, colour and graphics. Closed, confidential spaces contrast with more open areas, while the ever-present water serves as a common thread, most notably in the large pond that reflects the house. The entrance to the garden slips into a narrow passage along a shaded stream covered with duckweed, and continues through dense undergrowth and a 'nest' of bamboo. The Delomezes installed a series of wooden pontoons above the ferns, to allow the wet parts of the garden to be crossed. Emerging from these shadowy areas, the garden suddenly opens up to a new pond and a circular viewing terrace. There, a waterfall and its artwork, a Plexiglas cube, allow a different view of the garden, through this revealing prism. At the turn of a laurel alley, a productive vegetable garden in tones of red, green and black emerges, lush even as summer ends. Large mirrors reflect images that fragment and multiply the views, and also seem to split the space. This is one of the fantasies of this remarkable garden, where contemporary elements and unusual objects are boldly introduced. It is clear that its creators are happy to subvert the conventional approaches to garden design.

DEVONSHIRE, 12TH DUKE AND DUCHESS OF, WITH TOM STUART-SMITH, DAN PEARSON AND JAMES HITCHMOUGH

CHATSWORTH HOUSE
Bakewell, Derbyshire, England, 2015–21

Chatsworth is a historic garden of great stature, with a long tradition of integrating new with old. The 12th Duke and Duchess have continued this with input from three leading designers, who have effected the most significant transformation in the garden for 200 years. Dan Pearson redeveloped the Trout Stream and Jack Pond (2015–20), while Tom Stuart-Smith contributed to three projects (2018–21): developing a 'more comprehensive, naturalistic and ecologically inspired' planting of the 1.2-hectare (3-acre) Rock Garden originally created by the estate's influential head gardener Joseph Paxton in 1842; revamping the Maze borders with additional yew topiary and more traditional herbaceous planting; and producing a masterplan for a central, previously underdeveloped 6 hectares (15 acres), now named 'Arcadia'. Here, four meadow-like glades contain more than 300,000 new plants and trees. The Rabbit Glade is a tapestry of spring flowers followed by *Geranium*, *Heuchera* and other low-growing gems. The wet glade, known as the Bog Garden, exploits moisture from nearby streams to support swamp cypress, *Rodgersia*, *Gunnera* and ferns, among other damp-loving species. The Meadow Glade is the work of James Hitchmough, University of Sheffield professor emeritus, who designed a seed mix of more than 70 perennials to flower from March to July. Finally, the 100 Steps Glade (pictured); its planting forges links with the wider landscape, using perennials and grasses as well as shrubs, such as *Hydrangea* and *Euonymus*. Stuart-Smith (see p.277), Pearson (see p.224) and Hitchmough (see p.132) are just the latest notables to have their work grace these remarkable gardens.

ERIK DHONT

BONEMHOEVE
Damme, West Flanders, Belgium, 2005

Experiencing the transformative power of a garden, according to landscape architect Erik Dhont, is 'like flying away in your mind'. Following the sight lines of artistically mown pathways 'drawn' by a gardener, or studying the flickering reflections of pollarded willows on the surface of a pond, we release our cares. Dhont, who founded his eponymous firm in 1989, is renowned for his deep knowledge of the cultural history of Belgium and for the integration of modernist aesthetics with a commitment to ecological design. At Bonemhoeve, a 26-hectare (62-acre) estate garden in northwestern Belgium, the mission called for preserving privacy around a restored farmhouse while respecting the rural landscape of canals. Existing poplar and lime trees were thinned or pruned, while new trees, including *Quercus robur* (English oak), *Ilex aquifolium* (holly) and *Cornus mas* (Cornelian cherry), were planted. Canals and ponds were reclaimed and replanted. Site-specific works of contemporary art, including sculptures by Richard Long, Antony Gormley, Thomas Houeago, and Angus King, juxtapose stone and bronze against the ephemerality of plants. Since 2013, head gardener Gijsbert Smid has extended Dhont's plan to transform Bonemhoeve from an intensively fertilized and pesticide-treated site to an ecologically managed estate that includes an organic vegetable garden, orchards, unique topiary and beds brimming with successive perennials. Smid says he has become fused with his pruning shears, reshaping the garden and creating living sculptures that evolve each year. Birds, insects and works of art are equally accommodated throughout this exuberant refuge of nature and culture.

ROY DIBLIK

LOUIS SULLIVAN ARCH
Chicago, Illinois, United States, 2009

Located beside the Modern Wing of the Art Institute of Chicago is a garden designed by Midwestern plantsman Roy Diblik, one of the most influential and prominent plantspeople in the United States today. He cofounded the legendary plant nursery North Wind in Burlington, Wisconsin, which is a leading light in American horticulture. Diblik, who had planted the North and South courtyards at the Art Institute in 2007, was asked in 2008 to create a planting design that would 'carry the emotions' of the famous Lurie Garden in nearby Millennium Park (2004) by Piet Oudolf and GGN. Inspired in addition by French artist Pierre Bonnard's painting *Earthly Paradise* (1916–20), which is in the Art Institute's collection, Diblik designed a plant palette that echoed its colourful tones. The planting design includes a mix of short, textural grasses, including *Sporobolus heterolepis* (prairie dropseed) and *Molinia caerulea* subsp. *arundinacea* 'Transparent', that form a matrix, around which are woven such colourful perennials as *Sanguisorba tenuifolia* var. *tenuifolia*, *Lobelia siphilitica*, *Echinacea* 'North Wind' and *Penstemon* 'Pocahontas', which repeat and blend, creating patterns that flow through the space. There were some initial problems with lawn-grass seed that was germinating and appearing in the planting, but once this was addressed the scheme flourished, and it continues to inspire visitors to the gallery.

PAGE DICKEY AND BOSCO SCHELL

CHURCH HOUSE
Falls Village, Connecticut, United States, 2015–

Page Dickey, an acclaimed garden designer and prolific author of numerous award-winning gardening books, and her husband, the equally avid gardener Bosco Schell, have created a stunning 7-hectare (17-acre) garden on their property in the foothills of the Berkshire mountains. After leaving their well-known home and garden of more than thirty years, Duck Hill in Westchester County, New York, the couple began anew at Church House, a meeting house dating from 1793. This new garden in the bucolic countryside of northwest Connecticut was guided by the existing landscape, especially its breathtaking mountain views. The emphasis is on wildness and on leaving open space and sky to maintain those majestic views. Inspiration came from entomologist and ecologist Douglas Tallamy's philosophy of bringing nature home, such that lawns give way to meadows, becoming welcoming habitats for birds, butterflies and bees. Much of the property is uncultivated, with woodlands and fen given permission to be wild. The plant palette is mostly native, which suits the challenging alkaline limestone, allowing *Quercus muehlenbergii* (chinquapin oaks), sedges, grasses and numerous wildflowers to thrive. The organically managed garden also includes an orchard, a small greenhouse and a cutting garden, with low stone walls, gravel pathways and paths mown through the meadows. Around the house, beds and borders planted with native wildflowers bring the wildness of the woods closer to home. The custodians of Church House are passionate stewards of the land, inviting all manner of wildlife to share their garden.

**DIDIER DESIGN STUDIO
WITH PHYTO STUDIO AND
LAKE FLATO ARCHITECTS**

**POLLINATOR AND
BIRD GARDEN**
The Arboretum at Penn State, State College,
Pennsylvania, United States, 2022

Flipping the script on the standard pollinator garden, this 1.4-hectare (3½-acre) creation presents a startlingly immersive new prototype. Instead of bringing wildlife *back*, this public garden is about bringing people *into* the world of pollinators, even into the private chamber of a stylized beehive. The journey begins with a walk towards an immense sculptural disc, tilted slightly upwards and teeming with plant life. Moving around its elevated base, the visitor is at eye level with myriad wild bees, hoverflies, wasps and honeybees buzzing from flower to flower. With each step forward, the multilayered landscape unfolds in an intimate reveal designed to open our eyes to what insects and birds need to survive at a time of global climate crisis. Visitors can learn more by entering the beehive-like structure, or look out of the nearby birdhouse (designed as part of this multifaceted project by Lake Flato Architects) to observe songbirds in flight, foraging for insects over the boulder-lined pond. The design evolved from the science, with lead landscape architect Emmanuel Didier and planting designer Claudia West of Phyto Studio collaborating with entomologists at the Center for Pollinator Research and the ornithology department at Penn State University to construct an ecosystem comprising ultra-diverse habitat and a sequence of model gardens. From engineered soil types to variable water sources and from shrubs and trees to flowers, each selection supports specific populations of flora and fauna. This smart pollinator and bird garden is now a living laboratory for the landgrant university itself, even as students and visitors discover the timeless joys of simply hanging out with birds, microbes and bees.

HELEN DILLON

THE DILLON GARDEN
Dublin, Republic of Ireland, 1974–2016

In 1973 Helen Dillon and her husband, Val, laid out their now famous 0.2-hectare (½-acre) garden in the smart Dublin neighbourhood of Ranelagh. Helen, an irrepressible gardener, has shared her carefree approach not only through many books and television appearances, but also by opening the gates to her personal garden. From the beginning she embraced change and experimentation, drawing inspiration from many sources. She once wrote, 'Don't be afraid of the colour orange,' and has lived by her lessons, always encouraging people to find pleasure in their gardens, while also rehabilitating seemingly unfashionable plants, such as *Alstroemeria*, through her enthusiasm. In the mid-1990s she made the bold decision to replace the lawn with a dramatic 28-metre-long (92-foot) pool inspired by the Islamic design she had seen at the Alhambra palace in Granada, Spain. As well as her long, flower-filled borders, on either side of this reflective stage she arranged many hundreds of pots that Val described as a cast of players to be rotated and reimagined throughout the year. In 2005 she redesigned the entrance to the house to include a grove of *Betula utilis* subsp. *albosinensis* (Chinese red-barked birch), informed by her experience of Russian birch woods. This comparatively understated front garden did little to prepare the visitor for the riot of colour and form in the main garden, but was all the more successful for it. In 2016 the Dillons decided to downsize and sell their Ranelagh home and the joyful garden to allow for fresh creative input in a new garden.

D.I.R.T. STUDIO WITH PRINCE CONCEPTS

CORE CITY PARK
Detroit, Michigan, United States, 2019

This privately owned, public park was home to the Detroit Fire Department's Engine 12 and Ladder 9 from the 1890s until the firehouse was razed in the 1970s, and evolved over time into an abandoned, overgrown car park. However, in an unusual move, property developer Philip Kafka, founder and president of Prince Concepts, saw the power of the landscape and launched a project to regenerate it, creating a mixed-use commercial plaza and green space. He enlisted landscape architect Julie Bargmann of D.I.R.T. Studio (Dump It Right There – reflecting Bargmann's resourceful approach) to design a 743-square-metre (8,000-square-foot) pocket park at its centre. Her concept was to turn the space into an urban woodland. D.I.R.T. was assisted by architect Ishtiaq Rafiuddin of Undecorated and Lincoln MacKensie of Mack Landscaping. Most of the construction materials were salvaged from the site, including sections of the demolished fire station, such as the original cornerstone inscribed with the year 1893. Bargmann's aim was to preserve the original identity and accentuate the existing landscape. No engineers were used and no construction documents were produced, only beautiful hand drawings as needed during digging. The 'woodland' comprises a leafy canopy of eighty-seven trees, including *Cornus florida* (flowering dogwood) and *Gleditsia triacanthos* (honey locust). Scattered understorey plantings of ferns, native violets and irises emerge from a pathless expanse of crushed black slag, a byproduct of local steelmaking. The plants mingle with such found relics as reclaimed bricks and concrete slabs for seating, to celebrate Detroit's natural and urban elements.

DOXIADIS+

LANDSCAPES OF COHABITATION
Antiparos, Greece, 2004–

In 2002 Greek landscape architect Thomas Doxiadis, founder of Doxiadis+, and his colleague Terpsithea Kremali were commissioned to landscape areas ranging between 1 and 30 hectares (2.5 and 74 acres) around a development of low-density housing on a steep, wedge-shaped hillside on the island of Antiparos. The result – for which Doxiadis+ reached the finals of the 2018 Rosa Barba International Landscape Architecture Prize – blends almost seamlessly with the established local ecosystem, which is low-growing, windswept and stunningly beautiful. Great care was taken to avoid the destruction of the site during the construction, and excavated earth was reused to restore existing drystone terracing on the lower slopes. The challenge was to organize durable, drought-tolerant plantings that would be visible from many angles, showing each small variation to best advantage. New access roads, barely seen, follow the contours of the gradual incline overlooking the Aegean Sea, amid a succession of varied tapestries. The lower reaches are slightly lusher than the scrubland above. New plantings close to the houses provide a tended garden, and inspection reveals an enrichment of the plant selection in these areas. The fractal, interweaving patterns of spontaneous vegetation are imitated by planting in percentage mixes, so that what is dominant in one area becomes minor in the next. Further afield, more space is allowed for natural re-vegetation between the plants, colonized by such natives as *Centaurea spinosa* and *Calendula arvensis* (field marigold), as well as for areas seeded with agricultural crops and native shrubs. Where possible the local juniper (*Juniperus macrocarpa*) was preserved to further blend with the surroundings.

MONIQUE AND THIERRY DRONET

LE JARDIN DE BERCHIGRANGES
Granges-Aumontzey, Lorraine, France, 1984–

Nestled high in the Vosges mountains of eastern France, Le Jardin de Berchigranges is a lush and botanically diverse paradise. The garden has a powerful emotional effect on visitors, who not infrequently are moved to tears upon their first sight of the 3-hectare (7½-acre) garden, developed as an ongoing project by Monique and Thierry Dronet over decades. The garden presents its visitors with contrasts between clipped hedges, dense perennial borders and wildly experimental meadow planting. Bold innovation is key, Thierry having been a lifelong researcher and practitioner of ecological building techniques and Monique having a background in running a nursery for cottage-garden plants. The older, more 'conventional' parts of the garden, defined by lawn and borders, give way to experimentation down the slope that dominates the site. The wet local climate has led the Dronets to develop a shaded moss garden, while the local availability of decay-resistant *Robinia* timber has led them to make some unusual wooden ravines, which sprout ferns and other plants. The Bohemian Meadow is a surprisingly successful blend of the kind of perennials normally seen only in border plantings and local flora; late-summer perennials flourish among native grasses – a feat that is rarely managed, and here almost certainly thanks to the short growing season, which limits the growth of the grass. Le Jardin de Berchigranges is undoubtedly a true horticultural high-wire act, but one that works thanks to the knowledge and continued dedication of its creators, and their unique partnership. They clearly know just how close to the edge they can go.

NIGEL DUNNETT

BEECH GARDENS
Barbican Centre, London, England, 2013–16

The decision to build the 16-hectare (40-acre) Barbican Centre was as bold as its Brutalist architecture. The residential blocks of various heights, set on a podium, were designed by architectural firm Chamberlin, Powell and Bon and constructed between 1965 and 1976. Designed to bring life back to a part of the City of London devastated in the World War II, the green spaces between the buildings are integral to the masterplan. Residents and visitors navigate the traffic-free estate via paved walkways and plazas, and there are three ornamental gardens: the Lake Terrace, the Conservatory and the Beech Gardens. Elevated above street level on the estate podium, the Beech Gardens are effectively an accessible roof garden. By 2013 the original high-maintenance planting of a traditional mix of trees, shrubs and flower beds was in need of structural work, and Nigel Dunnett – a planting designer renowned for his innovative approach and expertise in designing high impact ecological planting (such as for the London 2012 Queen Elizabeth Olympic Park) – was commissioned to create sustainable plant communities defined by the distinct microclimates. Steppe planting includes species adapted to the exposed, dry conditions, and multi-stemmed trees and compact shrubs bring structure, height and mid-layer definition to some areas. A selection of plants based on form and foliage shape ensures diversity of texture, enlivened by season-long waves of vibrant flowers. Brick paths meander through naturalistic planting, and the visitor can sit and reflect in quiet areas among planting and small pools. This is a wonderful example of contemporary planting design adding human scale to a large space.

ISABEL DUPRAT

RAMP HOUSE GARDEN
São Paulo, Brazil, 2014

Integrating architecture with its surroundings and the natural landscape is a fundamental principle of landscape architecture for influential Brazilian designer Isabel Duprat. After graduating, she obtained an internship with world-famous Brazilian landscape architect Roberto Burle Marx, and gained experience of public urban projects during several years working in São Paulo's parks department, before founding her own practice in 1983. For this residential project, her wish to retain the existing beautiful specimen of *Cenostigma pluviosum* (*sibipiruna* or partridgewood) meant the architect had to change the position of the new house, building above the level of the old structure to protect the tree's roots. The garden takes its name from the ramp that was required as a result of this plant-driven decision. Duprat brings such attention to detail and respect for nature to every project she undertakes. The 850-square-metre (9,000-square-foot) site was formerly overlooked by tall buildings that reduced privacy and appeared to diminish the scale of the space. Duprat designs with light in mind, and here patterns of sunlight, shade and the contrasts between them play a significant role. She designed the pool to be a reflecting surface to illuminate a potentially dark area. Pale paving echoes changes in the tone of the sky over the course of the day. The layers of lush vegetation were chosen for architectural form, foliage shape and suitability to the site conditions, and the sun's enhancing effect on foliage colour and texture adds vibrancy.

RICK ECKERSLEY

MUSK COTTAGE
Flinders, Mornington Peninsula, Victoria, Australia, 2006–14

'I tried to make a quintessentially Australian garden,' says garden designer Rick Eckersley of his former 4-hectare (10-acre) garden at Musk Cottage, south of Melbourne. With help from friend and former colleague Myles Broad, Eckersley spent about eight years creating the garden, which balances deep sensitivity to place with exuberance and playfulness. As founder of Eckersley Garden Architecture, Eckersley has been influential in Australian landscape design for more than forty years. His own garden offered him the opportunity to experiment, free from the constraints of working for clients. 'I wanted to break new territory but stay within the profile of the Australian landscape,' he says. 'I just tipped it upside down, pulled it apart and restitched it.' The first clue to the garden's unique character is the huge pine tree reclining across the entry path. Walking underneath its arcing trunk is like entering a portal, where the familiar becomes unlikely. As if on cue, a grid of black-trunked ironbark trees (*Eucalyptus sideroxylon*) punctuate snaking clouds of clipped privet, while the sinuous gravel path expands and contracts as it draws the visitor in. The spaces are huge, but the scale is intimate. It is a garden for meandering, where close attention is repeatedly rewarded by small surprises: plant combinations, sculptural elements, vistas concealed and revealed. Not only is this surprising – and important – garden a clear expression of Eckersley's idiosyncratic approach to planting and design, but also it paints a vision of what a truly Australian garden might be.

AUSTIN EISCHEID

KINGWOOD CENTER GARDENS
Mansfield, Ohio, United States, 2020

Kingwood Center Gardens opened to the public in the 1950s and has grown significantly since, gaining a reputation for offering visitors 'transformative experiences'. Following a period of fundraising, renovations were carried out that included the addition of new areas. The Grand Perennial Garden was installed in the spring of 2020 and includes the New Perennial Meadow, which covers an area of 557 square metres (6,000 square feet), and represents an idealized meadow of perennials from all over the world. The masterplan for this area came from landscape architecture firm Terra Design Studio. Referencing the work of Dutch plantsman Piet Oudolf (see p.101 and p.216), kidney-shaped lawns are surrounded with planting by Oudolf protégé Austin Eischeid. Species of *Molinia* and *Sanguisorba* reach over the path, brushing against passers-by and enveloping them from the moment they enter the garden. In the centre the planting is lower, comprising a matrix that includes *Sesleria* and *Eragrostis* – more contrived in feeling but with the aim of opening out the area and encouraging people to picnic on the grass. Eischeid describes a path that leads to the estate's 1920s mansion, Kingwood Hall, as a 'grassy walkway where visitors can glide through a matrix' of planting. The surrounding trees posed a challenge, and so for this matrix he wanted to repeat plants that could tolerate both sun and shade, for continuity and cohesion. Here he used *Astilbe* 'Delft Lace', *Calamagrostis* × *acutiflora* 'Karl Foerster', *Amsonia tabernaemontana*, *Heliopsis helianthoides* var. *scabra* 'Summer Nights', *Deschampsia cespitosa* 'Goldtau' and *Sesleria autumnalis* in an exuberant, textured tapestry that delights the eye.

HELEN ELKS-SMITH

PRIVATE GARDEN
near Winchester, Hampshire, England, 2018

A simple, coherent design by Helen Elks-Smith gives this striking contemporary house within a 2,400-square-metre (25,800-square-foot) walled garden a sense of place. Elks-Smith, who set up her award-winning practice in 2005, calls on her background in mathematics to foreground spatially led design, blending technical expertise with artistic vision. Here, she felt a pared-down design was needed to resolve the connection between two attention-grabbing features: the house and the listed garden wall. Materials are limited to basalt paving for the two terraces, two linear reflecting pools, and through-flowing hardwood decking that connects the different spaces for dining and relaxing. The restrained palette of plants consists of carefully selected forms that link the garden to the adjacent trees. Existing trees were retained, and plants that added height were key. By borrowing and repeating plant forms, Elks-Smith aimed to bring everything into scale. Grasses – among them *Calamagrostis × acutiflora* 'Karl Foerster' – and perennials including *Veronicastrum virginicum* 'Album' and *Acanthus spinosus* (spiny bear's breeches) emphasize the vertical, while mound-shaped shrubs, including *Choisya ternata* (Mexican orange blossom), santolina and *Salvia officinalis* (sage), ensure softness. The palette of bronze, purple, russet and pink, seen in the amber bark of *Prunus maackii* (Manchurian cherry), the soft pinks of *Molinia caerulea* subsp. *caerulea* 'Moorhexe' (purple moor grass), coppery *Digitalis parviflora* (foxglove) and the deep maroon *Sanguisorba* 'Joni', tones with the house's cladding of red cedar and the hue of the original walls. All these considerations allow the garden to clothe the strong lines of house and wall with a unifying calm.

ELYSIAN LANDSCAPES

STORE FRONTAGE FOR BALENCIAGA
West Hollywood, California, United States, 2008

Fashion house Balenciaga is particularly popular among young people, who are drawn to the bold, unique aesthetic of its statement pieces that combine avant-garde design with high-fashion sensibility. Communicating a brand philosophy through the store's environment is often the first layer of experience for a customer, and it was the task of Judy Kameon, founding partner of multidisciplinary design studio Elysian Landscapes, to create a strong first impression when asked to landscape this West Hollywood store entrance. Inspired by the Balenciaga website, which described the interior of the store as a 'lunar landscape', the design encompassed a 1,365-square-metre (14,700-square-foot) street frontage that combines influences from the botanic garden in Oaxaca (see p.294), the Museo Anahuacalli in Mexico City and the film *Blade Runner* (1982). This creative fusion was interpreted through tall, ghostly cacti and succulents in tones of blue and silver, and *Strelitzia nicolai* (giant bird of paradise) floating on a sea of black gravel washing around lava boulders among islands of tawny-leaved *Kalanchoe beharensis* (felt bush), creamy-yellow and pale blue–green *Euphorbia ammak* 'Variegata' (giant milk bush), and silvery-spined *Cleistocactus strausii* (silver torch). Architectural plants were chosen for the shady areas, including clump-forming *Liriope muscari* (lilyturf) and fragrant *Pelargonium tomentosum* (peppermint-scented geranium), while raised concrete planters, designed to mimic the display cases inside the store, are filled with silvery succulents instead of the company's coveted handbags and footwear. The building itself, covered in vines and almost completely consumed by nature, clashes with this minimalist lunar landscape.

ENZO ENEA

ENEA TREE MUSEUM
Rapperswil-Jona, St Gallen, Switzerland, 2010

Founded in 2010, and designed by Swiss landscape architect and artist Enzo Enea, the Enea Tree Museum is set within a spacious 7.5-hectare (18-acre) park on the shore of Lake Zurich. The oval open-air museum is a refuge for salvaged trees, on a property that is also home to the Enea Landscape Architecture headquarters. The meticulously curated selection of approximately fifty tree specimens represents more than twenty-five species that Enea has collected over a period of nearly thirty years. He rescued the trees exclusively from the local climate zone, all of which were marked for felling. Arranged in a series of 'rooms', each specimen is treated and exhibited as preciously as any museum object, with delicate landscape work highlighting its unique attributes and beauty. Tall walls crafted from Italian sandstone frame each tree, where they are carefully positioned to maintain views of open sky and showcase their magnificent structural forms. As is typical of Enea's garden, the design highlights each tree individually, creating depth while contributing to a balanced microclimate. Specimens range in age from forty to more than a hundred years old, and in size from 4.5 to 12 metres (15–40 feet), and include English yew, weeping willow, Japanese maple, Scotch pine and bald cypress. Sculptures by contemporary artists engage with the theme of nature, standing alongside the trees and reviving the age-old dialogue between art and nature. The Tree Museum embodies Enea's vision, allowing him, for the first time, to seamlessly integrate landscape, botany, architecture, art and design.

EMILY ERLAM

EXPERIMENTAL STATION
Dungeness, Kent, England, 2013

Dungeness is a large shingle headland on the southeastern coast of England, in Kent. This unusual location became better known after filmmaker and writer Derek Jarman created a garden, Prospect Cottage, there in the 1980s, in the shadow of the nuclear power station. This 400-square-metre (4,300-square-foot) garden by landscape designer Emily Erlam sits within an area known as the Experimental Station, a place where marine equipment was once tested. Her clients requested a garden inspired by Prospect Cottage and by Piet Oudolf's perennial planting style (see p.101 and p.216), since they imagined that the enduring seedheads so characteristic of Oudolf's planting would provide good winter interest. The climate of Dungeness proved very challenging – extremely windy and very dry – and Erlam had to work hard to find a plant palette that would tolerate it. She focused on plants that would provide a good skeletal structure in winter, and created planting zones to mimic the landforms seen on the windswept beach, while being careful to avoid encouraging pernicious weeds. Clean soil, combined with a mulch of rotted manure and heavy gravel, helped to prevent the weeds. Some plants that Erlam initially thought badly placed earned their keep, for example *Persicaria* 'Darjeeling', which 'looked a bit twee when it was first planted' but turned into a brilliant brown mat in the winter months. The plant community has developed year on year, bringing an unusual character to the garden and setting off the seedheads elegantly.

ESTUDIO OME

FOREST GARDEN
Valle de Bravo, Mexico City, Mexico, 2020

Susana Rojas Saviñón and Hortense Blanchard founded their design studio in 2018 and the Forest Garden – one of their earliest projects – won a Landezine International Landscape Award. As they considered the wooded, steeply sloping, 1.2-hectare (3-acre) landscape surrounding the house designed by architect Rozana Montiel, they asked themselves, 'How do you live with the forest?' Strict parameters stated that only 1 per cent of vegetation per hectare could be non-native, and that any irrigation could be only with captured rainwater. It was the latter restriction that guided the pair towards creating a series of glades, their sizes largely determined by how much open garden the irrigation would allow. Each glade takes on a different character, revealing varying degrees of intervention where the boundary between natural landscape and garden is blurred to a greater or lesser extent. A secluded pool dominates one area, while another, the 'productive garden', feels clearly defined, with woven branches creating raised planters ringed by a boundary of fruit trees. However, in other areas native trees, such as *Arbutus xalapensis* (Texas madrone) and *Quercus rugosa* (netleaf oak), were planted to soften the edges and bring the forest in. The slope of the garden, while presenting its own challenge, means that as visitors travel between and emerge into each glade they are greeted with a new prospect. This is a garden of gentle interventions created by two designers who have embraced the site's limitations to encourage exploration and a new way of inhabiting the landscape.

FIELD OPERATIONS IN COLLABORATION WITH DILLER SCOFIDIO + RENFRO AND PIET OUDOLF

THE HIGH LINE
New York, New York, United States, 2009–19

The High Line is not the first example of disused urban infrastructure repurposed into an elevated linear park. That honour goes to the Promenade Plantée in Paris (1993), which runs for 5 kilometres (3 miles) from the Bastille to the Bois de Vincennes. But Manhattan's continuous greenway, at nearly 2.5 kilometres (1½ miles) long and opened in three phases (2009, 2014 and 2019), is arguably the most famous. It is also a wonderful testament to the positive impact of community action. It was the Friends of the High Line that prevented the demolition of the rail line – originally a spur of the West Side Elevated Line (which operated from 1934 until the 1980s) – and acted as the catalyst for its renaissance, commissioning the project along with the City of New York. The original transformation team has overseen the project since 2004, including design lead James Corner at Field Operations, architects Diller Scofidio + Renfro and planting designer Piet Oudolf (see p.216). New infrastructure installed on the original raised iron framework deliberately remembers the previous use, and Oudolf's planting was inspired by what had naturally colonized during the quarter-century of dereliction. However, he deliberately did not copy this but rather echoed its emotion, selecting plants for suitability, seasonality and visual appeal. Today the park nurtures more than 500 plant species in sixteen garden zones ranging from grasslands and wildflowers to wetland and woodland, each adapted to the particular microclimate (sun, shade, water, wind and so on) created by the adjacent cityscape. The High Line's success has inspired a national network of kindred projects, among them Philadelphia's Rail Park, the first phase of which opened in 2018.

ALASDAIR FORBES

PLAZ METAXU
near Tiverton, Devon, England, 1992–

The garden of retired art historian Alasdair Forbes is a modern revival of the intellectual garden traditions of the 18th century, when philosophy and symbolism shaped landscapes and were actively discussed. Spanning 13 hectares (32 acres) in a north Devon valley, it fits effortlessly into its pastoral surroundings. Forbes has crafted it with a light touch, but as the visitor explores they find more and more subtle signs that this is no ordinary landscape. Plaz Metaxu means 'the place between', reflecting Taoist and Buddhist ideas about the balance of space and form, and Forbes sees the valley as a dialogue between its sides, guiding the viewer through layers of meaning framed by hedges of hornbeam, beech and yew. Each part of the garden is named after a Classical deity, and designed to allude to the character and mythology of that deity. The visitor is encouraged to start at the Hermes courtyard, the gravel surface of which contrasts with the lush green elsewhere. Clipped hedges structure the space near the house, while further out, mysterious standing stones and inscriptions blend with grass, shrubs and trees around the central lake. Visitors interpret the garden as they wander: intellectuals find symbolism, classicists enjoy the mythological references, and children revel in the twists and turns. Forbes maintains the garden's intricate features himself, with only one day of help each week from a local man, Cyril Harris. The design, inspired by art history, poetry and philosophy, makes Plaz Metaxu a deeply thoughtful and beautiful place, blending art with a cultural landscape without disturbing its essence. The two inscriptions in the Corenzuela glade pictured are from Rainer Maria Rilke's *Sonnets to Orpheus*.

ANDREA AND PETER FORREST

MORITAKI
Blenheim | Waiharakeke, Marlborough, South Island, New Zealand, 2002–

Moritaki (the Japanese word for waterfall) is a truly enchanting private garden tucked away in the suburbs of Blenheim | Waiharakeke, a small town in the heart of the wine-producing area of Marlborough. The owners of this 0.34-hectare (just under 1-acre) garden, Andrea and Peter Forrest, set out to create a plot containing exclusively plants that are native to New Zealand. Keen gardeners, but with no experience of garden design, they enlisted Japanese garden designer Hiro Yoshida to assist them with the water-feature area of the garden. Moritaki does not pretend to be a Japanese garden, and since the Forrests were adamant from the start that it should be planted only with natives, Yoshida would suggest a desirable size and spread for a plant and its location, and they would make the selection. After twenty-two years, the garden is now fully established and has become a haven for bird life – and Yoshida has become a family friend. The planting includes *Dacrydium cupressinum* (rimu), *Podocarpus totara* (tōtara), *Sophora chathamica* (coastal kōwhai) and *S. microphylla* (small-leaved kōwhai), the kōwhais being an essential choice, since they are the national flower of New Zealand. This exquisite garden is a wonderful demonstration of what can be achieved using only native plants. Despite being so close to the town centre, it transports you to another place, a magical woodland complete with trickling mountain stream.

ELLIOTT FORSYTH AND THE ERSKINE FAMILY

CAMBO GARDENS
St Andrews, Fife, Scotland, 19th century, 2000–

The Cambo estate near St Andrews on the east coast of Scotland has belonged to the Erskine family since 1670 and is now managed by Cambo Heritage Trust, a charity set up to advance horticulture, heritage and cultural activity on the estate. Beside the large Georgian house sits a remarkable 1-hectare (2½-acre) walled garden dating back to the 19th century. This gently sloping site, enclosed by tall stone walls, was most recently developed by former head gardener Elliott Forsyth (who worked at the gardens from 2000 to 2018) and today is a paradise for garden-lovers. Featuring innovative schemes inspired by contemporary Dutch and German naturalistic plantings of grasses and perennials, alongside an orna-mental potager and a cutting garden, it offers a masterclass in creating harmony, rhythm and interest in a large space. It is also a treasure trove of rare and unusual plants suited to the colder climes of Scotland, many of which are available to buy on the estate. The fast-flowing Cambo Burn runs through the centre of the walled garden, and the sound of water combined with two little bridges and a summerhouse add even more to this outstandingly beautiful and original place. Beyond the walled garden, myriad pathways follow the course of the burn through the 28 hectares (70 acres) of ancient woodland to a spectacular sandy beach. Highly regarded for its snowdrops (it boasts more than 200 cultivars), Cambo also has a fine collection of historic roses, magnificent herbaceous borders, and North American prairie plantings that last until late into the season and ensure this historic garden offers contemporary relevance and inspiration.

FUTURE GREEN STUDIO, DANIEL BOULUD, ISAY WEINFELD AND KOHN PEDERSEN FOX

LE PAVILLON
New York, New York, United States, 2021

One of the tallest and newest skyscrapers in New York City, developer SL Green's One Vanderbilt reaches 427 metres (1,401 feet). One floor up is Le Pavillon, a Michelin-starred restaurant run by internationally renowned French chef Daniel Boulud. Brazilian architect Isay Weinfeld, architectural practice Kohn Pedersen Fox and award-winning Brooklyn-based landscape architecture firm Future Green Studio collaborated to realize Boulud's vision of a lush indoor garden that transforms dining into a bucolic experience. Within the 1,022-square-metre (11,000-square-foot) space, tall ceilings and a glass curtain wall create the illusion of an outdoor terrace. Grow lights designed by Dot Dash add ambient, natural-looking light. Nearly half of the dining area serves as a garden, and a winding, plant-lined path meanders around the tables. Future Green curated a plant palette of about twenty low-light species to evoke a New York woodland, and some 1,000 plants were installed and are maintained by landscaping firm Blondie's Treehouse, aided by a sophisticated irrigation system. A dozen black-olive trees 6 metres (20 feet) tall anchor and frame the space. Imported from Florida, they are not the familiar Mediterranean fruit trees, but rather the compact *Terminalia buceras* 'Shady Lady'. A shrub layer includes evergreen *Podocarpus macrophyllus* (plum yew) and *Heptapleurum arboricola* (syn. *Schefflera arboricola*; umbrella tree), while various ferns, *Saxifraga stolonifera* (strawberry begonia), *Peperomia tetragona* (parallel peperomia), *Zamioculcas zamiifolia* (ZZ plant) and *Aspidistra elatior* (cast-iron plant) form the groundcover. Although almost all are tropical, the plants were chosen for traits that mimic local flora for this grand, parklike eatery.

FERGUS GARRETT AND CHRISTOPHER LLOYD

OLD ROSE GARDEN AT GREAT DIXTER
Northiam, East Sussex, England, 1993–

In 1993 gardener and writer Christopher Lloyd made the controversial decision to remove his parents' rose garden, installed by architect Edwin Lutyens almost eighty years earlier, and replace it with an exotic riot of colour. This former cattle yard is small at just 240 square metres (2,580 square feet), surrounded by tall hedges and bounded on one side by a timber-framed cow shed. The roses had struggled with replant sickness for years, and Lloyd revelled in their destruction, as he wrote in *Country Life*: 'The noise of tearing old rose roots . . . was music to my ears.' He and his head gardener, Fergus Garrett, devised a new scheme that foregrounded the brightly coloured dahlias and cannas that were at the time largely disdained, causing consternation among the gardening public. Since Lloyd's death in 2006, Garrett has established Great Dixter as one of the UK's foremost gardens, renowned for its experimental, exuberant plantings. He has taken the Old Rose Garden in a greener direction, embracing the contrasts of exotic foliage and inspired by the paintings of Henri Rousseau to create a jungle that is more about light and texture than bright colour. He has even worked in conifers, their unique forms at home among the bold foliage of *Arundo donax* (giant reed) and *Tetrapanax papyrifer* (rice-paper plant). There are still some roses, as a nod to the past, but each year more of the garden is bedded out with tender plants that must be removed before the frosts. This allows constant invention of which Lloyd would surely approve.

JENNIFER GAY

KIRADIKEA
Corfu, Greece, 2014

At just over a hectare (3 acres), this garden on the Greek island of Corfu surrounds a stone-clad house, designed by French architect Emmanuel Choupis of MXarchitecture, and is set on a hillside overlooking the Ionian Sea. Jennifer Gay established her landscape architecture practice in Greece in 2004 and specializes in summer-dry gardens inspired by the wild Greek landscape of native olive trees and garrigue vegetation (known in Greece as *phrygana*). She typically works with shrubs and succulents, using plants from other Mediterranean zones to extend the flowering season and add drama. Gay's team maintains many of her gardens and regularly sources plants from French dry-garden expert Olivier Filippi (see p.12). At Kiradikea, gentle terraces settle the buildings into the hillside and three green roofs lessen its impact even further. The edges of the plot are blurred by cypress, carob and oak underplanted with native species, while around the house horticultural interest is heightened with a colourful mix including lavender, *Gaura*, *Centranthus*, *Cistus* and *Salvia*. Existing olive trees are pruned to emphasize their sculptural forms, adding to the contrasting textures, colours and shapes that combine to create a naturalistic yet painterly composition. Corfu has up to three times more rainfall than the rest of Greece, but summer drought is still a challenge. To help the plants survive, Gay uses concealed water tanks and gravel mulches, and trims young plants regularly so that their roots have less top growth to support. This sustainable approach mimics the 'goat-nibbled landscape' (as named by Filippi), a guiding principle of the contemporary Mediterranean garden.

GGN

PRIVATE GARDEN
Seattle, Washington, United States, 2019

Growing up on a logging road near forestry land in rural Washington state, Shannon Nichol experienced the 'shock of seeing forests which I'd played in just the day before, completely cleared the next day by logging operations'. However, she also witnessed rejuvenation as the land healed itself. Wildflowers emerged and saplings sprouted; 'It was like a miracle.' Those early encounters forged her later career in landscape design while nurturing a respect for the regionally native plants that are often dismissed as weeds. Her design firm, GGN Ltd, is connected with massive, prominent public projects, including San Francisco's India Basin Waterfront Park and Chicago's Lurie Garden. But when she was approached to transform a small 627-square-metre (6,750-square-foot) private urban plot in Seattle using native plants, Nichol eagerly accepted the challenge, seeing her goal as 'to work with regionally native plants and convert the community to the concept'. In keeping with the sleek, contemporary residence, stacked bespoke concrete-block planters are softened by native plants inserted as if they had sprouted there naturally. Concrete blocks are not the only innovative containers, however; giant, hollowed-out ancient *Thuja* (cedar) stumps were reclaimed as planters. Along pathways, directly sown native wild strawberries and violets create carpet-like groundcover accented by the bolt-upright fronds of *Polystichum munitum* (Western sword fern), while a sunken area takes planting inspiration from forest bogs and streams. The result is lush but also familiar, regenerating an oasis in urban Seattle.

CHRIS GHYSELEN

TUIN OOSTVELD
Oedelem, West Flanders, Belgium, 1989–

The garden of Chris Ghyselen, about 10 kilometres (6 miles) from Bruges, is a tapestry of colour and texture encircled by the geometry of neighbouring farmland. Ghyselen – one of Belgium's most distinguished garden designers – is renowned for his contribution to the development of new cultivars of *Persicaria*, *Brunnera* and *Sylphia*. He has developed his own garden, the 4,500-square-metre (48,400-square-foot) Tuin Oostveld, as a sanctuary and plant laboratory for more than thirty-five years. Its spine is a wavy, tightly clipped hornbeam hedge that encloses a prairie-style double border overflowing with long-flowering perennials. As the seasons turn, the palette evolves from subtle hues to the lemon-yellows, burgundies and pink-lavenders of *Helianthus* 'Carine', *Bistorta amplexicaulis* (syn. *Persicaria amplexicaulis*) 'Blackfield', *Symphyotrichum* (syn. *Aster*) 'Vasterival' and *Geranium* 'Anne Thomson' (which is named after Ghyselen's wife). In the lawn and wildflower meadow beyond, grasses in paisley-shaped beds – including *Sorghastrum nutans* 'Indian Steel' and *Molinia caerulea* subsp. *caerulea* 'Edith Dudszus' – add linear movement that is punctuated by *Succisella inflexa* 'Frosted Pearls' and *Knautia macedonica*, which also provide nourishment for butterflies and bees. Over the years Ghyselen has simplified the maintenance of the garden. Plants remain standing throughout the winter unless frost knocks them back. In early spring, everything is cut back before new growth emerges. He also assesses the plants at that point, replacing some with new, more interesting choices, and dividing others for replanting, ensuring both novelty and continuity in this magical sustainable garden.

GILLESPIES

ELEPHANT PARK
Elephant and Castle, London, England, 2021

A landmark mixed-use development designed with the aim of carbon net zero status when it is completed, Elephant Park comprises new housing, community spaces, restaurants, cafes and 4.5 hectares (11 acres) of new green streetscapes and cycle routes. Masterminded by construction and real estate firm Lendlease, the park at its heart is a 0.8-hectare (2-acre) green space designed by urban design and landscape architect firm Gillespies. The park's design retained twenty-seven mature trees, which give the area an established appeal and provide cool shade in this urban environment.

A further nineteen trees were planted, chosen for their resilience and their contribution to biodiversity. Hardscaping is refreshingly minimal, with paths of crushed gravel that offer a variety of routes, many weaving through the planting and allowing visitors an immersive and exploratory journey. Dynamic plantings include resilient ornamental grasses, a sub-layer of shrubs and seasonal perennials to give year-round interest, increase diversity and mitigate climate extremes, and rain gardens are incorporated to allow water to filter back into the ground rather than overwhelm drains. For younger users, the main attraction is Elephant Springs, a fully accessible adventure playscape of rocky outcrops, fountains, waterslides and sandy beaches. Crafted from tactile, non-slip Italian porphyry stone, it mimics a natural landscape, inviting safe exploration and play. Elephant Park is a hard-working example of contemporary urban development with engaging and considered planting that gives this newly emerging community a sense of place.

LUCIANO GIUBBILEI

FABBRICA
Pienza, Val d'Orcia, Tuscany, Italy, 2018

In 2015 the owners of this historic estate in southern Tuscany read about how Italian garden designer Luciano Giubbilei (originally from nearby Siena) had spent time with Fergus Garrett at Great Dixter (see p.106) in East Sussex, England, perfecting his knowledge of perennials. Admirers of Giubbilei's work, they invited him to Tuscany to design their garden. This project was Giubbilei's first design commission back in his homeland, after having trained and worked for several years in London. He had an open design brief, and the clients were safe in the knowledge that he would create a contemporary garden that would fit seamlessly into the surrounding landscape and enhance the historic buildings of this former monastery. Giubbilei took inspiration from the local, ancient landscape of Val d'Orcia, in particular Monte Amiata, which is the highest mountain in Tuscany and an ancient (now dormant) volcano. On this elevated site, 470 metres (1,540 feet) above sea level, winters can be very cold and summers very hot. The wider garden is a blend of formal and informal spaces, including an *orto* (kitchen garden). The 'Mediterranean' garden sits between the buildings, with breathtaking views out into the landscape. Here informal drifts of perennials – including *Iris* 'Medici Prince', *Artemisia* 'Powis Castle', *Helichrysum italicum* (curry plant), *Salvia nemorosa* 'Amethyst', *Clinopodium nepeta* (syn. *Calamintha nepeta*; lesser calamint) and *Stachys byzantina* (lamb's ears) – are planted in gravel. Softly mounded and in a colour palette of predominantly silver, burgundy, blue and purple, they mimic the contours and hues of the hills beyond.

JAMES GOLDEN

FEDERAL TWIST
near Stockton, New Jersey, United States, 2004–

When James Golden and his husband, Phillip Saperia, bought a property in New Jersey in 2004, their first intervention in its 0.6-hectare (1½-acre) garden was to call in a tree surgeon. That year they removed eighty *Juniperus virginiana*, which revealed that they had 'something approaching the world's worst soil'. Neither had any garden experience, and they had no idea what would grow. Golden was strongly inspired by the work of Piet Oudolf (see p.101 and p.216) but initial experiments, he admits wryly, involved 'watching many plants die'. A deer fence made all the difference, and they quickly realized it would be a grassy garden, with *Miscanthus* an early success. Today, winding paths lead away from the 1960s house through an immersive, extremely green garden that blends in with its surroundings. Golden used to refer to Federal Twist as a prairie garden but now readily admits that, being surrounded and populated by trees, it is a woodland-edge garden. He has an increasing fascination with woody plants and observes how they respond to a changing climate. *Lindera angustifolia* (willow-leafed spicebush), for example, recently came through three months of drought without any care. However, increasingly mild winters have resulted in the once-loved *Miscanthus* self-seeding to the point of becoming a nuisance. Golden won't be doing the weeding himself — he freely admits his dislike for the toil of gardening — preferring a more cerebral approach. While his knees may not be muddy the connection Golden has with his garden remains a profound and emotional one.

GRANT ASSOCIATES

GARDENS BY THE BAY
Marina Bay, Singapore, 2012

One of the most Instagrammed gardens in the world, Gardens by the Bay is a green jewel among the skyscrapers of downtown Marina Bay, Singapore. Built entirely on reclaimed land, this botanical wonder is a remarkable feat of engineering and environmental sustainability, a fusion of nature and technology. The effort – of which this is part – to turn Singapore into a 'city within a garden' was made possible by the Garden City movement (a response to industrialization and urbanization) and the vision of former prime minister Lee Kuan Yew. Designed by landscape architects Grant Associates (led by founder and director Andrew Grant), the public park is a 101-hectare (250-acre) tropical paradise (with Gustafson Porter + Bowman responsible for ongoing work on the Bay East Garden). Various themed gardens demonstrate exceptional garden craft and floral artistry while highlighting relationships between cultures and plants and the significance of plants in the age of climate change and biodiversity loss. A grove of eighteen towering mechanical 'Supertrees', each rising between 25 and 50 metres (82–164 feet), dominates the landscape. These colourful, eye-catching vertical gardens house tropical plants including bromeliads, orchids, ferns and climbers, much like epiphytes growing on tall forest trees. Two large, cooled, glass-domed conservatories, designed by architectural practice WilkinsonEyre, are futuristic; the Flower Dome features Mediterranean and semi-arid regional flora, while the Cloud Forest contains high-altitude habitats and exotic plants from tropical and temperate rainforests, cloaked in mist and fog, and an aerial walkway, the OCBC Skyway, offers breathtaking, picture-perfect views of the lush garden.

GREEN OVER GREY

MOUNTAIN & TREES, WAVES & PEBBLES
Guildford, Surrey, British Columbia, Canada, 2014

This green wall project by living-wall design firm Green over Grey (founded by Mike Weinmaster and Patrick Poiraud in 2008) has transformed a busy overpass near Vancouver, British Columbia, from a bleak slab of road infrastructure into a lush vertical garden. The largest green wall in North America, it incorporates more than 930 square metres (10,000 square feet) of vegetation, with 120 unique plant species and over 50,000 individual plants that are mostly native to British Columbia and suited to the conditions. Environmental sustainability, ecological habitat and biodiversity were important considerations for this fully hydroponic, energy-efficient vertical garden, leading to Gold LEED certification for excellence in sustainability. It was built entirely from recycled materials and serves as a carbon sink. Inspired by the abundant natural beauty of the province, its organic, swirling patterns in numerous shades of green evoke each element of the title. Weinmaster, its chief designer, was also inspired by the whimsical natural forms found in the landscape paintings of 19th-century Canadian artist Lawren Harris. The green wall, itself an eye-catching work of art, is double-sided, with exposure to east and west. The west face seen while driving east towards the mountains, represents mountains and trees. The east face (pictured), seen when driving west in the direction of the coast, represents waves and pebbles. This extraordinary suspended garden, completed for Guildford Town Centre, provides a much-needed, verdant visual treat for commuting drivers.

GREEN INC

BOTSWANA INNOVATION HUB
Gaborone, Botswana, 2019

Designed by the South African landscape architecture firm GREENinc, founded in 1995 by Stuart Glen, this is one of two spacious internal courtyards that form part of the Botswana Innovation Hub Science and Technology Park in the country's capital, Gaborone. The 57-hectare (140-acre) hub is at the cutting edge of green technology in science and education, and its creators were insistent that both the building and the landscaping design reflect that status. The courtyard design is primarily influenced by the semi-arid Kalahari Desert and Okavango Delta landscapes of Botswana, and uses local native species, particularly succulents that can grow both on the green roofs and in the large timber-clad planters in the courtyard. These containers of lush vegetation – which are heavily mulched after planting to ensure that they retain what little moisture there is – divide the courtyard into intimate gathering spaces. At the southern end of the space is an amphitheatre for staging outdoor events and presentations. Since the city's average annual rainfall is just 457 millimetres (18 inches), the garden relies on water capture. Large ponds add character to the landscape but are primarily there to help attenuate heavy rainfall, while run-off from the green roof is funnelled underground to be stored. It is this harvested water that irrigates the densely planted courtyards, while the deliberate selection of drought-resistant plants for the roof means that no irrigation is required.

JUAN GRIMM

BAHÍA AZUL
Los Vilos, Chile, 1996

Juan Grimm trained as an architect in his native Chile before becoming a landscape architect, a change prompted by his strong empathy with nature. Bahía Azul is his own holiday home, a place of relaxation but also of learning; its 0.4-hectare (1-acre) garden his laboratory for nearly thirty years. There he experiments with plants, observing how they grow, and how much sun and water they need to thrive in the exposed conditions on the north coastal edge of central Chile. Sustainability and working with native ecologies are founding principles of his landscape designs, and his selections for each design are based on native vegetation that has naturally adapted resilience to local conditions. While his wide-ranging portfolio includes public parks, commercial projects and private gardens, this garden exemplifies his design ethos. During his first ten years at Bahía Azul, Grimm built paths and a greenhouse, planted trees along a boundary with a neighbouring property, and began planting the native shrub vegetation. Nature has played a major role in shaping this garden; storms destroyed the boundary trees, but the shrubs have matured into organic shapes that shroud rocks and walls. Time on site is as important to Grimm as time spent working on plans in the studio. 'Creating a garden is always artificial, but it should be more than a collection of plants,' he says. He believes that a garden comes to life and many decisions are made when you actually handle the plants – making selection that are based on native vegetation that has naturally adapted resilience to the specific location you are working in. For Grimm, it is the development of a garden over time that is key to its use and enjoyment.

GRIMSHAW WITH SIR TIM SMIT AND JONATHAN BALL

EDEN PROJECT
Bodelva, Cornwall, England, 2001

The most dramatic thing about the Eden Project – the brainchild of entrepreneur and businessman Sir Tim Smit, with cofounder architect Jonathan Ball – is not the plants that are grown there but what they are growing in. Nestling against the back wall of a disused china-clay mine is a sequence of eight interlinked transparent domes designed by architectural practice Grimshaw (led by prominent architect and company founder Sir Nicholas Grimshaw). Based on the geodesic system made famous by the Montreal Biosphere (1967) by American architect Richard Buckminster Fuller, the domes are formed from hundreds of hexagonal and pentagonal ethylene tetrafluoroethylene (ETFE) inflated cells supported by a tubular-steel frame. On seeing the initial model, Sir Tim recalls, 'we loved it, because it felt natural – a biological response to our needs, but forged in materials that would allow us to explore the cultivation of plants in a way never before attempted'. The domes make up two biome buildings joined by a link building. The Rainforest Biome covers 1.6 hectares (4 acres), is 55 metres (180 feet) high and features more than 1,000 species from the humid tropics, including Southeast Asia, West Africa and South America. The Mediterranean Biome covers 0.7 hectares (1¾ acres), is 35 metres (115 feet) high and houses plant collections from the Mediterranean Basin, California, South Africa and Western Australia. Both biomes have education and conservation as the cornerstones of their existence, and they focus on wild plants and those used for economic purposes. Creating a picturesque setting, the Outdoor Gardens feature botanical collections of temperate and local Cornish species.

JELLE GRINTJES

PRIVATE GARDEN
Herwen, Gelderland, The Netherlands, 2020–

With the lease about to expire, garden designer Jelle Grintjes transplanted his previous garden lock, stock and barrel to its new home on this roughly rectangular 0.5-hectare (1¼-acre) plot some 30 kilometres (18 miles) east of Nijmegen, close to the German border. It comprises a large pond in the southwestern corner and ten or so informal, amorphously shaped island beds of different sizes among which wind grassy paths, their edges blurred by overhanging plants. The beds are filled with more than 50,000 bulbs and almost 20,000 perennial plants and grasses arranged in the Dutch Wave style. Also known as the New Perennial movement, this synthesis of new ideas drawing on art and philosophy, horticulture and naturalistic planting design arose in the early 1980s primarily through the work of such key figures as philosopher Rob Leopold, painter/plantsman Ton ter Linden (see p.168), and plantsmen/designers Henk Gerritsen and Piet Oudolf (see p.101 and p.216). Grintjes's approach hinges on year-round interest, and thus relies on much more than flowers. Swaying ornamental grasses, unusual plant forms and leaf shapes, colourful berries, interesting-looking seed pods and attractive winter forms are all just as important, and are used throughout his designs. Moreover, the naturalistic planting arrangement, a loose assemblage of small groups or drifts, ensures variety in all seasons. Another key element is time, as Grintjes notes: 'I let nature take its course. A design doesn't have to look exactly the same in ten years' time. My gardens only become more beautiful and natural over time.'

ALEXANDRE GRIVKO

LES JARDINS D'ÉTRETAT
Étretat, Normandy, France, 2015

Les Jardins d'Étretat, originally created for French actress Madame Thébault in the vertiginous landscape of the 'Alabaster Coast' in northern France, is where Claude Monet created a series of paintings and sketches known as 'Les Falaises d'Étretat' (The Cliffs of Étretat). In 2015 the house and gardens – the latter subsequently extended to their current 1.5 hectares (3¾ acres) – were bought by Alexandre Grivko, art director and chief landscape architect of garden-design and landscape company Il Nature, which is renowned for interpreting classic styles of Renaissance and Baroque topiary in large-scale compositions with a contemporary twist. At Étretat this theme binds seven gardens, various contemporary artworks and 2 kilometres (1¼ miles) of paths as they cascade towards the sea. In Jardin Émotions, shrubs shaped into mollusc shells honour Étretat's oyster farm (founded by Marie Antoinette); they are juxtaposed with a series of moon-faced sculptures by Samuel Salcedo entitled 'Gouttes de Pluie' (Drops of Rain), depicting raw, unfiltered emotional states. In Jardin Impressions, topiary waves and whirlpools rise and descend, representing the movement of the sea. Jardin Zen, dotted with white rhododendrons, includes the sound installation of pendulous terracotta sculptures by Russian artist Sergey Katran. Shaped to relect the sound waves for the word 'Art' in 125 languages, each word is played on a continuous loop. This avant-garde experimental garden connecting past, present and future holds two Michelin stars in the *Guide Michelin Voyage & Culture*.

GROUND STUDIO LANDSCAPE ARCHITECTURE   FALCON RIDGE

Salinas, California, United States, 2007

As design director of Ground Studio Landscape Architecture, Australian-born Bernard Trainor has conveyed his practical understanding of horticulture (he worked for a time with English plantswoman Beth Chatto) and passion for landscape through some of California's defining gardens. He moved to the United States in 1995, his vision to create landscapes related to the hills, valleys and coastal cliffs of northern California. Tucked into a rugged hillside, in an area where the client had spent much of his childhood roaming and exploring, the outdoor space at Falcon Ridge was required to celebrate the tension between the inhospitable nature of the land and its sensitivities. Moving about the 1.2 hectare (3 acre) site demands engagement as you step between levels and over offset accordion slabs. Smooth concrete is contrasted with rough boulders that affirm a sense of belonging to the land. Surrounded by native coast live oaks (*Quercus agrifolia*), the planting palette is minimal: scrubby *Juncus*, prostrate *Ceanothus* and groundcover *Dymondia margaretae* (silver carpet) mingle with succulents, shrubby manzanitas, *Salvia lanceolata* and upright *Restio*. The colours are muted, relying on long-lasting greens rather than a succession of bright flowers. Water is key to Trainor's designs, often in linear pools (as here) or troughs that lead the eye beyond the garden. Trainor's work, along with that of his four partners and team of designers at Ground Studio, speaks of the success of form, colour, light and simplicity, grounded in hands-on practicality. Trainor, who is also a talented painter and sculptor, says he is searching for a new, much-needed paradigm for how to exist as part of the natural world.

GROW TO KNOW WITH GEORGE KING ARCHITECTS

RE-GREEN NORTH KENSINGTON
London, England, 2024

A pocket park designed for the London Festival of Architecture 2024 and created from upcycled oil drums, with internal paths and seats of recycled plastic, this is a space where the community can explore, play, relax and connect with nature. Sited on a street corner in North Kensington, the semi-permanent installation was codesigned by George King Architects with Grow to Know — a not-for-profit changemaking and placemaking collective, seeking local, national and global joy and justice. Grow to Know was founded as a personal response to the Grenfell Tower tragedy of 2017, when a fire broke out in a nearby high-rise block of flats, as a commitment to future generations by activist Tayshan Hayden-Smith. The oil drum planters celebrate the Notting Hill Carnival held locally, which features steel pans – their origin stemming from the way discarded metal, such as oil drums and dustbins, was repurposed as musical instruments in 1930's Trinidad. The pastel colours nod to Notting Hill's houses, which are increasingly out of reach to the local community. There is also a statement on behalf of sustainability; objects that once contained a polluting substance, oil, has been transformed into a beautiful community garden – a subliminal reminder of the intersection between society and environment, and the opportunities and solutions that are channelled through community and nature. The garden contains a range of plants, among them *Kniphofia* (red-hot pokers), *Agapanthus*, tactile *Nassella tenuissima* (syn. *Stipa tenuissima*; Mexican feather grass), pines and *Cotinus* (smoke bush), alongside edibles such as strawberries, rosemary and an apple tree as a showcase of the beauty and ease of growing food locally.

SIMON AND MONIQUE GUDGEON

SCULPTURE BY THE LAKES
Pallington Lakes, Dorchester, England, 2011

Having moved to rural Dorset, southern England, in search of more studio space, sculptor Simon Gudgeon and his wife, Monique, gradually set about transforming a series of former fishing lakes into one of the UK's most beautiful open-air sculpture parks. Inspired by Simon's experience of placing his own monumental sculptures in gardens and parks around the world, and informed by Monique's horticultural training, they wanted to create a place of immersive natural beauty, where art would initiate an emotional response. The park, which has been accredited as a botanic garden, entices visitors to wander through 10.5 hectares (26 acres) of sensitively and imaginatively curated nature. Sculpture by the Lakes is a safe haven for more than 1,000 rare trees and shrubs, many of them under threat in the wild. With half of the land under some form of water, this is a mediative, calming journey, a silent conversation with nature and art. Choice sculptures, trees, ponds, riverbanks, wildflower meadows and woodland lie beyond the textural mass of perennial grasses and neatly sculpted topiary forms that radiate from the couple's house, and a network of informal trails leads into the wider landscape. This sustainably managed project champions gardens as habitat for wildlife, promotes the conservation of endangered species and offers a retreat for visitors. It is also the Gudgeon's home garden and only design project, a response to time spent with the land.

GUSTAFSON PORTER + BOWMAN

PARQUE CENTRAL
Valencia, Spain, 2019

This first phase of the Parque Central project repurposes 11.5 hectares (28½ acres) of disused railway tracks and industrial land into a city-centre park that will eventually cover 23 hectares (nearly 57 acres) and reconnect fractured neighbourhoods. It is being undertaken by award-winning landscape practice Gustafson Porter + Bowman, founded in 1997 by Kathryn Gustafson (see overleaf) and architect Neil Porter, later joined by partner Mary Bowman. Taking the form of five large, sculpted 'bowls' inspired by the region's traditional ceramics, the park consists of varied, multi-level gardens: the Children's Garden, the Flower Garden, the Orchard Garden (illustrated), the Romantic Garden and the Demetrio Ribes Arts Plaza. Designed to provide green spaces for a range of activities, age groups and uses, they all refer to three quintessential Valencian characteristics: water, food and the Mediterranean landscape. Hard landscaping uses a range of materials, including the Calatorao limestone typical of the city, as well as granite and marble, while the planting, in a patchwork of asymmetrical beds, imbues each area with its own character. Using 1,000 trees, 85,000 shrubs and 70 perennial taxa – either native to or tolerant of the Mediterranean climate – the planting design reflects the region's cultural and natural landscapes. Water – an ingenious unifying element that encourages visitors to move through and explore the park in a sensual journey of discovery – is manifest in a variety of guises, reflecting water in the local natural landscape: the Albufera de València (a large freshwater lagoon), the Mediterranean Sea and the River Turia.

KATHRYN GUSTAFSON

LES JARDINS DE L'IMAGINAIRE
Terrasson-Lavilledieu, France, 1996

From its beginning, the site of this public park – 6 hectares (15 acres) of steeply sloping woodland in a river valley next to the old town – included old terraces and drystone walls from its agricultural past. Into this already picturesque setting acclaimed landscape architect Kathryn Gustafson (see p.123), who is known for her impactful landscapes, wove thirteen gardens. Each expresses a different aspect of garden history, but the design style and form are contemporary, even biomorphic. In its intellectual depth, the design responds to the region's culture, history and landscape, and the visitor's experience of the gardens is fluid in a way that goes beyond the diverse use of water. The Garden of the Elements (illustrated) is a balance between nature and cultivation in which a golden ribbon winding through the trees invites one on to the path of imagination. Other gardens include the Sacred Grove, the Green Theatre, the Green Tunnel (covered in wisteria, clematis, jasmine and other climbers), a Rose Garden of 1,600 rose types and 360 climbing roses, and a Topiary Garden. Water is the unifying element (although wind plays a role in the Axis of the Winds); it runs through the Sacred Grove, cascades in Fountains Way, is depicted on the sculptures of The Rivers and is naturally the focus of the Water Gardens. In this last, most iconic area, jets play and rills run, encouraging the visitor to interact with this element. The park's greenhouse, designed by British architect Ian Ritchie, is a creative encounter between rough-hewn local Terrasson stone and sophisticated glass and metal.

JOHN GWYNNE AND MIKEL FOLCARELLI

POLLINATOR GARDEN
Sakonnet Garden, Little Compton, Rhode Island, United States, 2014–

At Sakonnet Garden, naturalist and landscape architect John Gwynne and interior designer Mikel Folcarelli have since the 1970s been forging a world-class collection of plants in a labyrinth of intricate 'rooms'. It was in 2014, when a lepidopterist friend alerted them to the dramatic plunge in local butterfly populations, that they determined to create habitat and food for insects within their 2-hectare (5-acre) parcel. Inspired by Le Jardin Plume in Normandy (see p.234), they removed invasive species on a flat 0.2 hectares (½ acre) and planted a giant square with paths. The original planting list for the insects' all-you-can-eat buffet matched plants and clientele specifically, until it was discovered that only the caterpillars cared. For bees and butterflies, a nectar- and pollen-rich mix of natives and exotics worked admirably. The challenge was to keep it coming throughout the season. The smorgasbord begins slowly with *Taraxacum officinale* (dandelion), *Eranthis hyemalis* (winter aconite), crocuses and *Camassia*, building to a chorus of meadow plants that is especially impressive in the Avenue of the Giants, with its verbascums and umbellifers. Popularity-contest winners include *Pycnanthemum* (mountain mint), *Asclepias* (milkweed), *Verbena bonariensis*, fennel, *Phlox*, *Vernonia* (ironweed) and tall New England asters. To protect eggs, pupae and insects, stem and leaf debris is left in place all winter. Perennials with hollow stems are cut down to 30 centimetres (1 foot), their tops loosely stacked into rustic fencing. Boardwalk paths are purposefully slender and immersive. 'The Pollinator Garden touches you, both physically and emotionally,' says Gwynne.

ALEX HANAZAKI

GMC GARDEN
Bragança Paulista, Brazil, 2013

This exemplary private garden integrates contemporary architecture with the natural landscape beyond. Its precision and simplicity reflect the approach for which Alex Hanazaki (who founded his practice, Hanazaki, in 1998) is renowned, and reflect the clients' wish for a low-maintenance garden in which less is more. Hanazaki is one of Brazil's leading landscape designers, whose work is influenced by his Japanese ancestry, Brazil's unique cultural diversity and native flora, and the importance of the interaction of people with nature. Site-specific plans and the use of local materials give his projects context. Here, a ground plan of bold geometric lines set out over 0.9 hectares (2¼ acres) defines terraces sculpted from the site's natural topography. The plateau is divided by a grid of edged lawns, planted areas, and a grass path bridge spanning a sunken void, all adding textural contrasts. Natural patterns of light and shade enliven the garden, and at night, LEDs emphasize the lines of the grid. Allées of trained trees bring shade and height, creating a visual link with trees in the surrounding natural landscape, while plumes of ornamental grasses contribute finer texture and a sense of movement. The garden boundary is defined by hedging where privacy is needed, but in other places it is open to views out. Two cantilevered belvederes enjoy a prospect over the lower garden (which includes a football pitch) and the landscape beyond.

HARRIS BUGG STUDIO

THE KITCHEN GARDEN
RHS Garden Bridgewater, Salford, Greater Manchester, England, 2021

For the restored Kitchen Garden at the heart of the Royal Horticultural Society's fifth – and newest – UK garden, the society chose an innovative, immersive design that reimagines the traditional kitchen garden with its neat rows of productive plants. Here visitors to the garden, designed by landscape architects Charlotte Harris and Hugo Bugg (of Harris Bugg Studio, established 2017), wander through a patchwork of more than 100 beds of varying size and shape, planted to provide ideas for their own growing spaces. Keen to reflect the heritage of the site, which lies alongside the Bridgewater Canal (a transport highway during the Industrial Revolution), the designers took inspiration from the canal's route to establish the main paths through the 0.7-hectare (1¾-acre) garden. The pattern produced by contemporary field boundaries became the blueprint for the beds, which are accessed by narrower gravel pathways. The historic walls are ideal for training pear trees, apples, apricots, plums and cherries, while the garden itself is divided into three zones: an intensively productive area mixing traditional techniques with newer ones, such as no-dig; a herbal area; and edible forests (a multi-layered system in which plants stabilize and nourish the soil with little or no input from the gardener), their canopies provided by such fruit-bearing trees as sea buckthorn (*Hippophae rhamnoides*), crab apple (*Malus sylvestris*), medlar (*Mespilus germanica*) and Japanese pepper (*Zanthoxylum piperitum*). The designers also embraced this holistic way of growing in Roots in the Sky, a projected 0.6-hectare (nearly 1½-acre) rooftop forest on an office building in Southwark, London.

HEATHERWICK STUDIO WITH MNLA

LITTLE ISLAND
New York, New York, United States, 2021

Little Island, a park nestled off the West Side of Manhattan, exemplifies Heatherwick Studio's renowned passion for creating 'non-boring' buildings. Founded by British designer Thomas Heatherwick in 1994, the studio's multidisciplinary approach is evident in this project, which was nearly a decade in the making, and showcases a striking visual complexity. The 1-hectare (nearly 2½-acre) pocket park is set on the Hudson River atop a series of gigantic concrete piles topped with tulip-shaped 'pots' that crowd together to form an undulating surface. At its lowest it is just 4.5 metres (14¾ feet) above the water, at its highest 19 metres (just over 62 feet). The forest of piles echoes the remnants of historic riverside piers, while their height was as much a way of elevating the park above flood-risk levels (much of the riverside was inundated following Superstorm Sandy in 2012) as it was about bringing variation to the city's flat topography. The project's landscape architects, MNLA (Mathews Nielsen Landscape Architects), needed a robust palette of plants to cope with the exposed conditions, but were able to use the differing shapes and heights of the 'pots' to create microclimates that allowed distinctly planted areas as well as more open spaces for performance and gathering. Planting includes 35 species of tree, 65 different shrubs and 290 types of grass, perennial, vine and bulb chosen to mitigate wind and noise, stabilize the soil and appeal through the seasons, while allowing varied views back across the city from the meandering path and key stopping points.

ANDRÉ HELLER

ANIMA
Ourika Valley, Morocco, 2016

Eye-catching Anima is the outcome of six years of hard work by the influential multimedia artist André Heller: actor, chansonnier, circus revivalist, poet, sculptor, singer, songwriter, theme-park designer and writer, among many other things. Nestled in the foothills of the High Atlas mountains some 30 kilometres (18 miles) southeast of Marrakech, it is intended to be a 'magical place of sensuality, of wonder, of contemplation, of joy, of healing and of inspiration for people of all ages who want to experience the unforgettable'. The garden is all about colour – including many shades of green foliage – and form. Tree-shaded paths meander through three richly planted hectares (nearly 7½ acres), encountering here and there buildings and water features, and always in close contact with botanical delights. Ranging from cacti and succulents to subtropical palms, the collection is varied and exciting, but competing with it for attention and providing a sympathetic yet contrasting juxtaposition are the sculptures by such luminaries as Keith Haring, Pablo Picasso and Auguste Rodin, set amid the flora. This is not art meets nature, but rather a harmonious conjoining of organic and inorganic art to be enjoyed separately and together, all set against the stunning backdrop of kingfisher-blue skies and angular, often snow-capped peaks. Heller is also the driving force behind the garden of the Fondazione André Heller, a whimsical mix of botanic garden (containing about 3,000 species) and contemporary art (by Haring, Rodin, Fernand Léger, Roy Lichtenstein and others) on the western shore of Lake Garda, Italy.

DANIEL J. HINKLEY

WINDCLIFF
Indianola, Washington, United States, 2000

When horticultural collector, nurseryman and lecturer Daniel J. Hinkley acquired Windcliff with his husband, the architect Robert Jones, in 2000, it was a cataclysmic location, but not a garden. On a cliff overlooking Puget Sound, with a view of distant Mount Rainier, the 2.6-hectare (6½-acre) private property was primarily turf when they arrived, and Hinkley's vision was to eliminate these swathes of grass immediately. 'It was previously all about the view,' he explains. 'My goal was to invite wildlife back in.' Now, with only about 500 square metres (5,400 square feet) of grass remaining, he has achieved that goal. From there, Windcliff redefined the concept of a collector's garden. Hinkley's style evolved beyond the basic perennial border, gravitating towards a 'habitat-like planting'. Having hobnobbed with world-class designers, such as Penelope Hobhouse and Graham Stuart Thomas, he knows the principles of design: repetition, textural interplay and juxtaposing forms (including sculptural highlights). Although Windcliff is not the first garden to embrace a meadow-like configuration, Hinkley's matrix uniquely enlists rare plants collected during professional plant-hunting trips around the globe. He primarily collected seeds, which (following approval by the United States Department of Agriculture) were grown into 5-centimetre (2-inch) plugs before being let loose in the landscape. With no soil amendment, the goal is to achieve a designed fabric rather than merely a museum collection. What started with a eucalyptus and Leyland cypress screen between Windcliff and its neighbours has grown into a dramatic scene where botanical rarities romp together like nowhere else on Earth, framing a view to die for.

JAMES HITCHMOUGH

GRASSLANDS GARDEN
Horniman Museum and Gardens, London, England, 2018

Set over 6.5 hectares (16 acres), including a meadow, a nature trail and a sunken garden, and with views north across the London skyline, the Horniman Museum and Gardens (founded 1901) aims through its diverse collections 'to connect us all with global cultures and the natural environment, encouraging us to shape a positive future for the world we all share'. As part of recent developments, James Hitchmough (London 2012 Olympic Park designer and University of Sheffield professor emeritus) designed the 400-square-metre (3,400-square-foot) Grasslands Garden as a continuation of the World Gallery, which celebrates the beauty and diversity of cultures. Assisted by Wesley Shaw, then head of horticulture at the Horniman, more than 5,000 perennials were planted in a naturalistic style, in celebration of two critically threatened natural habitats: North American prairie and central South African grassland. The flower display peaks across the summer months, and the plants (many of which were raised onsite) are arranged by height, creating an undulating, immersive display that is most effective when breezes ripple over the garden. Here, as in his other designs, Hitchmough's aim has been to draw on natural ecological systems to create a stunning wildflower planting that also encourages and supports local wildlife. Since 2021 Errol Reuben Fernandes has overseen the Horniman Gardens, introducing more sustainable approaches to the Horniman's traditional planting schemes. Among these are a micro-forest to screen and filter pollution from the busy road, and extensive xerophytic planting of species that are well adapted to thrive in dry conditions, to promote better understanding of their uses.

HOCKER

CISTERCIAN ABBEY AND CHAPEL
Irving, Texas, United States, 2015–

As an alumnus of the Cistercian Abbey Preparatory School, David Hocker has a special relationship with the 33-hectare (82-acre) campus not far from the urban sprawl of Irving, Texas. Recently, the Cistercian Order has attracted not only an influx of new monks, but also an interest in holistic land stewardship has been deeply expressed. 'They've really embraced the land,' Hocker noticed; 'they see how valuable it is, especially as the urban area expands.' Simultaneously, members of the community are exploring spacemaking while strengthening their commitment as caretakers, gardeners, beekeepers and so on. And that's where the designer's eponymous landscape architecture studio (founded in 2005), comes in. Hocker splits his year between Tuscany and Texas, and both environments have influenced the firm's design ethos, fusing nature and garden. The 1,000-square-metre (10,800-square-foot) garden at the abbey is a soft handshake between wilderness and minimalistic design, with sleek, angular, low-slung stone retaining walls creating space and purpose for outdoor areas while steering wayfinding, moving the monks outside. Native wildflowers were sown into grass-based meadows that feel God-given; native trees, such as *Prosopis glandulosa* (mesquite), were reinstated to forge a landscape so natural that it seems almost unedited. Closer to the buildings, reasons to access the outdoors for meetings and other purposes were increased by the presence of shade trees, such as *Acer buergerianum* (trident maple). 'The monks' land stewardship has become part of their identity,' Hocker notes, and the evolution is ongoing. What's next? A walled garden – in Hocker's words, 'A *hortus conclusus* with a spin.'

DOUGLAS HOERR

GARDEN IN THE ROUND
Lake Forest, Illinois, United States, 1991

In 1991, after a two-year sabbatical shadowing eminent British designers Beth Chatto and John Brookes in their own private gardens, landscape architect Doug Hoerr was contacted to tackle a drastic renovation. What existed on the private suburban site of just over 1,000 square metres (about 10,900 square feet) was a formal, no-nonsense landscape primarily for ornamentation, and the homeowners sought to eliminate the straight-lined, dahlia-filled parterres. Not a sprig of boxwood remains. Hoerr envisioned a curvaceous, naturalistic garden of rounded forms radiating from the Spanish-style house. Flowing out in lieu of a terrace, but visible from an interior sunroom, are amphitheatre-like steps and gravel beds in homage to the council rings of legendary local Midwest designer Jens Jensen. Those expanded beds hold a bounty of plant collections reflecting the homeowners' devotion to horticulture and providing strong silhouettes and year-around intrigue, nestling against the house to submerge the sunroom in the botanical experience. Moving outwards, lawn frames a wildlife pond (expanded far beyond the pocket pool originally envisioned by the clients), mirroring the tableau of shrubs and trees along its shores. Pathways through wooded areas planted with native redbuds and dogwoods lead around the house via stepping stones of local limestone. 'Everything flows together,' says Hoerr, 'becoming more naturalistic as it moves away from the house.' More radically, the garden reimagined a new, all-embracing dialogue where people, home, landscape and horticulture integrate as a whole. Hoerr established his firm Hoerr Schaudt in 2008 and this design approach has continued to inform the firm's ethos.

SEAN HOGAN

VON SCHLEGELL GARDEN
Portland, Oregon, United States, 2011

Sean Hogan is a botanist and nurseryman whose expert knowledge of the rich, diverse flora of the cordilleras (mountain chains) of the American West has led to striking work focusing on the region's native plants. Indeed, his nursery, Cistus (founded in 1996 with his late partner Parker Sanderson), is renowned for celebrating underused but locally appropriate species. This 1.2-hectare (3-acre) plot astride a ridge above Portland, Oregon, uses what Hogan calls 'Willamette Valley iconic . . . a native-esque planting palette . . . evoking what used to be here'. A range of evergreen native shrubs has been chosen to occupy space at all levels, with an emphasis on foliage interest for the winter as well as the dry summer. There is a lower layer of vegetation, some grasslike plants, a few perennials and, in the shadier areas, ferns. A green roof is planted with low-growing, grey-leaved plants. Water for irrigation is currently plentiful in the city, but in planning this garden Hogan looked to minimize the need for it, hence the selection of species that are adapted to survive dry summers. Key plants here – and in an increasing number of gardens in the region – are *Arbutus menziesii* (Pacific madrone) and the related *Arctostaphylos* (manzanitas). These small trees and shrubs have distinctive silvery leaves and rich cinnamon-coloured bark, on display through an open, bendy branching habit. Icons of the regional flora, they are easily killed by irrigation during the dry season, but here they flourish and point towards a more sustainable regional style.

HOLLANDER DESIGN

FARM FIELDS
Bridgehampton, New York, United States, 2021

Hollander Design, established in 1991 by Edmund Hollander and Maryanne Connelly, has acquired a reputation for making meaningful connections between landscape and 'home'. The studio was already familiar with the Farm Fields property, having worked on a previous project there. The new clients extended the home with a contemporary shingle-style house (designed by architect Thomas Kligerman in collaboration with designer Haynes-Roberts) and asked Hollander to settle the new house into its 6-hectare (15-acre) plot. While working previously on the garden, Hollander had with serendipitous foresight established a nursery there in conjunction with agriculturally reserved land. So, when the time came to weave gardens around the new house, he could harvest trees from the onsite nursery to form the rich bosques of catalpas and pollarded planes that segment the spaces. Hollander took his cue from the surroundings, identifying the planting's role as softening but also speaking to the modernity of the architecture. The garden draws you from one part to the next, starting with a reflecting pool in front and working through allées of lavender and hydrangea to a pergola and swimming pool at the back. To encourage that travel long, narrow, irregularly placed thermal bluestone planks align with the linearity of the home. Plantings are choreographed to fill the year with glowing moments as mini meadows of alliums dance above sedges, and Japanese anemone forms thickets corralled by boxwood. Hollander explains of this poignantly poetic design, 'In the still of the evening, the fragrances of summersweet [*Clethra alnifolia*] and 'Casa Blanca' lilies combine with roses around the firepit. We're striving to create magic.'

AMANDA AND PHIL HONEY

CAISSON GARDENS
Combe Hay, Bath, Somerset, England, 2010–

This wonderfully romantic garden that combines history with a contemporary twist is set in the rolling hills just south of Bath, southwestern England. Caisson House was built in 1800 as head office for the chief engineer of the Somerset Coal Canal Company; at the time in North Somerset there were more than eighty working collieries producing 100,000 tonnes of coal every year. It was there that a revolutionary lock system named 'Caisson' was devised, but it sadly failed, and soon afterwards trains took over as the main transportation for the coal. Caisson Gardens still contain an incredible fifteen (now dry) locks, their towering walls host to a variety of native plants including mosses and ferns; walking along the canal bed you can appreciate the incredible stonework of the past. Formal areas of contemporary planting surround the house, with a fusion of topiary and colourful perennials. As you move into the wider landscape it gradually becomes more informal, and wildflower meadows buzzing with life lead towards the encircling woodland. An interwoven stonework rill weaves its way down the slope from the house towards a large pond that is enveloped with banks of dramatic planting. Since 2010 the owners, Amanda and Phil Honey, have lovingly restored this garden, taking great care to pay tribute to the industrial heritage of the site but allowing their exquisite contemporary design to gently bring the garden into the 21st century. Their aim was to create a timeless landscape that was not only sustainable but also a haven for wildlife.

HOOD DESIGN STUDIO

AFRICAN ANCESTORS MEMORIAL GARDEN
International African American Museum, Charleston, South Carolina, United States, 2023

In 2015 architect Henry N. Cobb contacted designer, artist and educator Walter J. Hood to create a garden for the International African American Museum in Charleston. Cobb felt the project needed the voice of Hood, who set up his design studio in 1992 and is known for using cultural and historical narratives to give public spaces new resonance. Situated on Gadsden's Wharf, where many enslaved people first arrived in America, the museum sits on columns in accordance with hurricane building regulations, and Hood's richly symbolic 1-hectare (2½-acre) garden flows around it.

When Hood began the design, Charleston was reeling from the assault on Black culture of the Emanuel African Methodist Episcopal Church massacre. Against that backdrop, Hood's landscape 'expresses the grief and turmoil' of the Black experience in America. The Tide Tribute Fountain floods life-size figures laid head to toe etched in tabby concrete, depicting the cramped conditions during the turbulent ocean passage. Nearby, oversized shrouded statues kneel on a boardwalk between reflective granite walls. A meadow of *Anthoxanthum nitens* (sweet grass) honours the African American contribution to basketmaking, beside serpentine walls of pierced brick representing the brickmaking and bricklaying tasks undertaken by enslaved Americans. Walls of numbered badges – once compulsory identification for Black people in Charleston – shelter seating in homage to Toni Morrison's Bench by the Road Project, and lines from Maya Angelou's poem *Still I Rise* are etched in stone. Below a palm grove, the land undulates, symbolizing dunes as well as African Americans' shaping of the land. It's all part of Hood's aim to 'give our heritage a visual and physical truth'.

JIHAE HWANG

MOVING SEEDS
Seoul Botanic Park, Seoul, South Korea, 2018

With a background in fine arts, Korean-born and London-based Jihae Hwang considers herself a garden designer and environmental artist who approaches gardens from the viewpoint of conceptual art. *Moving Seeds* was created for the inauguration of the Seoul Botanic Park on 1 October 2018. Positioned in the crutch of two perpendicular paths, a sinuous central area surfaced with sand enables access to and through the 800-square-metre (8,600 square-foot) garden while bringing the visitor close to the juxtaposed planting areas. Hwang explains that the garden – which pays tribute to the Korean farmers who once sowed the seeds that sustained this land – 'links the deep core of the Earth with the edges of the sky, and becomes another form of universal language, granting new strength for life anew for humanity every day'. The seeds themselves are represented by fifteen wooden benches made from randomly sized pine trunks forming a stick-like structure. Each is treated with traditional lacquer made from *Toxicodendron vernicifluum* (the Chinese lacquer tree) using the Korean *ottchil* technique, and to add a sculptural, interactive element, each bench moves in response to the weight of the sitter. The planting was inspired by wildflowers that grow naturally in fields, farms and along roadsides and are often dismissed as weeds, while the design evokes the process by which the breeze brought by the river nourishes the plants and helps them to spread, drawing a visual narrative of their growth year by year.

ROBERT IRWIN

CENTRAL GARDEN AT THE GETTY CENTER
Los Angeles, California, United States, 1997

Robert Irwin was a leading figure in Light and Space art of the 1960s, the only wholly original art movement to begin in Los Angeles. He made site-specific installations that explored the reordering of the physical, sensory and temporal experience of the space to which they were now integral. For the 1.2-hectare (3-acre) Central Garden – one of five at the Getty Center, and his first piece of garden design – Irwin saw it as his duty to make a contemporary 'sculpture in the form of a garden aspiring to be art'. A tree-lined stream crisscrossed by a walkway descends to a plaza, where stylized tree-shaped trellises support bougainvillea. The stream continues through the plaza to tumble down a cascade into a circular pool in which a maze of azaleas 'floats'. Juxtaposed is a collection of speciality gardens, with all elements carefully selected to accentuate the interplay of colour, light and reflection. Irwin carved his declaration, 'Always changing, never twice the same', into a stepping stone as a reminder of his beliefs in the experiential relationship between art and viewer, and the ever-changing, evolving, living nature of a garden. It is a statement that applies to all gardens exactly because they are an experiential, organic art form. But, as Irwin also observed, 'Art shows you the world in ways you haven't seen it before; it brings you back to look at it again.' It certainly does here.

KAZUYUKI ISHIHARA

MIHARA GARDEN
Mihara, Nagasaki City, Japan, 2020–

Before turning his green fingers to the design of gardens, Nagasaki-native Kazuyuki Ishihara trained in *ikenobo*, one of the oldest schools of the ancient art of ikebana (Japanese flower-arranging). He now has fourteen Chelsea Flower Show medals to his name (including four for Best in Category), and was even dubbed 'a magician of greenery' by Queen Elizabeth II in 2010. Tucked into a hillside, the Mihara Garden in his home city has been described as 'a healing space of magical flowers and greenery'. It makes use of the best of the traditional Japanese approaches to design, offering a masterclass in the selection, positioning and manicuring of specimen plants and blending them with rocks and water to generate the illusion of a nature more perfect than nature itself. When the garden is illuminated at night and filled with artificial mist, the effect is ethereal, creating almost another garden entirely, especially when viewed from above. But within it there is also the interesting juxtaposition of a Western-inspired garden, in which many Japanese plants not usually seen in local gardens are planted in arrangements unfamiliar to Japanese gardeners. The garden also boasts a number of facilities, including a tea room, vegetable garden, a bonsai landscape and a gallery, all of which create a unique destination offering visitors a space for relaxation and the appreciation of natural beauty.

YUKIYO IZUMI

TASHIRO-NO-MORI
Tokachi, Hokkaido, Japan, 1994–

This 5.6-hectare (14-acre) woodland surrounding a traditional-style thatched cottage on Hokkaido, the northern island of Japan, is a labour of love for its creator, retired antiques dealer Yukiyo Izumi, who has spent years transforming a forest degraded by invasive native bamboo into a haven for native plants. Through persistent clearing, he has enabled slow-growing woodland species to recover their numbers and thrive. Izumi-san has also grown some species from seed, planting them out then waiting patiently for them to flower, set seed and begin to spread. He focuses on 'addition by subtraction', clearing domineering plants, such as *Sasa* (bamboo), and allowing smaller, more delicate species to survive. Now, in springtime, there are drifts of wildflowers, such as pink *Glaucidium palmatum* (a distant relative of the poppy), along with several species of *Trillium* (wake robin), anemones, *Erythronium japonicum* (dog's-tooth violet) and *Corydalis ambigua*. Micro-habitats created by a stream and the undulating terrain enable a variety of plant life to flourish, from *Hydrangea serrata* in damp areas to species of *Hemerocallis* (daylily) under some of the oaks. In brighter areas, the vigorous local herbaceous flora flourishes, which Izumi-san also manages, but less severely than the *Sasa*. The garden is essentially an all-too-rare example of habitat restoration in which gardening techniques have been used to revive a pre-deforestation landscape, turning it from something approaching a bamboo monoculture into a lush, thriving ecosystem. Tashiro-no-Mori stands as a beautiful testament to a striking combination of human intervention and the resilience of nature.

SHEILA JACK

PRIVATE GARDEN
London, England, 2023

Once-languishing urban gardens that used to feel limited in scope are increasingly being realized as precious outdoor space for owners who consider themselves lucky to have access to nature and its restorative qualities. Couple this with a contemporary preference for large-windowed extensions that connect indoors with outdoors and the challenge is set for clever garden solutions. Garden designer Sheila Jack set up her studio in 2017, having formerly worked as an art director for magazines including *Vogue* and *Harper's Bazaar*. Her eye for a well-designed page is now turned on gardens and often sees her collaborating with architects. A recent transformational extension to a Victorian terrace by Neil Dusheiko Architects left a long narrow, 126-square-metre (1,350-square-foot) garden requiring a similar makeover for its visionary clients. Jack has achieved a room-like quality using horizontal and vertical rectangles to create a series of spaces and encourage exploration through the length of the garden. Leading from the house, a tactile 'lawn' of *Soleirolia soleirolii* (mind-your-own-business) is grounded by oversized boulders and mounded evergreen conifers, while a bespoke raised wooden pathway seemingly floats over planting towards a brick terrace. Here, a concrete bench becomes a destination to sit and look over the raised Corten-steel reflecting pool. A missed-brick wall functions as both architectural form and dividing screen, allowing dappled light through and glimpses of a further seating area beyond. Influenced by Tom Stuart-Smith's (see p.81 and p.277) sophisticated take on texture and form, Jack has tuned her own approach to an accomplished melding of soft planting and stylized hardscaping.

JAMES DOYLE DESIGN ASSOCIATES

PRIVATE GARDEN
Highland Park, Dallas, Texas, United States, 2022

'Good design starts with solutions,' says Justin Quinn of James Doyle Design Associates (JDDA) about the evolution of this property in Highland Park. Known for its elegant, inventive, functional designs, JDDA was unfazed by a brief that included a sauna, a plunge pool, a lap pool and two lounging areas embraced by a generous living space and a cabana/garage, on a 0.3-hectare (¾-acre) plot. Led by Quinn and James Doyle, the team delivered the requested spaces with panache. Although it might seem counter-intuitive, to avoid a cluttered scene they divided the small space into 'rooms' delineated by low-growing hedges that reflect the classic, expressive lines of Alex Eskenasy's architecture. The one exception is a colourful herbaceous border that defines the pool and softens the scene while increasing natural habitat. Grade changes also define spaces. A sunken lounging area behind the newly constructed cabana uses limestone to remain faithful to the local vernacular. Beauty is big, but underground issues were also a focus. Beyond space-saving solutions and layout, JDDA also carefully weighed and conserved what was happening below the soil surface. Dallas is built on clay and limestone, and water flow can be a problem. Rather than adding impermeable surfaces with pool coping and poolside paving, they minimalized masonry in favour of green solutions. Instead of surface drains, a sandy soil mix sends stormwater percolating slowly down into the soil. In the lounging area, crushed stone underfoot absorbs precipitation. The result reflects the sleekness of the house and serves the ecosystem, without feeling minimalistic.

PETER JANKE

HORTUS
Hilden, North Rhine-Westphalia, Germany, 2005–

Since 2005 designer Peter Janke has been developing an intricate garden of 1.4 hectares (3½ acres) around a busy nursery, near Düsseldorf in western Germany. Inspired in his early years by British plantswoman Beth Chatto, in whose Essex nursery and garden he worked for a time, Janke has sought to combine an obsession with plants with ecological design. He and his husband, Michael Frinke, have amassed more than 4,500 different plants with which they exploit the garden's various microclimates, always keeping in mind Chatto's dictum of 'right plant, right place'. The garden sits on primarily acidic sand, with pockets of clay, and Janke was keen to work with what they had, rather than amending the soil. Embracing the ground's free-draining nature, he established a dry garden that has never been irrigated since its creation almost twenty years ago. The herbaceous planting is generally loose and naturalistic, but it contrasts pleasingly with the clipped formality and structure provided by Janke's love of topiary. There is also a strong sense of geometry. One enters the garden along a cypress avenue, and further lines of plants, such as *Miscanthus*, divide the garden areas, which include colour-themed silver and bronze gardens. With such a huge range of plants, there is interest at every time of the year, and Janke hopes his garden will inspire people to create more environmentally sensitive plantings.

BETTINA JAUGSTETTER

ABB FACTORY
Ladenburg, Mannheim, Germany, 2010

An industrial site at the eastern edge of the German city of Mannheim for ABB, an energy and automation technology company, has been unexpectedly transformed by a striking, naturalistic planting design by Bettina Jaugstetter. Covering 2,000 square metres (21,500 square feet), the vegetation contrasts sharply with the modern structures of steel and glass. Jaugstetter's planting is a site-specific version of what is known in Germany as 'mixed planting', a style developed in the 1990s whereby a planting formula is established for a particular aesthetic or set of site conditions, and can then be rolled out for whatever size is needed. The positions of plants within the mix is essentially randomized, adding spontaneity. Seven planting formulas were developed for this project, each comprising a mix of structure, companion and groundcover plants so that all space is filled effectively and impact is made through varying colour, form and texture. Grasses and species with attractive seedheads provide continuity across the site, while short-lived species add early visual interest before slower-growing, longer-lived plants take their place. The mix was designed to evolve, and the company embraced the idea of seasonal changes, bringing a dynamic, more residential feel. Areas around the entrances are designed for the strongest impact, while other spaces, such as car parks and walkways, are wilder. Jaugstetter's approach balances structure with flexibility, allowing for changes based on environmental conditions or maintenance capacity. For the staff, the planting system provides unexpected contact with flowers and plants, rendering this very ordinary industrial environment a workplace of great natural beauty.

CHARLES JENCKS

CELLS OF LIFE
Jupiter Artland, near Edinburgh, Scotland, 2003–10

Charles Jencks (1939–2019), who studied English literature and architecture at Harvard University, was also a pioneer of 'landforming', a soil-based art using a synthesis of sculpture, garden design and conceptual thought. When art philanthropists Nicky and Robert Wilson decided to transform the 40-hectare (100-acre) parkland surrounding their home at Bonnington House into the vast contemporary sculpture park Jupiter Artland, Jencks was the first artist from whom they commissioned a permanent artwork. Inspired by the early stages of cell division through the process of mitosis (whereby a cell divides to produce two genetically identical daughter cells), Jencks created eight landforms that range in height from a few metres to more than 20 metres (65 feet), a connecting causeway surrounding four lakes, plus bridges and a parterre for the display of sculptures, which together became *Cells of Life*. It took several years to realize his complex vision, as large mounds based on prehistoric earthworks were carefully sculpted into layered spirals from a pattern marked out using pegs and spray paint. Thousands of tons of earth were shifted by machinery and manual labour before finally being sown with grass. Curved concrete seats within the design bear models of cells surrounded by naturally formed Liesegang bands of cement usually found between layers of sedimentary rocks, their concentric circles mimicking the organelles inside these units of life. This remarkable piece of land art is a testament not only to Jencks's extraordinary vision but also to the skill of the machinery operatives and landscapers who turned his micro-concept into macro-reality.

SALLY JOHANNSOHN

PRIVATE GARDEN
near Hobart, Tasmania, Australia, 1988–

On 3.2 hectares (8 acres) of land around a delightful 1870s stone house near Hobart in Tasmania, Sally Johannsohn and her husband, Andrew Darby, have spent over thirty years creating a magical garden brimming with interesting and unusual plants. In the foothills of kunanyi (Mount Wellington's original name, bestowed by Aboriginal Tasmanians), with fertile volcanic soil, a spring and a backdrop of tall eucalyptus opening to views over Storm Bay, the garden's natural amphitheatre shelters it from the elements. Johannsohn, a trained florist and self-confessed plant obsessive, has visited gardens and wild spaces around the globe and evidently has developed a great talent for combining form, texture and colour. Having found it difficult to buy the plants she coveted, she even set up a small nursery, aptly named Plant Hunters. The layout of the garden was inspired by the organic shapes found in the work of artist Joan Miró, sculptor Alexander Calder and the contour lines of the area, so the pathways are meandering, and the timber benches and stone walls curvaceous. Distinct microclimates, including a wetland area, a woodland and open sunny spaces, allow Johannsohn to grow a wide range of plants, and her preference is for saturated colours balanced by green foliage. Planted in drifts and repeats, bulbs, grasses and a careful edit of annuals and self-seeding perennials maximize seasonal interest, ensuring that there is always much to see and learn in this original garden. Johannsohn is currently simplifying the garden and planting Tasmanian rainforest and alpine trees and shrubs to combine with the more exotic species.

PHILLIP JOHNSON

CHELSEA AUSTRALIAN GARDEN AT OLINDA
Dandenong Ranges Botanic Garden, Olinda, Victoria, Australia, 2023

When Phillip Johnson's design for an Australian garden at the RHS Chelsea Flower Show 2013 was awarded Best in Show, he had a dream to bring it back to Australia. He envisioned a design in the tradition of a grand botanic garden that connected people with nature and instilled a sense of awe in the face of Australia's vast range of native plants. A decade later the garden was reimagined on an underused golf course at just under 1 hectare (nearly 2 acres) – twenty-eight times its show-garden size – opening officially in June 2023 as part of the Dandenong Ranges Botanic Garden. Showcasing the diversity of Australian flora through the use of more than 400 species, it was awarded the 2024 World Urban Parks Outstanding New Park Project Award. Situated on First Nations Wurundjeri Country, it combines Johnson's underpinning design principles, which are to increase biodiversity and connect people back to Country and the beauty of nature while using Australian plants in a sustainable design. The opportunity to direct the construction ensured his vision was undiluted. Water as the focus of healing habitats is at the crux of Johnson's designs, and designed billabongs (pools) softened by tree ferns are his gardens' soul. Over 100 rare and endangered species, including a collection of thirty Wollemi pine (*Wollemia nobilis*), can be appreciated from the paths that wind through the garden. Architectural Queensland bottle trees (*Brachychiton rupestris*), grass trees (*Xanthorrhoea glauca*) and the *Waratah Studio* sculpture provide structure in this outstanding and inspirational garden.

JANE JONES

PRIVATE GARDEN
Portsea, Victoria, Australia, 2019–

It is often in the most challenging environments that a designer's talents are best realized. Jane Jones – whose work displays a unique approach to form, function and location – drew on more than twenty years of experience as a landscape designer when she began a project on a 0.5-hectare (just over 1-acre) block bordered by the Mornington Peninsula National Park, on the traditional lands of the Bunurong people. In this wild marine environment the soil is essentially sand and the scrubby vegetation dominated by the twisted forms of *Melaleuca lanceolata* (moonah) and *Gaudium laevigatum* (syn. *Leptospermum laevigatum*; coastal tea tree). In a highly crafted garden with both informal and tightly clipped planting, the decision to echo the sculptural character of the coastal vegetation is inspired. Near the house, existing tea trees were cloud-pruned, as were specimens of *Olea europaea* (European olives), which were underplanted with clipped *Westringia fruticosa* (coastal rosemary) and *Viburnum tinus* (laurestinus). At the front entrance, striking *Furcraea parmentieri* (syn. *F. bedinghausii*) and tall, slender *Cupressus sempervirens* 'Glauca' (Mediterranean cypress) punctuate a mix of low shrubs, perennials and succulents. Stone and gravel paths lead through a tapestry of feathery ornamental grasses, including *Pennisetum*, which contrast with tightly clipped spheres throughout the garden, where the planting palette includes *Casuarina glauca* 'Green Wave', *Eryngium* (sea holly), *Elaeagnus × submacrophylla* (syn. *E.* × *ebbingei*) and *Limonium peregrinum* (pink statice). This elegant garden was designed to be viewed from any room of the house, and – now double its original size – has drawn glowing accolades.

COLM JOSEPH

WALLED GARDEN
Suffolk, England, 2022

The 20th century witnessed the decline of many walled gardens, but the 21st century has seen once-neglected plots reborn as, for example, community projects, specialist nurseries, heritage enterprises and restaurants, often with noted architects and garden designers at the forefront of their success. Such is the story with this walled garden to a former country estate in Suffolk. Designer Colm Joseph was commissioned to create a garden wrapping around a contemporary house as part of a residential development. He set out to give the property its own sense of place that took advantage of the enclosing walls, but also looked beyond and connected to its location. The 650-square-metre (7,000-square-foot) plot has been divided into an entrance garden, a gravelled area of perennials with terrace and seating, a wildflower meadow and a kitchen garden. Entering the property, a path weaves through a minimalist planting of tall *Calamagrostis × acutiflora* 'Karl Foerster', its form and colouring – particularly in the winter – inspired by reed beds in the nearby estuary. Eight clipped cylinders of *Fagus sylvatica* (beech) give this area structure and definition. Moving to the back of the house, mingled naturalistic perennials are set against the old wall, itself left unadorned in celebration of its heritage and form. Clipped hedging provides screening while trees including pine, birch and beech provide a link to the treescape beyond. Joseph's designs are carefully considered, and his restrained use of simple, crisp hardscaping against naturalistic planting is key to the harmony of his gardens.

JULIE MOIR MESSERVY DESIGN STUDIO IN COLLABORATION WITH YO-YO MA

TORONTO MUSIC GARDEN
Queen's Quay West, Toronto, Canada, 1999

It all started with a note from famed cellist Yo-Yo Ma, asking whether you can make music into a garden. This most brilliant reply is a green jewel of forest glades, glacial stone, flowing pathways and a natural amphitheatre, set on the waterfront of Canada's largest city. It is the masterwork of landscape designer Julie Moir Messervy, taking her cues from Ma's sublime interpretation of Bach's first cello suite. The original site was a 1.2-hectare (3-acre) sliver of land between a major road and a lake. Messervy reshaped the land into three mounded hills and overlaid them with six free-flowing garden rooms, each evoking the tempo and spirit of a dance from Bach's suite. You enter through the Prelude, where a wide concrete pathway is brushed to swirl and eddy like a stream around islets of bolt-upright hackberry trees (*Celtis occidentalis*) with boulders set below like notes on a musical stave. Other garden rooms frame fern-like scrolls and bass clefs to create a journey of contemplation as they branch into benches, glades and views. The centre of the garden spirals up through waves of ornamental grasses to the raised Courante with a tall maypole at its heart. The nearby Menuett garden is crowned by an airy pavilion wreathed in ivy, and visitors seated on grassy steps enjoy summertime musical performances in the Gigue garden below. Connected to the greater landscape, yet offering private moments too, this garden is finely attuned to its surroundings and the nature of big-city life.

JUNYA ISHIGAMI + ASSOCIATES

GARDEN MIZUNIWA
Tochigi, Japan, 2018

A hypnotizing clash of nature and artifice, this sinuous, fairy-tale 'meadow' has been conjured by relocating organic material from a wooded site earmarked for the construction of an artist retreat and hotel. Award-winning architect Junya Ishigami (formerly of celebrated architectural firm SANAA and who established his own studio in 2004), was entrusted with the creation of a garden to accompany the development, and chose to populate it entirely with ingredients sourced from the construction site. Over a four-year period 318 mature trees were painstakingly transplanted and arranged in close proximity, graceful and immaculate, accompanied by 160 serpentine ponds fed by a nearby sluice and maintained with an existing system of irrigation. The undulating, mesmerizing Water Garden covers 1.6 hectares (4 acres) and was inspired by the location's bygone capacity as a rice paddy; its shimmering pools conferring a sprightly allure even in snowbound winter. The ground is laid with gentle *koke* (moss), and selective access is enabled with irregular stepping stones, all taken from the site. Aiming not to create something entirely new, Ishigami focused on the effective use of the found environment – rearranged, disentangled and glorified – and 'let the passage of time create a garden'. Wildlife has moved in, and the pools have become habitats for insects, aquatic plants and animals. The disarming, idealized living tableau raises pertinent questions relating to custodianship, perfectionism, reuse, sustainability, fabrication and the wild. The garden was granted the inaugural Obel Award, for outstanding architectural contributions to human development, in 2019.

RAYMOND JUNGLES

MASÍA EOLO
El Valle de Anton, Panama, 2015

Florida-based – and aptly named – garden designer Raymond Jungles has specialized in creating lush plantscapes in tropical areas of the Americas and the Caribbean. Two of his earliest influences are Mexican designer Luis Barragan and Brazilian designer Roberto Burle Marx, and in his enriching, intelligible designs Jungles has always followed the latter's advice to 'be curious'. But he has fused this with his own mantra, 'live in harmony,' for his gardens are as much concerned with ecosystem restoration, natural stewardship and sustainability as they are with delightful and arresting aesthetics. This award-winning garden was forged out of an inauspicious 1.5-hectare (3¾-acre) plot, a former chicken farm, devoid of trees and with irregular contours. But what a setting! Nestled within a verdant volcanic crater, cool at altitude, its sides cloaked in primary forest, it enjoys wonderful sight lines out into the landscape, and Jungles used these 'borrowed' vistas to dictate the land-forming contours and the position of the dwelling. The lake and its cascades form a rainwater harvest and mitigation system, and they have also increased the habitat range and thus the biodiversity of the garden. This and the visual impact are enhanced by the lavish tapestries of locally sourced (not wild-collected) native plants that give the garden not only its richness, but also a seamless transition into the wider habitat. But this is more than just views. There are trails that lead the visitor out from the designed naturalistic garden into the genuine wilderness of unspoiled forest and up into the alpine flora of the crater's rim.

MARC PETER KEANE

EMPTY RIVER
Kyoto, Japan, 2023

While studying landscape architecture at Cornell University, Marc Peter Keane found his niche in approaching the garden as art. That led him to Japan for what he had planned to be a year's stint, but he became so immersed in Japanese garden design that eighteen years slipped by before he returned to the United States for a one-year teaching assignment. Another eighteen years passed before Keane returned permanently to Japan in 2019, and there he remains, creating what he calls Poem Gardens: 'Poetry is the distillation of language and these gardens are the distillation of concepts.' The courtyard garden he created at Hōnen-in Temple in Kyoto exemplifies his art. Designed to embody the Buddhist concept of emptiness while symbolizing the carbon cycle, Keane embellished a 48-square-metre (517-square-foot) space overlooked on two sides by verandas and nurturing 200-year-old camellias set in white gravel. He wove through the space a curvaceous dry river of carefully laid charcoal sticks, then – for continuity and to soften the places where the 'river' begins and ends – he planted *Pieris*, *Aspidistra*, *Ardisia* and *Dryopteris*. 'Carbon is cycling through nature, never staying in one form permanently,' explains Keane. 'It exemplifies the constant flux of the world and the concept of emptiness.' The choice of motif was also, in part, to reference carbon's effect on global climate change – just one way in which the garden's message becomes pertinent to our times. Simple yet infinitely complex, the Empty River distils a profound environmental and artistic statement into a memorable visual scene. It truly is poetry.

BROOK KLAUSING AND REBECCA MCMACKIN

BROOKLYN MUSEUM GARDEN
Brooklyn, New York, United States, 2023

A reimagined entrance plaza for the Brooklyn Museum's Beaux-Arts building, designed in 1897 by influential architectural firm McKim, Mead & White, was transformed into a public garden to welcome both people and pollinators by landscape designer Brook Klausing and ecological horticulturist Rebecca McMackin. The minimalist entry pavilion by architect James Polshek (2004) consists of a semicircular glass enclosure surrounded by a large outdoor amphitheatre of terraced lawn. Working within the crescent, Klausing and McMackin envisioned the space as a beautiful, biodiverse, ecologically beneficial meadow. They replaced the lawn with a mix of native plants, including wildflowers for bees, host plants for butterflies, and species that would provide seed for birds. To keep the pollinator-friendly design open and inviting to passersby, paths were created so that people can engage with the plants. Inspired by Deborah Kass's playful *OY/YO* sculpture (2015) – the only vertical element in the garden – McMackin selected the plant palette carefully, choosing mostly yellow and white flowers for spring and summer, including *Penstemon* and *Coreopsis*. *Asclepias* (milkweed) plays an important part in the scheme, planted close to simple wooden benches scattered throughout the garden, so as to bring people and butterflies into close contact. In the autumn, colours shift as purple asters come into bloom and provide vital late-season sustenance for wildlife. In addition to wildflowers, shrubs, such as *Ilex verticillata* (winterberry) and *Clethra alnifolia* (sweet pepperbush), are used as anchors, and native grasses, including *Panicum virgatum* (switchgrass) and *Schizachyrium scoparium* (little bluestem), provide structure and year-round interest.

JACQUELINE VAN DER KLOET

DE THEETUIN
Weesp, Amsterdam, The Netherlands, 1983–

De Theetuin (The Tea Garden), nestled within a 17th-century fortress in a small town near Amsterdam, is a tranquil place. Concealed behind towering beech hedges and designed around a pond enclosed by a hedge of *Thuja* (western red cedar), it unfolds in meandering paths, offering surprises at every turn. The 1,000-square-metre (10,760-square-foot) plot was intended as a garden for visitors, and conceived as a place to enjoy and learn about plants, inspired by English garden-visiting and the culture of having tea at the end of a visit. Although created by the garden's three adjoining households, it is foremost the display and experimental garden of leading garden designer and bulb expert, Jacqueline van der Kloet. Her planting philosophy is in many ways classically Dutch, blending structure with spontaneity, the clipped hedges framing informal perennial borders, but here the role of bulbs breaks with Dutch tradition. Having been asked to trial bulbs, van der Kloet developed a way of integrating them with perennials and other plants, often to dramatic and innovative artistic effect. She has been commissioned by many public gardens worldwide, including Keukenhof, the Netherlands' top display garden, and the Lurie Garden in Chicago, where she worked to complement Piet Oudolf's plantings. De Theetuin is naturally at its most colourful in the spring, but van der Kloet also promotes the role of summer bulbs, such as alliums, martagon lilies and nerines. In the winter, the role of clipped shrubs in the design comes to the fore.

**PETER KORN AND
JULIA ANDERSSON**

KLINTA TRÄDGÅRD
Höör, near Malmö, Sweden, 2015–

In 2015 Julia Andersson and Peter Korn moved to the south of Sweden to create a new ecologically driven garden on 1.4 hectares (3½ acres) of land. A nurseryman and landscape designer, Korn was already known for his pioneering approach to growing plants in pure sand, and this new garden allowed him to experiment further. Counter-intuitively, the structure of sand maintains a consistent humidity, so plants require little to no watering. 'Think of a beach,' Peter explains, 'where the surface is too hot to walk upon, but dig in your toes and it's always cool and moist.' In sand fewer nutrients are available, so plants don't grow so tall; this means less staking and keeps overly vigorous plants in check, but the growth is also slower and stronger, resulting in more resilient plants. Andersson and Korn, who employ this technique for public plantings, wanted to produce their own sand-grown plants to avoid the problem of transplant shock in conventionally grown plants. At Klinta there is space for a nursery to produce these plants, but the couple have also developed a shared garden of distinct spaces, with Korn's the more exposed and exclusively sandy, and Julia's the shadier, more naturally moist areas. The planting style is abundant and colourful, intermingling a large number of grasses with flowering perennials. Even though both Andersson and Korn are fanatical plantspeople with a range of unusual treasures, they do not discriminate against common garden plants, including self-seeding *Valeriana officinalis* and *Echium vulgare*, if they are also beautiful and serve an ecological function. Combining organic methods with habitat creation and diverse planting, this unique garden has encouraged a huge range of insect life.

PRADIP KRISHEN AND THE INDIAN ECOLOGICAL RESTORATION ALLIANCE

RAO JODHA DESERT ROCK PARK

Jodhpur, Rajasthan, India, 2006–

In the shadow of Jodhpur's Mehrangarh Fort, Rao Jodha Desert Rock Park is a 30-hectare (74-acre) testament to ecological restoration. The land, once degraded and overrun by mesquite (an invasive shrub of American origin), has been transformed into a habitat for more than 200 species of native desert plant, alongside diverse birds and animals. The restoration was led by India's Ecological Restoration Alliance with the input of leading conservationist Pradip Krishen. The immediate focus was on eradicating mesquite – mostly by hand, enabled by local people using traditional quarrying techniques – in a process that took seven years. Livestock-grazing was stopped and native species reintroduced. Locally native plants had to be sought over a wide range, throughout the Thar desert region; seeds were collected, grown on in a nursery, planted and mulched to conserve water. The attempts to establish them in the harsh conditions were carefully documented so that each success or failure added to growing knowledge of the necessary planting techniques. By the end, success rates were almost 100 per cent. Grasses are an important component, as well as trees (which can access water through deep roots), succulents and ephemerals (species that grow and flower during a brief period after rain). Visitors can explore winding sandstone paths and marvel at restored cultural landmarks, including a stepwell, a Jain temple and a pavilion. The visitors' centre includes geological exhibits and field guides, and runs naturalist-led tours of this immersive park that illustrates the potential of conservation to revive neglected terrain.

LAGUARDIA DESIGN GROUP

OCEANFRONT GARDEN
Sagaponack, New York, United States, 1998–

In 1969 a pilot flying over Long Island looked down on a 12-hectare (30-acre) oceanside potato field and decided to purchase the plot. He commissioned architect Norman Jaffe (1932–1993) to build an iconic, modern shingle-style saltbox house on the site, to evoke the original potato barns. All was bucolic until 1998, when a violent storm decimated the dunes. Architect and landscape architect Christopher LaGuardia, who is renowned for his sympathetic blending of architecture and landscape, and had worked with Jaffe before setting up his own studio in 1992, was called in to save the house. His solution was to move the building back 122 metres (400 feet), and he solved the conundrum of obtaining the 23,000 cubic metres (30,000 cubic yards) of fill needed to settle it on a floodplain by excavating a 'borrow pit'. This resulted in a uniquely shaped 0.6-hectare (1½-acre) wildlife-attracting pond. Along its shores, he installed an ecosystem of blueberries, bayberries, winterberries and Eastern red cedar with stands of native hibiscus to create a vanishing shoreline. Using the redistributed soil, LaGuardia rebuilt the dunes in east/west-orientated chevrons to replicate the undulations created by waves, clothing them in *Calamagrostis breviligulata* (American beach grass) 'as a gesture to the original dunes and to evoke the sculptural quality of the house'. Away from the water, the landscape transitions into a warm- and cool-season mixed tall-grass meadow. The project may originally have been about creating resiliency, but it has also resulted in a garden of incredible beauty.

ANDREW LAIDLAW

GUILFOYLE'S VOLCANO
Melbourne Gardens, Melbourne, Victoria, Australia, 2010

Guilfoyle's Volcano covers an area of about 4,000 square metres (43,000 square feet) on the southeastern edge within the Royal Botanic Gardens' Melbourne location. The highest point in the gardens, it features a body of water constructed in 1872 by the creator of the gardens, botanist William Guilfoyle. It is designed to store 1 million litres (about 264,200 gallons) of water, which is then fed by gravity around the gardens. The brief for the gardens' landscape architect Andrew Laidlaw in 2010 was to work creatively with Guilfoyle's historic theme – the volcanic landscapes of the South Pacific – to rework the disused and run-down feature. The resulting garden was designed for maximum visual impact and still functions as an integral part of the overall system of water management. Five circular floating islands designed to resemble Monet's waterlily paintings are planted with native and exotic plants that treat the water as it passes through their roots; they are cut back each year and the trimmings used as compost. Guilfoyle's Volcano provides all-ability access and platforms that allow views of the surrounding city. Seasonal interest is created using annual and biennial planting, including the spectacular *Echium wildpretii* (tower of jewels) and *Swainsona formosa* (Sturt's desert pea). The planting framework features a mixture of exotic and Australian arid and succulent plants that, in their colours and forms, bring to mind a volcanic scene. Set out in drifts around the main cone, they simplify the palette and reinforce the circular form of the feature.

LARRY WEANER LANDSCAPE ASSOCIATES

THE BOWER
Shermans Dale, Pennsylvania, United States, 2020

On a slope in the Appalachian Mountains just north of Pennsylvania's capital city, Harrisburg, Bill and Jane Allis have converted their 14.5-hectare (36-acre) rural farm into a native plant garden and sculpture park that opened to the public in 2021. In 2019 the Allises enlisted landscape architecture firm Oehme, van Sweden (see p.207) to develop a masterplan for the site, and the following year they commissioned Larry Weaner Landscape Associates to produce a horticultural plan focusing on ecology, and to implement the design. Turning their homestead of fifty years into a sanctuary where art and nature would coexist harmoniously was a lifelong dream for the Allises, who were further driven by the COVID-19 pandemic to create an accessible open space for solace-seekers. This involved creating a landscape of open meadow and woodland featuring an abundance of wild and introduced native plants, complemented with large-scale sculptures and land art. Larry Weaner, an ecology-based landscape designer known for working with native plants and integrating ecological principles and naturalistic designs that benefit wildlife, revitalized 2.5 hectares (6 acres) of existing meadow, introducing native wildflowers and grasses, greatly diversifying the ecological landscape. Along with the enhanced natural meadow habitat, large garden beds with drifts of herbaceous perennials, a series of small wetland pools, shrubs and forest combine gracefully with sculptures, providing an immersive experience in which to learn about the benefits of native plants and the importance of biodiversity. The garden features work by artists who take direct inspiration from The Bower's landscape.

LATZ + PARTNER

LANDSCHAFTSPARK DUISBURG-NORD
Duisburg-Meiderich, Germany, 1990–2002

A post-industrial wasteland in Germany's Ruhr Valley now forms a visionary green space and adventure playground attracting more than one million visitors every year. Duisburg Nord Landscape Park is no ordinary park; it is a sprawling, 180-hectare (445-acre) site framing the colossal remnants of the Thyssen Steelworks and Coal Plant, which shut down in 1985 after eighty-seven years. Its gradual revitalization was part of a region-wide initiative to convert the rust belt into parkland. In 1990 landscape architect firm Latz + Partner (founded by Peter Latz) came up with an innovative strategy to repurpose the site and rewild the landscape while leaving its rusted bones exposed, but it took twelve years of systematic diagnosis and problem-solving to effect a site-wide metamorphosis. The seven-storey Blast Furnace 5 and its girder catwalks now overlook a performance space in the Piazza Metallica. Its giant concrete fuel tank has been repurposed into the largest diving tank in Europe, railway beds are now visitor pathways, and flowering trees and other vegetation have been planted to decontaminate the ground. The polluted canal was drained, treated and refilled with rainwater, and a network of walking trails and cycle paths surrounds a vast wildlife refuge. Each evening a laser show brings the industrial core of the site back to life. The park revolutionized the architectural game plan for post-industrial sites in Europe and beyond, directly inspiring such projects as the High Line in New York (see p.101) to resurrect the detritus of our industrial past into the ironclad promise of a greener urban future.

ARABELLA LENNOX-BOYD WITH FRANK GEHRY

MAGGIE'S DUNDEE
Ninewells Hospital, Dundee, Scotland, 2003

Founded by writer and garden designer Maggie Keswick Jencks (who died of cancer in 1995) and her late husband, Charles Jencks (see p.147), Maggie's Centres are an international network of drop-in centres that offer support to cancer sufferers. The first opened in Edinburgh in 1996. As part of her original concept, Keswick Jencks emphasized gardens, landscape and outdoor spaces to generate a calm, stress-reducing environment as an aid to healing. For Maggie's Dundee – the first wholly new centre – acclaimed architect Frank Gehry (see p.62) was commissioned to work alongside equally established, multi-award-winning garden designer Arabella Lennox-Boyd. For this, his first building in the United Kingdom, Gehry designed a white, cottage-like structure modelled on a traditional Scottish 'but and ben' dwelling. Complementing that visual simplicity, Lennox-Boyd realized 1.2 hectares (3 acres) of gardens, incorporating a circular garden surrounded by scented plants and flowering trees intended as a place of retreat for meditation and reflection. The most poignant element, however, is the set of three earthwork amphitheatre-like turf steps that frame and rise up from a circular labyrinth 33 metres (108 feet) in diameter. Picked out in water-washed cobbles, the pattern is based on the 13th-century example set into the nave of Chartres Cathedral, France, for the purpose of meditative reflection. Beyond it, a perimeter shelterbelt of native trees and shrubs, many of them flowering, encloses the grounds and screens the functional aspects of the nearby hospital. Also within the garden is Antony Gormley's sculpture *Another Time X*, adding another layer of artistic expression to this beautifully considered space.

MAYA LIN WITH TAN LIN

READING A GARDEN
Cleveland Public Library, Cleveland, Ohio,
United States, 1998

In collaboration with her brother the poet Tan Lin, celebrated American architect, designer and sculptor Maya Lin created a sculpture for the Eastman Reading Garden at the main branch of the Cleveland Public Library. The garden (renovated in 1998 by landscape architect Laurie Olin) is home to Maya Lin's site-specific stainless-steel, granite, crushed stone and bronze piece *Reading a Garden*, after Tan's poem of the same name. Lin is known for her minimalist style and in particular for designing the powerful National Vietnam Memorial in Washington, DC, and the Cleveland work is part of her *Ohio Trilogy* series of landscapes dedicated to her home state. A central L-shaped fountain sends a gently cascading stream of water over paving blocks of black granite inscribed with the text of the poem. Some of the type is written backwards or upside down, to be mirrored in the reflecting pool that gathers the waters. The non-linear nature of the abstract poem and its carefully placed text encourages movement as the words lead visitors through the garden, appearing on meandering paths of paving stones, on benches and walls, and on plaques in tree beds. The poem and its presentation encourage discovery, playful interaction and creative interpretation. The outdoor reading room includes a recessed seating area shaded by a grove of honey locust trees (*Gleditsia triacanthos*). It is a response both to the garden and to the cultural context of the library, focused on the idea of reading and offering a quiet retreat from the city streets.

TANJA LINCKE AND ANSELM REYLE WITH DAS RESERVAT

RUIN GARDEN
Berlin, Germany, 2014

In an 'uneasy' love letter to the Romantic movement of the late 18th century, husband and wife team, architect Tanja Lincke and artist Anselm Reyle, have shaped a living ruin from the detritus of Communist East Germany. In 2008, wishing to increase his studio space, Reyle acquired an 8,700-square-metre (93,600-square-foot) industrial site once occupied by the GDR's water police on Berlin's River Spree. Lincke's expertise amplified the location's possibilities and invigorated intentions, recalling and subverting the Romantic fascination with the emotive resonance of times past. Reyle and Lincke worked with design firm Das Reservat to achieve 'restoration' with a process of meticulous demolition, 'fraying' existing brickwork and preserving telling features, such as signage, decaying beams and a large rusting crane. They opted to retain only the outer walls of the former boathouse ('they became our hedges'), opening up the classically Romantic notion of creating a void, then pervading it with soft and tranquil nature. Piet Oudolf's work on the Manhattan High Line (see p.101), blending naturalistic planting with industrial surroundings, proved instructive. Pioneer plant species contribute to a restrained, authentic picture, and the seasons pass with salutary shifts in mood and colour. The couple's family home, designed by Lincke, now graces the site, as do their respective workspaces, and their output has evolved as a result of daily exposure to the natural, organic, ageing, reusable and mutable materials of their garden. Indeed, large shards of concrete formerly comprising the boathouse floor are rearranged into a sculpture echoing Romantic painter Caspar David Friedrich's *Das Eismeer* (Sea of Ice; 1823–4).

TON TER LINDEN WITH GERT TABAK

PRIVATE GARDEN
De Veenhoop, Friesland, The Netherlands, 2008–14

Raised slightly above the landscape, its impressionistic planting reflected in a kidney-shaped pond, the garden at De Veenhoop stood like an outpost overlooking green fields stretching to the horizon. It was in this remote village in the northern Dutch province of Friesland that artist and plantsman Ton ter Linden set up home with his creative and life partner, photographer Gert Tabak, in 2008 and created one of his most compelling landscapes. A key progenitor of the Dutch Wave in naturalistic design, ter Linden has been most influential for his first home garden in Ruinen. But it attracted so many admirers that he escaped to a quieter life further north at De Veenhoop. His own hero was renowned modernist garden designer Mien Ruys (1904–1999), and ter Linden's 3,200-square-metre (34,500-square-foot) garden reflected her architectural influence of wild planting in a strong design with pergolas, paths, water features and minimalist hedges. During his six years in De Veenhoop, he framed the back of the house with a central terrace leading along a boardwalk to the pond. The borders spilled out from both sides in June with a high-voltage profusion of red opium poppies, alliums, irises, roses, geraniums and aquilegias, with late summer fireworks still to come. This was design by subtraction, achieved by finely editing the plantings with a long asparagus knife, a practice ter Linden had picked up while watching the gardeners at work in the heemparks (naturalistic public parks) of Amstelveen. Ter Linden – who is known for his painting as the 'Dutch Monet' – approaches gardens as living art, and De Veenhoop was his northern masterpiece.

JOHN LITTLE

HILLDROP
Horndon on the Hill, Essex, England, 2010

Many people might not recognize Hilldrop – with its wildflowers growing out of heaps of rubble – as a garden. This 3,000-square-metre (32,300-square-foot) plot is, however, very much a garden, and one that makes a brave statement that we must rethink what we mean for our outside spaces. Here is convincing evidence that we can indeed create gardens and manage landscapes in a way that supports far more biodiversity than conventional approaches. Brownfield sites, born of human activity and disturbance, are often ignored or built over, although they host the many species that thrive in low-nutrient conditions, making them biodiversity hotspots. In his own garden, John Little aims to replicate the conditions found in these locations, with piles of rubble, sand, crushed ceramics and other materials almost devoid of nutrients. Denied the resources they need to spread, competitive plant species give way to a larger number of less strong-growing ones, so that space is left for invertebrates, especially solitary bees, to build nests in the ground. Little's creativity extends beyond plants, and insect habitats made from sand piles, gabion walls filled with rubble, and drilled posts provide additional encouragement to wildlife. His experiments demonstrate that small design tweaks can transform waste into a valuable habitat while remaining visually appealing. Most of the planting here uses native wildflowers, but some areas incorporate garden plants, too. The result is certainly wild, but colourful in early summer and, above all, a vibrant hub of life, providing evidence and inspiration for other gardeners and landscapers.

TODD LONGSTAFFE-GOWAN

PRIVATE GARDEN
London, England, 2014

Todd Longstaffe-Gowan is a master at combining historical and contemporary elements in his gardens, building on the legacy of the past yet creating imaginative, stylish spaces that feel fresh and modern. Hidden behind a row of tall Georgian houses in Kensington, this 18-metre-long (60-foot) London garden was inspired by the topiarized structures of 17th-century Dutch town gardens, with a framework of yew topiary anchoring the space. A gravel path curves through beds punctuated with tall cones of yew, drawing the visitor through to a simple circle of lawn and an elegant arched yew theatre. This provides the perfect stage set for a statue of a white stag, an antiques-shop find by the garden's artist owner. The strong architectural structure of the yew is set against textured planting, providing the dramatic tension that defines this garden and gives it its contemporary edge. Bold foliage plants, such as *Hydrangea aspera* and *Euphorbia × pasteurii*, provide a foil for a succession of jewel-like flowers, while a 6-metre-high (20-foot) south-facing wall near the house is clad thickly with more plants to take advantage of every inch of growing space. As well as using traditional climbers such as roses, ornamental vines and wisteria on this wall, Longstaffe-Gowan has experimented with training shrubs that are not often grown in this way, such as *Sambucus nigra* (elder) and *Buddleja alternifolia*. The garden's final hurrah is a secret enclosed seating area behind the yew theatre, adding the element of surprise that Longstaffe-Gowan believes is crucial in any garden.

RON LUTSKO

PRIVATE GARDEN
Portola Valley, California, United States, 2016

As both landscape designer and horticultural expert, Ron Lutsko (who founded his landscape design firm in 1981) is a pioneer of the American West Coast landscape architecture community, and renowned for producing sensitively designed landscapes that connect people to plants and the natural environment. The brief for this garden was to create a setting for the house that does not detract from its architecture, and the design satisfies that requirement while also reflecting Lutsko's design philosophy, which is shaped by his interest in and knowledge of ecosystems, sustainability, design, architecture and conceptual art. There is apparently no boundary to mark where the garden ends and the landscape begins, offering uninterrupted views of the surroundings. The design follows the topography of the site, using low concrete walls that reach out from the building to form a visual link with the hillside. Lutsko has worked on a range of residential, commercial, civic and institutional projects around the world. His underlying passion for sustainable horticulture and California's native landscapes has led to collaborative expertise in both visible and invisible elements of completed projects, from the management of stormwater, soil health, and the conservation of materials and resources to permeable paving systems, swales for filtration and water dispersion, and green roofs to capture water and recycle nutrients. He focuses on restoring landscapes by reintroducing site-specific native plants, drawing on his native plant nursery and selecting species that have proved sustainable in a particular microclimate and conditions.

SUE AND IAN MABBERLEY

NANT-Y-BEDD
near Abergavenny, Wales, 1980–

Nant-y-Bedd (Stream of the Grave), a 4-hectare (10-acre) organic garden in a woodland, is hidden in the Black Mountains at an altitude of 366 metres (1,200 feet). It is named after the stream that runs through it, beside which at the top of the mountain stand two Bronze Age burial mounds. Sue has gardened here for forty-four years, Ian for twenty-eight, in which time it has evolved into more than just a garden; with its varied, harmonious naturalistic planting it has become part of the wider landscape. The garden is split by its access road. On the northern side, surrounding the house, is the butterfly-filled Cottage Garden which features an eye-catching fern sculpture carved from an old Western red cedar. From there, an understated wooden bridge crosses the stream to the Edible Forest Garden. On the southern side the Potager Garden is carved out of the forest, its boundary a fern- and moss-encrusted drystone wall. A path winds through the woodland (containing Cedric – another characterful tree sculpture – a treehouse and the tranquil no-phones-allowed Silent Space) and a rope bridge traverses the stream again, its steep sides clothed with native ferns, leading to wilder areas. Alongside the bridge grow *Camassia leichtlinii* subsp. *suksdorfii* and *Narcissus poeticus*, leading to the serenity of the natural swimming pool with its fringe of native marginals and sheltering Douglas firs, some topping 36 metres (118 feet). From here, there are alpine-like views down over the Picnic Meadow, a picturesque valley of woodland pasture and wildflowers. This is a garden in which the dynamics of natural change are embraced.

T. J. MAHER

PATTHANA
Kiltegan, Co. Wicklow, Republic of Ireland, 2008–

The artist T. J. Maher made this garden with his husband, Simon Kirby, as time and a limited budget allowed them. *Patthana* denotes the Buddhist concept of bringing the attention to the present, and Maher has long had a great knowledge of and respect for the natural world: another Buddhist tenet. This and his delight in combining plants have driven the design of his joyful country garden. A cobbled courtyard is sheltered by a stone wall, sunny on one side, where pots create a blaze of colour from early spring to autumn, and shady on the other, where foliage plants thrive. The inner garden, enclosed by mature hawthorn trees, is a grassy terrace cut into by two oval beds to maximize the layered planting chosen with pollinators in mind. Simple species or single-flowered blooms are preferred, especially when it comes to dahlias, which Maher hybridizes in favourite shades of magenta, crimson and raspberry. In 2020 the couple purchased the adjoining field, extending the garden to just under 0.5 hectares (1 acre), and in this more exposed site, with a view of the church, they sculpted excess soil to echo the nearby mountains and created large beds filled with prairie-style plants, such as butterfly magnets *Echinacea* (coneflower) and *Verbena bonariensis*, and ornamental grasses, such as *Calamagrostis arundinacea* (also listed as *C. brachytricha*), which have space to sprawl and sway. A winding path leads to a torc-shaped planted mound encircling a peaceful seating area, and for further diversity the couple have added a variety of native and non-native plants to a meadow that already attracts numerous insects.

MARGARIDA MAIA

PRIVATE GARDEN
Rio Maior, Santarém, Portugal, 2016

'I started the garden here for my son's wedding, as I wanted to have the celebration at our house, and I wanted flowers for the event,' says Margarida Maia, who made this bold start some six years before she retired. Reading and making use of technical information is second nature to her after a career in the medical profession, so, as gardening became a passion, she recalls having to 'study, to find out all about plants and about soil'. The resulting 0.4 hectares (1 acre) is an exuberant array of perennials, grasses, shrubs and annuals, viewed from a central lawn around the house, which is on a hill surrounded by rolling countryside and eucalyptus plantations. Maia's inspiration is the New Perennial movement and the work of Piet Oudolf (see p.101 and p.216). A diversity of plants is held together by plentiful repetition, particularly of airy *Oenothera lindheimeri* (gaura), *Verbena bonariensis* and the grass *Muhlenbergia capillaris*. There is a small pond, and Italian cypresses create vertical drama. Morning mists are frequent on this hilltop site, and it is Maia's ability to use them as a foil for the colours and shapes of her planting that has created much of the magic in the smartphone photography that made her an Instagram sensation. The soil is a calcareous clay, so part of the challenge has been identifying plants that work and, indeed, sourcing them, but none of these difficulties dissuade Maia from planning more experimental planting in this sublime, exuberant garden.

MAKI AND ASSOCIATES

THE GARDEN OF TRANQUILITY
Aga Khan Centre, London, England, 2018

The late Japanese architect Fumihiko Maki was an expert in cultural design, including several museums and performing-arts centres worldwide. The Garden of Tranquility within the Aga Khan Centre (for which Maki was also architect) in London is itself architectural and draws spatial inspiration from Egyptian and Middle Eastern covered loggias. The Islamic influence is referenced also in the eight-pointed star motif used on the ceiling, enclosing glass walls and balustrade. The light, airy space and the smooth simplicity of line and material — pale limestone floor and polished marble benches — ooze serenity, while another sensory note of calm is sounded by the gentle murmuring of the central fountain. Its surround of black marble and, leading from it, the four perpendicular stripes of the same material set into the floor reference the archetypal form of the Islamic garden, the four-square *chahar bagh*. The Aga Khan Centre and its immediate environs are enlivened by a collection of ten roof, terrace and courtyard gardens, all melding echoes of historic Islamic architectural and garden styles with the contemporary. A further three are by Maki and Associates; there are also the rooftop Garden of Life by Madison Cox, the Garden of Light by Nelson Byrd Woltz, the Garden of Reflection by Vladimir Djurovic Landscape Architecture and, below the Garden of Tranquility, the Jellicoe Gardens by Tom Stuart-Smith and Townshend Landscape Architects, where the enclosing trees and informal meadow-like planting meld British and Persian influences.

VICTORIA MANOYLO

PRIVATE GARDEN
Moshchun, Kyiv, Ukraine, 2023

This garden was first planned in 2020 by landscape designer Victoria Manoylo for a young family, and built the following year. However, in March 2022 the village became a battleground during the Russian invasion, resulting in widespread destruction. The house and garden were burned down, along with neighbouring properties. Restoration efforts began in 2023, following the liberation of the village from Russian forces. The site borders a meadow and forest near a tributary of the Irpen River, within a wildlife-rich nature reserve. The 0.2-hectare (½-acre) garden slopes down to a reservoir and is irregularly shaped, with distinct zones: an entrance area with birches and conifers; a more formal garden with box and grasses near the house; a naturalistic lakeside garden with willows and perennials; and an orchard. Rebuilding took two years, and involved the planting of new trees amid the remnants of war, including shell fragments. Although it is now a sanctuary of greenery and harmony, the air-raid sirens and missile defence explosions are reminders of the conflict. The garden had another life as the inspiration for a show garden at the RHS Hampton Court Palace Garden Festival in England in 2022. In the show garden, titled 'What Does Not Burn', a fire-damaged building graphically illustrated the destruction but there were also signs of renewal, hope and resistance, with wildflowers, traditional cottage-garden flowers, barley (illustrating the importance of the agriculture for which Ukraine is universally known) and *rushniks*, the woven or embroidered decorative cloths that are a fundamental part of traditional Ukrainian culture.

ULA MARIA

GARDEN OF CHILDHOOD MEMORIES
Northampton, Northamptonshire, England, 2017

The garden that snagged Ula Maria the Young Designer of the Year award at the 2017 RHS Tatton Park Flower Show perfectly reflected the rich landscapes she loves to weave. Aroma, layering and sense of place are paramount to her style, explaining that 'soft layers of texture make a garden feel lived in'. Maria was inspired by the textures and colours of the multi-generational garden she grew up with in coastal Lithuania to create the winning garden, staging such herbs as *Salvia rosmarinus* (rosemary), *Stachys byzantina* (lamb's ears) and *Helichrysum italicum* (curry plant) beside sedums, *Centranthus ruber* 'Albus' and other uplifting plants. As the show wound down, attendees purchased a few flashier elements, but what to do with the more subtle ingredients? A call to Maria's father in Northampton brought an immediate adoption agreement. He was delighted to give the garden a home, where the herbs flourish in the lean, gritty soil. The whole family worked over three years to breathe further life into the adopted mini landscape (about 48 square metres/510 square feet), adding paving scavenged by Maria's brother – a landscaper – from demolition sites, plus fencing to screen distractions. 'The small scale adds to the richness of the experience,' says Maria. 'It's an invitation to explore.' She and her family need no longer rely on memory for their heritage garden – it lives on. She brings a similar approach to her clients' gardens, tapping into the essence of each owner's own formative experiences.

STEVE MARTINO

ARROYO RESIDENCE
Paradise Valley, Arizona, United States, 2009

Observing that 'when the power of water is shut off, your garden should not die', Steve Martino has for more than four decades pioneered desert landscapes in America's southwest. He was an early adopter of native plants, and his gardens are carefully contrived to showcase the colour, form and texture of these species, combined with the added vitality of the native fauna enticed in by the plantings. Another Martino characteristic is a dramatic juxtaposition of natural and ecological processes with artificial elements, as seen in this striking domestic garden. This may be within the garden itself – such as natural rock and native plants next to fire pits and brightly painted walls – but it applies equally to the garden as a whole and the borrowed desert landscape beyond. There is always a close integration of house and garden; the one opens to the other, while shade structures (arbours, pergolas, screens and so on) shelter the interior of the building from the harsh desert sunlight while also making the garden usable. Here, the strong forms and bright colours of the artificial elements harmonize yet contrast with those of flowers and architectonic plants, many of which are succulents. Some are planted in naturalistic settings, others in containers and raised beds. Life-giving water is used both in its still, mirroring state in pools, where it introduces a note of calm, and as eye-catching sheets of falling water, adding sound and energy to the dynamism of the garden as a whole.

FERNANDO MARTOS

PRIVATE GARDEN
El Casar, Guadalajara, Spain, 2010

Northeast of Madrid, landscape designer Fernando Martos has created a 2,800-square-metre (30,000-square-foot) garden that exemplifies the direction a new generation of Spanish garden designers is taking, breaking with traditional formality but still recognizing the primacy of form and texture. Such an approach is vital in the harsh steppe climate of central Spain. Martos, who trained at Madrid's Castillo de Batres school and was inspired by an internship at Newby Hall in Yorkshire, says, 'What I like about the English garden and what I want here is the loose, natural look, movement and seasonal changes, particularly with colour.' Striking at the heart of tradition, he finds 'the typical Mediterranean garden very static, it never changes'. By contrast, he wants 'to make gardens that look different every time you look at them', stressing that, for clients, 'change gets people excited'. Around a contemporary house, the planting is dominated by hummocks of *Cistus* (rock rose) and *Lavandula* (lavender), regularly pruned – a practice that imitates the nibbling of grazing animals – partly to ensure longevity. Grasses provide a strong but harmonious contrast, while in the spring and early summer there is plenty of flower colour. Sustainability is integral to the design, especially when it comes to water conservation. Deep planting holes encourage resilient root systems, mulching conserves soil moisture, and a discreet drip irrigation system provides water as it is needed.

JUAN MASEDO

PRIVATE GARDEN
Ibiza, Spain, 2018

Self-taught, with a passion for plants and armed only with experience, intuition and vision, Juan Masedo has established himself as the go-to garden designer on this delightful Balearic island, where, he says, 'natural harmony saves me from human noise'. This private 0.5-hectare (1¼-acre) garden belongs to an old country estate in the north of Ibiza, surrounded by native pine forest. Masedo restored the old drystone walls and terraces, adding winding paths and new outdoor spaces for alfresco dining and relaxing, surfaced with gravel that is also of local stone. Anchored around carob and olive trees, the naturalistic planting is elegant and vivacious, and consists of drought-tolerant Mediterranean species, including *Achillea* (yarrow), *Ballota* (horehound), *Helichrysum orientale* (immortelle), *Salvia rosmarinus* (rosemary) and *Santolina chamaecyparissus* (cotton lavender). The garden reveals Masedo's phased approach, whereby he first visits the site in order to recognize its character and what is already there. The 'inventory' taken, the next stage is to 'cast the main characters of the story', as he calls them, which are the trees and large shrubs. He does not use just any specimen, however, but carefully, specifically selects from perhaps hundreds of candidates in order that the chosen one will integrate with the *genus loci* (the spirit of the place), so that 'they look like they have been part of that old story'. Once the structure is created, the third and final phase is to add 'the nuances, colours, textures and perfumes', which he calls 'extras' but which 'add a lot of weight to the history as well'.

TOM MASSEY

PRIVATE GARDEN
Twickenham, London, England, 2020

For someone who set up his practice as recently as 2015 (garden design was a second career), Tom Massey has already had an impact on the horticultural scene, creating thought-provoking gardens at shows and for clients, and winning several awards along the way. He brings contemporary design and innovation to the fore, while rooting each project in ecological and sustainable principles, with resilience a key consideration. This garden in southwest London exemplifies his style. In response to the clients' request for an interesting, dynamic way to move from basement level to the top of a narrow, overlooked garden of just 250 square metres (2,700 square feet), Massey created a path of concrete cuboid steps that play to the style of a new glazed extension at the back of the Victorian terraced house. Overbearing × *Cuprocyparis leylandii* (Leyland cypress) trees were removed in favour of climbers and less dense screening trees, including *Amelanchier* × *lamarckii* (snowy mespilus) and productive pear trees. The 'cubist cliff path', as it became known, is flanked by dense woodland-style planting that screens the rest of the garden. From the top, zoned areas include a seating terrace, a lawn, a fire pit and a garden studio. Water is a key feature in Massey's gardens (his garden for WaterAid at the RHS Chelsea Flower Show in 2024 showcased sustainable water management), and here a water feature interacts with the steps, filling pools and running along Corten channels and chutes to animate the journey.

SHUNMYŌ MASUNO

YU-KYU-EN
Hofu City Crematorium, Hofu City, Japan, 2003

Saying farewell to a loved one is among the most painful of all life events, and the surroundings in which that farewell takes place have a powerful effect on the experience. It was with this understanding that Japan's leading garden designer, the Zen monk Shunmyō Masuno, approached the design of Yu-Kyu-En (Garden of Eternity) at the crematorium in Hofu City, on the southern coast of the island of Honshu. Masuno envisaged the garden as a sequence of compartments that would allow mourners to reflect on their loss. On entering the site and making their way to the crematorium, they pass the first garden, Tabidachi no Niwa (Garden of Departure), a modern interpretation of a *karesansui* viewing garden (illustrated) — a dry landscape garden in which stone, gravel or sand represent nature. Large stones at the back of the garden represent the afterlife, while green moss and a single tree at the front symbolize the life that has now passed; the boundary between life and death is marked by the 'River Styx', a path of white sand. Located between Tabidachi no Niwa and the crematorium, mourners enter Shoka no Niwa (Ascension Garden), with its large circular pond that reflects the sky, surrounded by gravel — comprising six curved, polished low gravel arcs — and a single rock representing the forty-nine days it takes the spirit to reach the afterlife. The final garden, Shizume no Niwa (Spirit Pacifying Garden), represents another change, with trees including a red maple and a pink azalea that celebrate being alive.

ARNE MAYNARD

PRIVATE GARDEN
near Petworth, West Sussex, England, 2022

It requires the confidence of a talented designer to take a restrained approach, and Arne Maynard's design for this 1.6-hectare (4-acre) plot is a masterclass in considered interventions. Surrounding a charming brick-and-flint house on the edge of the Petworth estate, the garden already felt like that of an English country farmhouse. The challenge was to build on this atmosphere while retaining the underlying humility. The garden sits on a slope, with the house and several converted farm buildings on the lower level. Water meadows, areas of long grass and an old orchard take up most of the site, with a more intensively gardened area within original stone and brick walls around the house. In the L-shaped front garden, low box hedging and an exuberance of cottage-garden favourites, including old-fashioned roses, delphiniums, peonies, dahlias, phlox, hollyhocks and lady's mantle, offer a wonderful sense of arrival. Wisteria, honeysuckle and roses adorn the walls and old brick paths are threaded with various low-growing plants. Beyond an established magnolia, an open area connects to a guest cottage, where cloud-pruned hedging brings structure. A swimming pool is backed by a series of undulating grass banks that lead up to the orchard and a modest vegetable patch. Maynard explains: 'Essentially, the whole project was about trying to replicate the country gardens of my childhood, which were ornamental, productive and much loved by their owners.' He has clearly succeeded; the design seems so perfectly natural that one could imagine it had evolved almost by itself.

CRISTINA MAZZUCCHELLI

CLOROFILLA KINDERGARTEN
Milan, Italy, 2013

In 2012 the Clorofilla Kindergarten in south-eastern Milan asked designer Cristina Mazzucchelli to provide an enchanting, educational space that would stimulate the senses of small children. Mazzucchelli has achieved this using fragrant, aromatic plants with soft textures that encourage the children to engage and interact. The teachers also use the plants to inform the youngsters about plants, nature and seeds. There are spaces to sit and learn and be totally immersed in nature, to watch the insects and enjoy the scents and sounds. This rooftop space of about 300 square metres (3,200 square feet), on a building that previously housed a convent, then theatre and latterly a cinema, had its limitations. It had arches that span the space, and it was important that the floor not be damaged by construction or penetrating roots, allowing water into the floors below. Since grass would not be a sensible option, Mazzucchelli brought unity and harmony to the built elements and the planting using stress-resistant coloured flooring that simulates a coloured carpet, and a plant palette that tones beautifully. With its continental climate, Milan is very hot in the summer and cold and wet in the winter, although neighbouring buildings help to reduce wind damage to this roof garden. One half of the garden is sunny and open, while the other is in shade. Raised beds ensure that the plants – which include *Salvia rosmarinus* (rosemary), *Agastache* 'Blue Fortune' (giant hyssop), *Senecio vira-vira* (dusty miller) and the fountain grass *Cenchrus alopecuroides* (also known as *Pennisetum alopecuroides*) – are at the children's eye level and safe from damage.

MICHAEL MCCOY

STONE HILL
Woodend North, Victoria, Australia, 2011–15

Michael McCoy, a garden designer with a deep understanding of botany and horticulture, is based at Woodend, Victoria, the traditional land of the Indigenous Dja Dja Wurrung people. In 2011 he began developing nearby Stone Hill for owners captivated by the New Perennial movement, a naturalistic garden style close to McCoy's heart. The 2-hectare (5-acre) garden is invisible from the strikingly minimalist house, so is a delight to be discovered. It comprises two parts, a perennial garden and a garden of predominantly tough rushes, sedges and grasses in an old quarry. The perennial garden is set in gravel and designed as an undulating surface to be looked over. The play of light is critical to its enjoyment, captured in magical fashion by light-catching plants, such as the grasses *Celtica gigantea* (syn. *Stipa gigantea*) and *Calamagrostis* × *acutiflora* 'Karl Foerster'. One key principle is deliberate repetition, so that clumps of the same species echo and re-echo in the distance. The garden requires little watering, and the selected plants thrive in the local conditions. McCoy's masterly choice of foliage and texture, the addition of bulbs for early spring display and his ongoing maintenance of the garden showcase his skill and training as a gardener. The publication of *Michael McCoy's Garden* in 2000 followed by *The Gardenist* in 2012 brought him to the attention of gardeners across Australia and set him on a trajectory that has included presenting the television series *Dream Gardens*. His design for Stone Hill has deservedly gained attention worldwide.

McGREGOR COXALL

WALAMA | BALLAST POINT PARK
Birchgrove, Sydney, New South Wales, Australia, 2009

Ballast Point, on the traditional lands of the Gadigal and Wangal people at the edge of Sydney Harbour, is named after its use in the early 19th century to quarry ballast for ships. A later marine villa was bought by the Texan Oil Company in 1928 and demolished to make way for oil tanks that were part of the first seaboard oil terminal in Australia. When it began closing by stages in the 1970s, a long community campaign agitated for the land to be returned to public use. Success came in 2002, and in 2006 landscape architects McGregor Coxall were commissioned to design the new 2.5-hectare (6-acre) park, which opened in 2009. The design integrates landforms and relics from the park's former uses into a multilayered, intellectually challenging, sophisticated public park in a broad and exceptionally beautiful setting. The park is arranged as a series of stepped platforms containing intimate spaces that form microclimates. The dialogue between the geometry of the industrial relics, raw concrete and gabion walls and re-created nature using the area's native flora demonstrates skill and sensitivity. Such nuanced interpretation of the former uses of the site required a high degree of creativity that has produced a benchmark in park design and an exemplar of a 21st-century approach to the transformation of old industrial sites into public parks (see pp. 61, 101, 164, 297). The words of 20th-century Australian poet John Tranter are etched in a harbourside concrete wall: 'Like us, water breathes and dances to and fro, between earth and sky.'

MICHAEL VAN VALKENBURGH ASSOCIATES

THE MONK'S GARDEN
Isabella Stewart Gardner Museum, Boston, Massachusetts, United States, 2013

American art collector and philanthropist Isabella Stewart Gardner founded her eponymous museum in Boston in 1903 for 'the education and enjoyment of the public forever'. Horticulture and plants have always played an important role there – from the building's original interior courtyard garden to stunning displays of flowers and botanical works of art – and this latest garden reflects the ongoing importance the museum places on landscape architecture. Designed by Michael Van Valkenburgh Associates, the Monk's Garden takes the form of a serene, contemporary woodland and provides an enchanting transition between the original central atrium and the new wing created by Italian architect Renzo Piano in 2012. The 700-square-metre (7,500-square-foot) garden is relatively narrow, yet – being enclosed on three sides by tall brick walls – ideal for creating an immersive experience. The design is inspired by the meandering layout of the galleries within the museum, and by the colours, textures and idiosyncratic nature of its collection. A looping pathway of dark brick offers visitors several ways of walking around and engaging with the space. In places the path widens to accommodate seating, which is carefully positioned to take in a particular vignette. Dextrously placed evergreens and deciduous trees rise above a varied, richly textured underplanting of shade-loving perennials. The brief was to create a gift for visitors, one that would draw them in for relaxation and contemplation, and this innovative approach achieves precisely that.

MIKYOUNG KIM DESIGN

FARRAR POND GARDEN
Lincoln, Massachusetts, United States, 2007

Mikyoung Kim's exploration of landscape architecture's restorative power is exemplified in this private garden project at Farrar Pond. Fully on board with the concept of a garden as an uplifting, contemplative and poetic experience, the clients wanted to celebrate the natural beauty and ecosystem of the site and its sense of place. The scene is achingly beautiful: 1.2 hectares (3 acres) within a necklace of pools adjacent to the famous Walden Pond that inspired 19th-century essayist Henry David Thoreau, graced by compressed hillocks and valleys (termed kames and kettles). The goal 'to let the land speak' exercised all Kim's talents, incorporating sculpture into a landscape interwoven with groves of native birches and oaks. The homeowners' request for a fence to contain their dogs fostered a unique sculpture, a spine-like creation of weathered steel running through the woods. 'It forms a woven language,' says Kim, 'marking the undulations in the land, highlighting the changes of season', while providing the soothing sense of a framework. Lawn was avoided in favour of native species and groundcover plants that tolerate foot/paw traffic, inlaid with blue-stone. The resulting organic sculpture and the multisensory health benefits of colour, smell, shape and texture ever-changing from season to season fulfil what Kim feels is a professional obligation to express art while nurturing a biophilic experience. This early project laid the groundwork for her later, highly influential work, notably the Crown Sky Garden for the Ann and Robert H. Lurie Children's Hospital in Chicago, commissioned in 2012. Both projects, though different in scale and context, reflect Kim's focus on creating spaces that heal and restore.

BILL AND DIANE MITCHELL

FIRE AND BEAUTY
Yallingup, Western Australia, Australia, 2012–

Since the 1990s extreme fire risk has threatened Bill and Diane Mitchell's home overlooking Smiths Beach, surrounded by the Leeuwin-Naturaliste National Park on the traditional lands of the Wadandi Noongar people. To mitigate this, they removed the predominantly Western Australian native garden around the house on this 10-hectare (25-acre) property and replanted with fire-retardant plants. The design evolved around the colour, form and texture of the plants. Bill, whose love of surfing is captured by a sculpture of a surfer on an artificial sand dune close to the house, became increasingly entranced with water-storing aloes and other succulents. The approach to the house through highly flammable native vegetation with carefully placed sculpture gives little hint of the artistic garden to come. A massive drought-tolerant Queensland bottle tree, *Brachychiton rupestris*, stands at the edge of the drive near the house, and from there the wonder of the fantastic xeriscape unfolds. Huge barrel-form cacti (*Kroenleinia grusonii*) and agaves impress the visitor immediately, and mass planting of about 560 specimens from 26 species of aloe provides the winter colour that inspired the garden's name. *Kalanchoe beharensis* (felt bush), *Dracaena draco* (dragon tree), *Beaucarnea recurvata* (ponytail palm) and *Aloidendron barberae* (tree aloe) provide sculptural form, while black- and green-leaved aeoniums jostle one another next to red-flowered euphorbias. This garden has been a wonderful artistic adventure. Bill, who will readily say that he didn't know much about gardens until relatively recently, has been totally caught by a succulent craze and created a wondrous garden.

TERESA MOLLER

PUNTA PITE
Papudo, Valparaíso Region, Chile, 2005

Often the simplest things are the most extraordinary, and this is the case for Chilean landscape architect Teresa Moller's innovative design for a 2-kilometre (1¼-mile) stretch of Pacific coastline about 160 kilometres (100 miles) north of Santiago. Having studied garden design at the New York Botanical Garden, Moller returned to Chile and established her studio in 1990. Her sensitive approach to location has allowed her to work in startlingly varied landscapes, including this stretch of coast, part of an 11-hectare (27-acre) strip of land jutting into the sea. Unusually, the property-developer owners commissioned the landscape before they began building high-end condominiums overlooking the sea. The layout of this extraordinary landscape intervention is uncompromisingly rectilinear; the shoreline is rocky and was previously almost impossible to navigate safely, but now path fragments and steps in the local granite allow safe access. No rock was removed, and only paths that were strictly necessary were laid. At one junction magnificent steps rise like a site-specific sculpture, the treads increasing in width as visitors make their way up. There are no signs to indicate the way, and in fact there are several possible routes, each offering a different viewpoint from which to contemplate the breathtaking site and the crashing waves. It took forty stonemasons some two years to complete the work, following lines marked out with string and fashioning each rock using just hammers and chisels. There is something profoundly poetic to this pared back yet ingenious design, which unquestionably holds its own against the powerful landscape.

MOSBACH PAYSAGISTES

MUSEUM PARK LOUVRE-LENS
Lens, Hauts-de-France, France, 2012

Located some 200 kilometres (125 miles) north of Paris, built on a 20 hectare (50-acre) former coal mine and co-designed by Japanese architects SANAA, New York studio Imrey Culbert and landscape architects Mosbach Paysagistes, the Louvre-Lens art museum opened in 2012. From the outset the building and designed landscape were seen as one entity. Architects and landscapers collaborated closely to create a park that integrates the city of Lens, an iconic cultural institution and the de-industrialized landscapes of both the site itself and the wider *bassin minier* (mining area), now a UNESCO World Heritage Site. The result, which pays homage to the past while emphasizing the revivification of the local ecosystem, is very effective. As intended by Catherine Mosbach (founder of design firm Mosbach Paysagistes), the museum extends into the landscape, and upon entering one is aware of the past: smooth concrete paths leading to the building follow old track lines that once connected the mine and the main rail network, now passing through wild meadow and native woodland. Scattered sward-covered, crescent-shaped hummocks echo in miniature the *terrils* (spoil heaps) of the wider *bassin minier*. Approaching the museum, oval-ish discs of concrete dot the grass, becoming closely packed before merging to form a forecourt that is itself a patchwork of smooth concrete (it looks wonderful when wet) pierced by amorphous flower beds. The resulting textures, imaginatively blended, are intriguing in their own right and contrast yet harmonize with those of the architecture.

MOX LANDSCAPE ARCHITECTURE

PRIVATE GARDEN
Ilyichevo, Leningradsky, Russia, 2015

Deep in the forest outside the old Russian capital of St Petersburg, a new rectilinear house required very specific landscaping to ensure that it fitted in with the coniferous forest that fills much of its 1.3-hectare (just over 3-acre) plot. This is just the sort of project that is relished by Yury Fomenko of St Petersburg-based firm MOX Landscape Architecture: creating a garden that acts as a liminal space, a buffer between the forest and the dramatic building. The house is reached through the trees via a weathered steel bridge clad in green tiles to blend in with the vegetation, and rooms look out over pine and birch trees in mossy surroundings (*MOX* is Russian for 'moss'). The planting around the house consists of topiary trimmed in precise geometric shapes to reflect the geometric building. Cyclamen and heather are planted in rectangular boxes, alongside other plants that can withstand the long, cold winters. A large hawthorn tree with a crown 4.5 metres (nearly 15 feet) tall stands at the front of the house, obscuring the view of the driveway slightly. At Christmastime, it is extravagantly decorated in berry-like red baubles that contrast with the snow-laden branches. A covered gallery with holes cut in the roof for the trunks of pine trees is reached via granite steps bordered by small, fern- and moss-covered hillocks, which soften the approach and highlight the contrast between formal planting and towering forest, which was left untouched by Fomenko and lends the project a mysterious yet romantic quality.

CAMILLE MULLER

PRIVATE GARDEN
Paris, France, 2002

The planting seen in this rooftop garden in western Paris is more typically found in the drier regions of the Mediterranean: perfumed dwarf shrubs and colourful annuals that require little maintenance. Overlooking the Auteuil racecourse and with a heart-stopping view of the Eiffel Tower, the 129-square-metre (1,388-square-foot) roof was dominated by two brick chimneys that could not be moved, so the ingenious solution of Paris-based landscape gardener Camille Muller was to reimagine them as sculptures. One he turned into a seating area with wooden benches shaded by steel *brise-soleils* through which grow honeysuckle and ivy; the other he surrounded with terracotta pots filled with hardy shrubs that can withstand the vagaries of the Parisian weather, from harsh sun to snow and wind. Large metal planters filled with grasses, shrubs and scented jasmine both screen the garden and keep visitors away from the edges of the roof. Muller, who trained with celebrated French gardener Gilles Clément (see p.61), has collaborated with several visual artists, and their influence is evident in the carefully constructed disorder of this rooftop. A dwarf Mediterranean pine partially obscures the view of the racecourse, while a pile of large oval stones provides an interesting juxtaposition with the distant Eiffel Tower. Although Muller designed the garden in 2002, when few people talked of water conservation and the changing climate, it is low-maintenance and environmentally friendly; the gravel paths allow water to drain away, while the treated wooden table and benches are also resistant to weather.

MUNICIPALITY OF AMSTERDAM AND TON MULLER

ORLYPLEIN SLOTERDIJK
Amsterdam, The Netherlands, 2014

As one of his first major public planting commissions, Ton Muller and his team was given the brief to reimagine Orlyplein, a large square of concrete dominating the entrance to Amsterdam's Sloterdijk railway station. Supported by designers Climmy Schneider and Iris van der Helm, Muller sought advice from master nurseryman Hans Kramer on the 1.4 hectares (3½ acres) of 'grey to green transformation' – fittingly, since when the station was built in the 1980s it controversially encroached upon a nature reserve, De Lange Bretten. The new park, intended as a 'green heart' for this built-up area, has stimulated a wider regeneration. New businesses have flourished and wildlife has increased dramatically, but there were practical benefits, too, such as soaking up the run-off that had often flooded the station buildings. Despite the Netherlands' infamous flatness, this park is on a small hill created by the varying levels of different train lines. Much of it is effectively a roof garden with soil only 30 centimetres (1 foot) deep, into which Muller planted a range of sun-loving perennials, such as *Rudbeckia*, *Coreopsis*, *Baptisia* and *Hemerocallis*. These tough plants have thrived, but others suffered. The original planting was about 60 per cent grasses, including many short forms of *Molinia*, but in the extreme drought of 2018 many grasses (including almost all *Molinia*) perished. Interestingly, the taller grass cultivars, such as *M. caerulea* subsp. *arundinacea* 'Skyracer', which Muller used as replacements, seem more drought-resistant. While the bold summer colours are always popular, Muller enjoys the autumn months most, describing how the turning foliage makes the park 'feel like a very natural space'.

MUÑOZ Y MOREU

JARDIN SECO
Ávila, Castile & León, Spain, 2021

With nature as their inspiration and impetus, Clara Muñoz-Rojas and Belén Moreu believe 'landscaping is an art and a tool that allows us to unite with nature', and look for 'beauty, inspiration, serenity, silence and harmony' in each landscape. But it was an encounter with the words and work of 'dry-gardening guru' and Mediterranean flora expert Olivier Filippi (see p.12) that awoke in them the importance of designing for low or no water requirements. The design of this 3,500-square-metre (37,700-square-foot) garden west of Madrid, with the Sierra de Gredos mountains as a 'borrowed' landscape, is an interpretation of the way the site spoke to the designers, while the naturalistic planting evokes the wild environment that surrounds the property. It relies on Mediterranean species: shrubs to impart structure, such as *Pistacia lentiscus* (mastic), *Myrtus communis* (common myrtle), *Phillyrea angustifolia* (narrow-leaved mock privet) and *P. latifolia* (green olive), intermingled with herbaceous perennials and ornamental grasses that bring movement and reflect the changing seasons. Since the garden faces all directions, there was the opportunity to structure the planting to take advantage of the different conditions. The north side is more prone to frost in the winter and cooler in the summer, so its use focuses on the summer and early autumn; the pool is also there. The south-facing area is warmer in the winter and spring, so is used more then. The whole demonstrates that garden-making with water-wise sustainability and informed plant choice as core tenets certainly does not mean giving up beauty.

DOMINICK MURPHY

SHEILSTOWN GARDEN
Knockananna, Co. Wicklow,
Republic of Ireland, 2006–

A derelict cottage hidden behind a line of spruces on a hillside where people have farmed for thousands of years was landscape architect Dominick Murphy's choice when he moved out of Dublin in 2006. His 3.6-hectare (9-acre) garden was to be carved out of the four fields surrounding the cottage and its outbuildings, but from the start he knew he must garden with a light touch: 'We're part of a bigger landscape here, and we have a responsibility to blend in.' He began by sketching a network of paths that would connect the various spaces: a gravel terrace beside the house, two traditional meadows, a woodland, a sunken walled garden, and a pond fed by an existing stream. Other elements that show this is a gardened space are views (often created by removing trees or shrubs), seating, the addition of gates, and areas of planting influenced by the naturalistic schemes of the late James van Sweden (see p.207). Murphy's choice of plants includes many that harmonize in both form and colour with the native species in the field and hedgerows beyond the garden. For example, *Corylus maxima* 'Purpurea' (purple hazel) and *Hamamelis mollis* (witch hazel) are used as 'one step ups' from the native hazel, while *Miscanthus sinensis* 'Gracillimus' and *Calamagrostis* grasses in the Walled Garden mirror the native grasses in the meadows. Murphy and his business partner Colum Sheanon established their studio, Murphy + Sheanon, in 2015, aiming through both private and commercial projects – and informed by Murphy's own experiences at Sheilstown Garden – to create an engagement between people and the landscape.

JEAN MUS

PRIVATE GARDEN
Saint-Jean-Cap-Ferrat, Côte d'Azur, France, 2015

This garden on the terraced hillsides of Saint-Jean-Cap-Ferrat, one of the most beautiful places on the French Riviera, was designed to offer a walk around a contemporary villa and its swimming pool. The celebrated French landscape designer Jean Mus knew how to make the most of the awkward 3,000-square-metre (32,300-square-foot) site on a steep, rocky slope falling away to the sea. He built stone walls to hold back the earth, creating three levels of terracing that maximize the planting space and opportunities. The upper level, at the entrance to the villa, is planted with stately cypresses, olive trees and palms. Further down, the swimming pool is backed by a wall of water and doubled by a mirror pool, the two separated by a clump of *Pittosporum*. The lower level is inspired more by wild vegetation and the scrubby landscape of its surroundings. Here, the planting mixes *Osmanthus*, *Myrtus*, *Euphorbia*, lavenders, rosemary and many other fragrant plants that stimulate the senses. The terraces are linked by stepping stones and stairs that disappear under bushes of *Helichrysum* surrounded by pine trees. The stairs are set in soft curves as much as possible, according to Mus's principles, so that there are no brutal angles to offend the eye. The garden thus gives what he calls 'a reading of the Mediterranean', forming a place of luxuriant planting for enjoyment and contemplation while evoking the local flora.

MVRDV

SEOULLO 7017 SKYGARDEN
Seoul, South Korea, 2017

High above the busy roads and railway station of Seoul, South Korea's densely populated capital, an artery of public paths is filled with greenery. Along the wide 'sky paths' sit circular planters of different sizes bursting with local plants. The elevated position of this urban garden reflects its origins in the 1970s, when the Seoul Station Overpass was built to enable cars to travel to the city's largest traditional market, Namdaemun Market, from the western neighbourhoods. By 2006, the 17-metre-high (56-foot) overpass had been condemned as unsafe and slated for demolition – a decision that was highly unpopular with the public. Instead, a design competition was held to repurpose the space, in a similar way to the New York High Line (see p.101) a few years later. The winning design, by Dutch architectural firm MVRDV (founded in 1993 by Winy Maas, Jacob van Rijs and Nathalie de Vries), proposed a flexible space with an elevated pedestrian walkway that would serve as a nursery, growing young trees that could then be planted elsewhere in the city. MVRDV created an arboreal library whereby species were planted in 'neighbourhoods' and arranged alphabetically according to the Korean alphabet. This not only allows visitors to navigate the Skygarden, but also links the 938-metre (3,077-foot) walkway to the various local neighbourhoods. The Skygarden remains a work in progress. The intention is for new arterial gardens to be added in response to demand, and that facilities, such as cafes, greenhouses or libraries, will eventually appear along its paths.

LISA NEGRI AND KEVIN PHILIP WILLIAMS

SUMMERHOME GARDEN
Denver, Colorado, United States, 2019–

Lisa Negri didn't think twice before buying the 500-square-metre (5,400-square-foot) plot next door in 2019, and her decision to tear down its 1920s bungalow was equally rapid. But what to do with the newly acquired space required more creativity. New to gardening, she had volunteered at Denver Botanic Gardens, where she met the gardens' horticulturist and designer Kevin Philip Williams. The pair had already designed a drought-tolerant hellstrip (verge) together (which received a wave of positive input from Negri's neighbours), and that triumph sparked the initiative to convert the newly vacant site into a garden. Beyond just another private planting, the concept evolved rapidly into a pocket park that would be open to the community, with an educational mission statement. The concept that seemed most apropos in a region that receives 20–38 vastly fluctuating centimetres (8–15 inches) of rain annually was to profile xeric (drought-tolerant) plants in a naturalistic setting. For his muse, Williams looked to scrublands where nature had reclaimed space. The planting is heavy on xeric shrubs (the ratio being 60 per cent shrubs to 40 per cent grasses and perennials), which serve as what Williams calls 'cornerstone plants, providing structure and support for the many other species in the garden'. Annuals are also used as temporary fillers between shrubs that will ultimately expand. 'It really plays well together,' says Negri of the evolving micro-park, which is maintained by neighbourhood volunteers; 'the community sees climate resilience at work.'

NELSON BYRD WOLTZ

PEABODY ESSEX MUSEUM
Salem, Massachusetts, United States, 2016–19

The Peabody Essex Museum was founded in 1799 to enable members of the East India Marine Society (an organization of Salem captains and supercargoes who had sailed beyond either the Cape of Good Hope or Cape Horn) to display artefacts procured during their travels. Today it houses extensive maritime, American and Asian art collections, and this very contemporary, unexpected 344-square-metre (3,700-square-foot) garden was made as part of a major expansion. Designed around the museum's story by influential practice Nelson Byrd Woltz, the garden offers the visitor an opportunity to reflect on what they have seen inside, while taking them on a three-'room' journey from North America to Asia. The key sensory themes are variety in material textures, movement and seasonal variation of planting, and the sound of water. Inviting exploration of the garden and inspired by various maritime processes, a sinuous strip of granite that is a deeper grey than the local stone paving meanders from inside the atrium through the garden rooms. The Native and Asiatic gardens are planted with species distinct to North America and Asia, while the Hybrid Convergence Garden contains species that occur in both (for example, rhododendrons); all three echo the cultural diversity, knowledge exchange and interdisciplinary innovation at the core of the museum's collections and mission. Water is introduced by a water wall in the Native Garden and the 'poetry fountain' in the Hybrid Convergence Garden. Here the water flows from two small pools at either end through sinuous rills reminiscent of those found in Chinese scholar gardens to mix – like cultures – in a central basin.

CLAUDIA NEVELL

NEVELL GARDEN
Coffs Harbour, New South Wales, Australia, 1993–

On the traditional lands of the Gumbaynggirr people of subtropical coastal northern New South Wales, landscape designer Claudia Nevell has developed her own 2,500-square-metre (27,000-square-foot) garden on a sloping suburban site. In a climate subject to sudden, heavy storms, the management of stormwater, drainage and erosion control were key considerations. Existing frangipanis and a large *Camphora officinarum* (syn. *Cinnamomum camphora*; camphor laurel) were retained and the slope divided into three level areas of lawn, supported by thickly planted banks, with gravel paths and stone steps to connect them. Nevell used mainly tropical foliage plants, including local rainforest species and tall palms – among them *Archontophoenix alexandrae* (Alexandra palm) and groves of *Livistona australis* (cabbage tree palm) – which give the garden the lush feel of an oasis. One exception to this tropical palette is the successful use of *Buxus microphylla* var. *microphylla* (Japanese box), clipped into balls and long rectangular blocks, which help to define areas of exuberant groundcover and native grasses. Tree aloes, cordylines and *Licuala ramsayi* (fan palm) are underplanted with bromeliads, the soft but sculptural *Agave attenuata* and groundcover species, such as *Trachelospermum jasminoides* 'Tricolor'. Change and experimentation are a constant, but bold feature plants used throughout the garden include *Doryanthes palmeri* (the native spear lily, with its sword-like leaves and the occasional spectacular scarlet-orange flowering spike), *Alcantarea imperialis* 'Rubra' (red bromeliad) and *Zamia furfuracea* (cardboard palm). Now mature, this exciting garden demonstrates Nevell's art as both designer and gardener.

BILL NOBLE

PRIVATE GARDEN
Norwich, Vermont, United States, 1991–

Bill Noble wasn't gardening professionally when he first moved to his 9-hectare (22-acre) property in central Vermont in 1991. However, that changed rapidly as he took up positions at the New Hampshire historic properties of Saint-Gaudens National Historical Park and The Fells, and subsequently at The Garden Conservancy (where he worked as director of preservation overseeing the restoration of significant American gardens). The gardens he encountered shaped his own land, but the deepest influence was the landscape and its past. It was a farm, and he wanted to preserve that essence – including the ghost of an old dairy barn, its foundations now planted with alpines and various groundcover plants sprinting along crevices. The house has a phenomenal view of the White Mountain foothills, but also a steep field behind. To frame the view and create drama where it might be appreciated from a deck, Noble converted a vegetable garden into a tapestry of rare shrubs and perennials backed by an allée of Lombardy poplars (*Populus nigra* 'Italica'). He has brought many treasures home from trips, with an emphasis on rhubarbs, willows, saxifrages, hydrangeas, phlox, hellebores, rodgersias, thymes and sedges. Native plants, including shrubs, play an important role, while the rhubarbs reinforce the farm flavour. With the help of gardening assistant Susan Howard, who has come weekly since 1996, the land is clothed in long, sinuous borders of cold-tolerant plants. Despite resembling nothing else in the neighbourhood, the garden feels brilliantly apropos of both its time and its place.

ULF NORDFJELL

PRIVATE GARDEN
near Umeå, Norrland, Sweden, 2010

Leading Swedish landscape architect Ulf Nordfjell has been gardening and observing nature in his family garden in sub-Arctic Sweden since he was a young boy. Surrounded by a forest of pines, rowan and birch, in an EU-designated Natura 2000 conservation area, the 800 square metres (8,600 square feet) of planted garden slopes down from the wooden house to the Öre River. In 2010 Nordfjell embarked on a bold redesign, inserting a strong architectural framework for planting that flourishes in the challenging climate – it is May when spring rushes in and the first snow falls towards the end of October – and introducing new elements, such as a contemporary glass, steel and timber pavilion, sawn granite steps and granite retaining blocks for the redesigned borders. His designs for city parks and private residences show a preference for natural materials and often feature structures and furniture from his own collection. They showcase planting that sits comfortably in the landscape, and here he retained a number of mature plants, including a hazel, apple trees, a gnarled hawthorn and a sentinel stand of shuttlecock ferns, which immediately ground the new planting. Nordfjell chose shrubs and trees from the Swedish E-mark plant system, which was developed by the Swedish University of Agricultural Science to identify species that are resilient and hardy as well as beautiful and/or productive. Clear-stemmed forms of *Amelanchier laevis* (smooth serviceberry) and *Viburnum opulus* (guelder rose) provide a microclimate for a succession of perennials, bulbs and annuals growing beneath them, resulting in a garden that is simultaneously of great horticultural interest and entirely at home in its pristine surroundings.

KELLY D. NORRIS

THREE OAKS
Des Moines, Iowa, United States, 2017–

Ecological gardener Kelly D. Norris feared he would never find the property of his dreams, but when this 2,415-square-metre (26,000-square-foot) site presented itself in 2017, he had to abandon his dreams of a bungalow-style house in favour of the optimal site. Set on a hill above a floodplain, 'it was a blank slate,' he recalls. The landscape designer and former director of horticulture and education for the Greater Des Moines Botanical Garden immediately began creating a site-specific garden. He describes himself as having 'an artist's heart and a scientist's head', and to satisfy both – and because he comes from the Midwest – prairies and meadows have always held his interest. To his neighbours' surprise, he began with the front garden. Meadow Nord, as he calls it, is now a dramatic, colourful and textural sweep of penstemons, grasses, *Liatris* (blazing star), *Echinacea* (coneflower) and *Prunella* (self-heal) under 1 metre (3 feet) tall, planted in the hardpan clay. Next, he focused on the passage running beside the house to create Long Look Prairie, harnessing the property's iconic oaks to frame the view. In 2021 his husband, horticulturist and entomologist David McKinney, joined him on the property to tackle the back garden and create The Romp (a matrix mosaic), the sloping Valley (a bioswale or planted run-off ditch), Exotica (a container corridor) and a gravel garden. All areas are intensively planted, with riveting results. 'Three Oaks is like a long-running sitcom,' says Norris. 'It's the same cast of characters, but it does something different every season.'

MARC NUCERA

LE TERRAIN
Noves, Provence, France, 1980s–

Le Terrain sits among rich farmland in the Durance River valley, Provence. These 1.2 hectares (3 acres) have served as garden, living space, workshop and gallery for tree sculptor Marc Nucera since the late 1980s. Having begun as a prizewinning olive-tree pruner, he joined forces with celebrated Provençal designer Nicole de Vésian and learned to work with the evolving growth rather than imposing outside shapes – the opposite of topiary – revealing the interacting qualities of wood, stone, plants, earth and sky. Today Le Terrain greets visitors with a broad circle of weathered building stones. Four plots are linked by intimate, meandering paving, inviting slow exploration. First comes an experimental orchard with fifteen varieties of fruit tree, where increasingly warm temperatures now let Nucera plant pepper trees, carobs and pistachios, as well as more familiar local varieties, such as walnut and olive. The second plot offers shady repose under hackberries (*Celtis australis*), sophoras and field maples. Massive seats carved from the trunks of plane trees could almost be reassembled into their original shape and resume their former life. The third area, set around a pool, evokes an oasis with yuccas and palms, but also includes garrigue species: *Quercus ilex* (holm oak), *Pistacia lentiscus* (mastic) and *Pinus helepensis* (Aleppo pines). The last plot distils local landscapes into a kitchen garden, alongside which sit Nucera's workshop and gallery. The garden is maintained simply, through one big winter clearance and the upkeep of paths and sitting spaces, and watering is limited to recently planted trees. Sculpture is beautifully sited among semi-wild vegetation, rich with wildlife.

ALEJANDRO O'NEILL

PRIVATE GARDEN
Cap d'Antibes, Côte d'Azur, France, 2019

This 1,200-square-metre (12,900-square-foot) private garden challenges conventional ideas of Mediterranean gardening by integrating an extensive plant palette into a finely balanced naturalistic design and employing strategic pruning to replicate natural environmental pressures. Uruguayan landscape designer Alejandro O'Neill's methods of 'goat pruning' and 'wind pruning' promote compact growth, enhance drought resilience and create a sense of controlled wildness. O'Neill's work demonstrates the dynamic possibilities of Mediterranean flora, using texture, height and seasonal shifts to create a planting style that is both ecologically sensitive and aesthetically rich. This garden, which innovatively incorporates a circular former water tank, merges two distinct Mediterranean ecosystems: garrigue and woodland. Subshrubs take a subtle role, forming a ground layer that makes way for taller, emergent herbaceous species, such as *Cephalaria ambrosioides*, which provide height without density. Rounded, stable shapes enhance the appearance of more sculptural plants, such as *Sarcopoterium spinosum* (thorny burnet). Small native trees, among them *Amelanchier ovalis* (snowy mespilus) and *Cercis siliquastrum* (Judas tree), provide essential shade. This layered approach is enriched by self-seeding plants that provide continuity and cohesion throughout, along with bulbs and annuals that subtly mark the seasons. The resulting impression is one of a light, airy aesthetic somewhat reminiscent of northern European cottage gardens, enlivened by the contrasts between lush greenery and stark, skeletal beauty.

OEHME, VAN SWEDEN

NATIVE PLANT GARDEN AT THE NEW YORK BOTANICAL GARDEN
New York, New York, United States, 2013

The American native garden is a style in ever-exciting flux. Beginning with the Midwestern prairie garden in the late 19th century, it has come to embrace all regional floras. The 1.4-hectare (3½-acre) Native Plant Garden at the New York Botanical Garden, developed by horticulturist Thomas H. Everett in the 1930s as The Wildflower Garden, was one of the nation's first but had degraded. A gift from the Leon Levy Foundation, the revitalization of the gently sloping site in 2013 was by Sheila Brady (director emeritus at Oehme, van Sweden), a strong advocate of regionalism in garden design. Continuing the long legacy of plant-led design of OvS (founded in 1977 by Wolfgang Oehme and James van Sweden, and credited with pioneering the 'New American Garden' style), this celebration of the northeastern flora uses almost 100,000 plants from more than 700 native taxa to emphasize colour, contrast, texture and seasonality. The planting harmonizes with the natural hydrology and topography – there are sloping ridges of old growth oak-hickory woodland, and outcrops of the local bedrock pop up throughout. The natural rock formations have become focal points within the four curated zones that represent local ecosystems: glade, meadow, wetland and woodland. The goal of improving the health of the Bronx River, which runs through the adjacent Thain Family Forest, inspired the series of three water basins, stone weirs and adjacent planting. The result is a year-round floral display that meets the objective of educating about the aesthetic and ecological value of native plants. Moreover, the whole garden is traversed by a fully accessible path, allowing everyone to enjoy the united beauties of native plants and contemporary design.

OJB LANDSCAPE ARCHITECTURE IN COLLABORATION WITH MARY IRISH

SUNNYLANDS CENTER & GARDENS
Rancho Mirage, California, United States, 2012

The name might evoke a twee 1950s retirement home, but Sunnylands, an 89-hectare (220-acre) estate in Rancho Mirage, California, is not only a masterpiece of mid-century modernism, but also features a noted contemporary garden. Once the home of billionaire publisher Walter Annenberg and his wife, Leonore, the original estate was designed in 1963 by architect A. Quincy Jones. From the 1960s to the 1980s the Annenbergs hosted royalty, Hollywood and eight US Presidents in lavish style at Sunnylands. In 2006, when it was decided to open a visitor centre, a 3.6-hectare (9-acre) garden was commissioned from landscape architect James Burnett and his studio OJB; it won the ASLA Honor Award in 2012, the year of its opening. Annenberg's collection of French Impressionist paintings inspired Burnett, and it is easy to detect their influence in the dot patterns of massed cactus and agaves and in the play of light and shade under the diaphanous canopies of palo verde and mesquite trees. Burnett is known for his urban designs, and at Sunnylands the calming geometry of long views, a circular open space, meandering walks and seating at the garden edges combine in an assured nod to the livable formality of the historic estate. Swathes of arid-landscape plants – added with the input of native plant expert Mary Irish – were, however, a timely departure from the original thirsty lawns and petunias. This creative distillation of a desert landscape is a template for sustainable, ecological planting and local distinctiveness.

OLIN

U.S. EMBASSY LONDON GARDENS
London, England, 2018

When U.S. Embassy London moved from its central location to its new Nine Elms home in southwest London, it presented a project with complex functional requirements. Back in 2009, when Philadelphia-based landscape- and urban-design firm OLIN joined the competition for the design, the 2-hectare (almost 5-acre) site was in an industrial area overpowered by Battersea Power Station (see p.280), which had yet to be renovated. The state-of-the-art building was seen as an anchor to further developments to the neighbourhood. As Hallie Boyce, the OLIN partner who led the landscape team, explains: 'We created a symbolic and multifunctional landscape and there were practical considerations of adaptation, security and accessibility [when] moving approximately 1,000 people daily into and around the embassy building.' They also had to factor in the 500-year flood level from the nearby River Thames. The solution was spiralling meadows with biodiverse plantings of grasses, native bulbs and perennials beside curvaceous walkways climbing gradually to the building's entrance. A pond shapes the pedestrian flow while addressing stormwater management and water reuse, and woodland plantings provide shade. Reference is made to the historic exchange between American and British botanists as well as the accord between the two nations. And horticulture continues inside with six gardens that portray themed plantings linked to regions in the United States. A handshake between countries, the embassy grounds have succeeded on all levels.

SUE OLIVER AND OTHERS

TE HENUI CEMETERY GARDEN
New Plymouth, Taranaki, North Island, New Zealand, 2009–

In many cultures, the pain of death is alleviated through flowers, yet commemorative posies among ranks of solemn gravestones and memorials offer little comfort to the bereaved. A perfect long-term antidote to such formality is to soften these unyielding forms with plants, filling a cemetery with the softness of foliage and the beauty and fragrance of flowers. With this in mind, local resident Sue Oliver, affectionately known as 'Cemetery Sue', who began tidying and planting neglected gravesites in 2009 and is now joined by other volunteers, has gradually transformed Te Henui cemetery into a garden of great serenity, bringing solace to the bereaved in all seasons. The spaces in and around the graves are filled with trees, shrubs, roses and herbaceous plants, which flow through the landscape in a fusion of naturalistic and cottage-garden style, while the framework of paths remains neatly mown. Plants are also allowed to self-seed and form large drifts, then edited as necessary. A benign climate allows a wide range of plants to flourish, from traditionally hardy species, such as roses and hydrangeas, to exotics, among them South African *Dierama* (angel's fishing rod), bulbs and echiums. The cemetery, which opened in 1861, also includes valuable elements of the social and cultural heritage of the New Plymouth and wider Taranaki areas, and a restoration programme that included the conservation and restoration of memorials won the local council a conservation award in 1992.

GABRIEL OROZCO

THE OROZCO GARDEN
South London Gallery, London, England, 2016

When invited to design his first garden, leading international artist Gabriel Orozco was tasked with transforming an unloved paved courtyard for the South London Gallery – in collaboration with 6a architects and horticulturists from Royal Botanic Gardens, Kew. His goal was to create an inspiring outdoor platform for the local community in this 1,000-square-metre (10,760-square-foot) plot behind the free contemporary art space. Orozco, celebrated for his artistic explorations of everyday objects, employed circles – a recurring motif in his work – as the foundation for his design, using the arc of a swing door on the adjacent building to establish his scale. Restricting himself to the familiar local building materials York stone and London brick, he conceived a sequence of circles and arcs formed in brick-shaped stone and arranged at different levels, from a sunken 'pond' to a terraced 'hill'. These geometric forms are linked by snaking paths to create various spaces, some intimate, others large enough to accommodate performances. The geometry of the garden is, over time, intentionally being obscured by the plants, which were chosen for their shape, form and colour, including creeping, tumbling *Cerastium tomentosum* (snow-in-summer) and *Erigeron karvinskianus* (Mexican fleabane), along with bushy, vigorous *Coronilla valentina* subsp. *glauca* (scorpion vetch) and *Salvia rosmarinus* (rosemary), which together create, in the words of gallery director Margot Heller, 'something wild and unruly and fantastic'.

LUIZ CARLOS ORSINI

INSTITUTO INHOTIM
Brumadinho, Minas Gerais, Brazil, 2006

Surrounded by dense tropical foliage, a concrete platform appears to float on a turquoise reflective pool in front of a concrete box, the Adriana Varejão pavilion. It all belongs to a much larger museum and sculpture park complex covering some 45 hectares (111 acres), deep within a 600-hectare (1,485-acre) ecological park encompassing the remnants of native Atlantic forest and *cerrado* (savannah) in the southeastern Brazilian state of Minas Gerais. For Luis Carlos Orsini, the third landscape designer to work at Inhotim following Roberto Burle Marx and Pedro Nehring, the challenge was how to integrate the complex's many galleries, pavilions and modern sculptures into the natural landscape and existing gardens. Orsini's design included sculptural plants to complement the Modernist structures: *Agave vilmoriniana* (octopus agave), *Beaucarnea recurvata* (ponytail palm), with its bulbous base and shock of tendrils, and succulents, among others. Splashes of colour come from drifts of cultivars of *Codiaeum variegatum* (Joseph's coat) and the angular flowers of *Strelitzia* (bird of paradise). As well as showcasing art from around the world, Inhotim features plants sourced from every continent. Since the park opened in 2006 – founded by the mining magnate and art collector Bernardo Paz – it has amassed the world's largest collection of palms (more than 1,500 species) and 4,300 rare botanical species. Water features heavily, with lakes, ponds and pools to cool the surroundings and provide reflective spaces.

ERIC OSSART AND ARNAUD MAURIÈRES

AZAREN
Tnine Ourika, Marrakech, Morocco, 2011

The Atlas Mountains provide an extraordinary backdrop to the three red rammed-earth pavilions of Azaren, 30 kilometres (19 miles) south of Marrakech. Their surroundings, completed in 2011 by peripatetic landscape-design duo Eric Ossart and Arnaud Maurières, consist of 8 hectares (20 acres) of experimental arid 'meadow' planting sweeping around the villas, dissected by paths and encircled by climate-toughened silvery olives. Ossart and Maurières set up their practice in Paris in 1989 and have been on a career-long quest to obtain climate-appropriate species for the Mediterranean and dry-climate gardens they have created. Early on, they determined to demonstrate that exuberant planting is possible without abundant water, and their book *Éloge de l'aridité* (In Praise of Aridity; 2016) is a manifesto for reimagining gardens with respect to local climate. In 2003 they moved to Taroudant in southern Morocco, and there, over the next ten years, they worked on projects that successfully combined rammed-earth architecture with dry-climate gardens capable of withstanding extreme conditions. At Azaran, where yearly rainfall averages little more than 230 millimetres (9 inches), many key species are chosen from Ossart's experimental plant selections resulting from a five-year survey to identify Moroccan natives suitable for cultivation. Vast drifts of impressive Saharan grasses mingle with African euphorbias and American agaves. Particularly striking are two ochre-coloured arches designed by the house's architect, Imaad Rahmouni, emerging from seas of silver-green *Agave americana* and the dusty purple *Pennisetum advena* 'Rubrum', a stunning combination that has provided inspiration to many.

PIET OUDOLF

OUDOLF GARDEN
Vitra Campus, Weil am Rhein, Baden-Württemberg, Germany, 2020

The Vitra Campus in southern Germany, envisioned by the eponymous furniture-design firm, is a wonderland of architectural innovation, featuring structures from the likes of Frank Gehry, Renzo Piano and Zaha Hadid. But one of the most recent additions to its pantheon is not a building at all; it is the wildly designed naturalistic meadow and looping pathways of the 0.4-hectare (1-acre) Oudolf Garden that forms the centre point for the starchitect-designed buildings clustered at its edges. The garden invites visitors to lose themselves in the sensorial beauty of a finely tuned display containing some 30,000 perennial plants, designed by the Dutch maestro at what may be the creative zenith of his fifty-year career. Here, Oudolf freely combines the controlled style of perennial block planting with a free grass-matrix planting at the core. His year-round approach highlights the importance he places on the dynamic nature of a garden as it evolves through the seasons. At the heart of the garden is a two-part sculpture by Ronan and Erwan Bouroullec with a circular steel ring around a lone *Zelkova serrata* tree and a water channel of white marble. Oudolf's signature circular mounds of grass and open gravel create fresh viewpoints across the meadow, looking back to the campus's architectural highlights, including the 2014 Vitra Slide Tower by Carsten Höller. The garden was planted during the COVID-19 pandemic by a team led by garden designer Bettina Jaugstetter (see p.146). The panoply of perennial meadows embodies the widely acknowledged zeitgeist of connecting us with the natural world through its avatar in the form of designed garden landscapes.

ROSS AND WENDY PALMER

WELTON HOUSE
Blenheim, South Island, New Zealand, 2003–

The garden at Welton House, the latest in a trio of collaborations between owner Wendy Palmer and her garden-designer brother Ross, is filled with theatrics. Set high on an ancient sand dune, with views of hills and mountains to one side and Cloudy Bay to the other, the 2.5-hectare (6-acre) site benefits from a range of soils, including fertile valley loam. Add a benign climate and there is an enviable palette of plants with which to conjure. Unexpected, vibrant, richly coloured plant associations take full advantage of this. Among the eclectic mix that surprises gardeners from cooler climes are tender epiphytic orchids, bromeliads and ferns growing outdoors on trees, New Zealand natives and permanent drifts of arid-zone succulents combined with hardy plants, including heritage roses and magnolias. From late winter, daffodils, tulips, primroses and magnolias bloom. Waves of sculpted *Corokia* – a fun, contemporary feature that provides structure and echoes the surrounding landscape – are interplanted with succulents, line the paths, and contrast with the formal swimming pool. Mature trees provide a sense of age, native woodland bestows a clear identity, and South African *Leucadendron* with its pincushion flowers evokes far-off lands. The big border is a fantastically coloured tapestry, starting with hellebores in the winter before orange cannas, *Imperata cylindrica* 'Rubra' (Japanese blood grass) and feathery *Calamagrostis × acutiflora* 'Karl Foerster' (feather reed grass) take over at the peak of summer. Heritage fruit and vegetables fill the kitchen garden, and seats throughout the garden allow visitors to pause and absorb the remarkable sights.

PAMELA BURTON & COMPANY

ROYAL OAKS RESIDENCE
Encino, California, United States, 1951, 2022

Because gardens are forever evolving, updates are often necessary, and rethinking was required for this unique Mid-century Modern treasure. The house was the work of acclaimed architect Richard Neutra (1892–1970), while the 0.2-hectare (½-acre) garden was the creation of his frequent collaborator, the landscape architect Garrett Eckbo (1910–2000). In 2022, seeing the potential to reclaim the historic beauty of the original landscape while adding recent ecological understanding, the current owners called in Mary Sager McFadden of Pamela Burton & Company. 'Light, air and continuity between inside and out are key,' says Sager McFadden of the Mid-century Modern tenets applied to the renovation. The studio rediscovered the original plan with the assistance of architectural historian Barbara Lamprecht, and now the garden swarms around the house, beginning with a water feature at the entrance. To reinterpret the garden in view of the evolution of the site, Sager McFadden removed non-native eucalyptus that was obstructing the view, and re-created the quintessential path of round concrete paving steps that begins in a lily pond and proceeds through the landscape. The remaining native live oaks, after which Encino is named, are now celebrated without competition from eucalyptus, while cycads beside the swimming pool were preserved and Italian cypresses added. The overgrown hillside is replanted with a pollinator-friendly weave of *Salvia*, *Ceanothus* (wild lilac), *Carex* and similar performers tripping down to a native meadow and new rose garden. Not only is the past brought into the present, but also the property's future is now strengthened.

PARKKIM

MOUNTAIN AND WATER
CJ Blossom Park, Gwanggyo, South Korea, 2017

In a constricted urban location at the foot of a mountain, the landscaping for the three circular towers that comprise the research and development headquarters of CJ Corp (one of South Korea's largest companies) required a different approach. The cutting-edge landscape-architecture firm PARKKIM, which was founded by Jungyoon Kim and Yoonjin Park in Rotterdam in 2004 and moved to Seoul in 2006, was brought in to overcome the challenges of the site and create a harmonious park that reflects the groundbreaking work taking place inside the buildings. PARKKIM created a series of hills and a large reflecting pond at the main entrance to cope with the heavy water run-off from the mountains during the rainy season, which has intensified in recent years owing to climate change. A rooftop garden has more undulating hills, while each of the lab buildings' roofs is home to hollow aluminium benches, with seasonal flowers filling the gaps between. Covering 11 hectares (27 acres), the site was broken up using white- and pink-blossoming cherry trees around the buildings, while a grove of pines sits on the steep slope with stone seats built into the hillside. Special attention was paid to marking each season by changes of colour in the planting, from the cherry blossom in the spring to the vibrant reds of South Korean maples in the autumn. PARKKIM's intention is to give the landscape a local context in a city that people often feel lacks a sense of space and specific Korean identity.

PARKS AND WILDLIFE COMMISSION OF THE NORTHERN TERRITORY

ALICE SPRINGS DESERT PARK
Mparntwe | Alice Springs, Northern Territory, Australia, 1997

The concept for Alice Springs Desert Park was formalized in 1994 with a masterplan prepared by the Conservation Commission of the Northern Territory (later the Parks and Wildlife Commission). The premise was simple: to address the fact that, despite 70 per cent of the nation's landmass being arid, there was no single site promoting Australia's desert landscapes, plants and animals. It drew on precedents of botanic gardens, zoos, wildlife parks, national parks and museums, given a contemporary edge by their distillation into a holistic evocation of Australia's arid zones. This was realized in a 54-hectare (133-acre) core within an overall buffer zone of 1,300 hectares (3,200 acres). The park, which opened in 1997, is shaped around three habitats: sand country, desert rivers and woodland. Existing vegetation was generously augmented by naturalistic plantings of arid-zone Australian species and the creation of several dedicated wildlife enclosures. The visitor's experience is sensory and compelling, promoting conservation as well as beauty. The site is of significant cultural importance to the local Arrernte people and includes parts of the 'Akngwelye Artnwere' and 'Yeperenye Altyerre' (Wild Dog and Caterpillar) Dreaming stories, so that traditional environmental management and use form a key interpretation. The skies here are generally clear, and as dawn breaks over Ntaripe | Heavitree Gap, the colours of foliage and flowers are slowly revealed, followed by the deeply contrasted shadows of midday, until dusk falls over the stunning backdrop of Tjoritja | West MacDonnell Ranges.

UMBERTO PASTI

GARDEN OF ROHUNA
Rehouna, Morocco, 2004–

In 2004 the plantsman, writer and Milanese native Umberto Pasti took a walk along the Moroccan coast to the south of Tangier. He fell asleep under a fig tree and woke knowing he had to make a house and garden on that stony hillside above the sea. The fig tree is now surrounded by just under a hectare (2 acres) of garden at Rehouna: romantic, untamed and a sanctuary for threatened native species including indigenous geophytes (plants with underground storage organs, such as bulbs and corms). From the outset Pasti's passionate desire to conserve and protect the increasingly rare native flora has provided a key planting theme and objective, and he has rescued thousands of specimens from development sites around Tangier. After two decades and with the help of many locals, the purchase of further land and the addition of huge quantities of topsoil and manure to enrich what was a treeless charcoal-burning area, the hillsides are a haven for native wildflowers. A tangled tapestry of greenery and shady trees combines with a sculptural jostle of native plants at the periphery and non-natives on stone-walled terraces next to the house. Pasti insists that 'a garden is all about the plants and the people, more than it is about design and aesthetics. It is real,' and evidence of this belief is melded with his storytelling. He has woven tales for the garden's named compartments, and attributed to each an imaginary character: 'The Englishman [Garden], for example, is a melancholy drunk,' while the Egyptian Garden is so called 'because when I sit there I feel as if I'm in Luxor'.

ANTHONY PAUL

COASTAL GARDEN
West Wittering, West Sussex, England, 2019

Anthony Paul – one of Britain's most innovative contemporary designers, with an international portfolio – explains that he is always 'looking for ways to enhance the space we are given, both aesthetically and environmentally'. At the mouth of Chichester Harbour on the south coast of England, against the sandy foreshore at West Wittering (where it is thought the Romans landed), this garden 'offers a seamless transition between the wildness of the coast and the more orderly space around the house,' says Paul. A tranquil pool on a raised terrace mirrors the sky and brings its weather into the garden; it also connects house and garden visually with the borrowed landscape (and moods) of the sea. Between them is a stout, pier-like fence of horizontally laid oak boards, cleverly angled at the end of the garden to give the impression of a wooden ship's hull while usefully deflecting wind and wave. The hard landscaping evokes a maritime feel (boulders beside paths resemble the coastline), and becomes less neat and structured further from the house, although flint is the unifying material, used for the house and filling the gabion walls of the garden. As if sculpted by the wind, the planting of maritime species is in drifts and mounds, with both familiar favourites, such as *Armeria maritima* (thrift), *Carpobrotus edulis* (sour fig) and *Crambe maritima* (sea kale), and more unusual Australasian coastal species, including *Corokia* × *virgata* 'Yellow Wonder', *Grevillea* 'Clearview David' and *Pittosporum crassifolium* (karo).

DAN PEARSON IN COLLABORATION WITH TAKANO LANDSCAPE PLANNING

TOKACHI MILLENNIUM FOREST
Kamikawa District, Hokkaido, Japan, 2008

This highly innovative conservation project on Japan's northernmost island of Hokkaido was the brainchild of newspaper magnate Mitsushige Hayashi. His ambition was to create a landscape for a thousand years to offset the carbon footprint of his business and to encourage Japan's predominantly urban population to reconnect with the wonders of nature. The masterplan for the 240-hectare (590-acre) site, in the foothills of the central mountain range, was created by leading UK landscape designer Dan Pearson, along with Hokkaido-based Takano Landscape Planning.

The plot has four main areas: an ornamental Meadow Garden, a landform Earth Garden, a wild Forest Garden and a productive Farm Garden. In the Meadow Garden (pictured), vast swathes of plants showcase a careful selection of indigenous Japanese species alongside ornamental perennials and grasses. Beautiful and soulful, it is a masterclass in naturalistic planting on a grand scale. Next to it is the Earth Garden with its immense, turfed landforms. Irresistible to both children and adults, their wave-like contours cleverly draw visitors out of the more ornamental areas towards the unfamiliar setting of the Forest Garden beyond, where numerous site-specific artworks can be discovered. The climate is harsh, with long, extremely cold winters and hot, humid summers, so it's not an easy place to garden. Fortunately, the site is sensitively managed by close collaboration between Pearson and the garden's team. Midori Shintani, the head gardener from the outset, moved on in 2024, but her tenure will play an important part in the garden's envisioned thousand-year life.

PAOLO PEJRONE

PRIVATE GARDEN
Monte Argentario, Tuscany, Italy, 1996–

'Lazy gardening' is the phrase Italy's most celebrated living landscape architect, Paolo Pejrone, uses to describe his designs. At Monte Argentario, a rocky promontory on the Tuscan coast, he applied his 'lazy' treatment to a 14-hectare (35-acre) garden within 35 hectares (86 acres) of *macchia* – partially wild, wooded landscape – sloping down to the Tyrrhenian Sea. The result is a garden that appears always to have existed among the natural vegetation. In this ongoing project, which he started in 1996, Pejrone planted hardy native Mediterranean herbs, such as lavender and rosemary, with olive, cypress and myrtle trees, interspersed with native lichens, mosses and orchids that need little nurturing. They have since grown within the existing vegetation on the steep, dry, rocky hillsides that are at the mercy of strong sea winds. Raised, treated wooden steps meander through the hillsides, while winding gravel paths take the visitor through carefully maintained evergreens that grow in small, tight groups. Pejrone eschews any form of pesticide; instead, it takes the efforts of eight full-time gardeners to keep the garden looking 'natural', and pruning is done three times a week. The original house and the modern structures that dot the estate meld into the garden, a blend that is achieved by covering the house with ivy and allowing its exteriors to flow into the garden. The approach reflects Pejrone's training as an architect before a life-changing meeting with his teacher, English garden designer Russell Page, in 1970. Lazy it is not.

ANTONIO PERAZZI

GIARDINO DI PIUCA
Greve, Tuscany, Italy, 1990s–

Enjoying stunning views over hills, Piuca is the personal garden of designer, botanist and writer Antonio Perazzi. Looking out over the gentle meadows, the sculptural islands of tall grass in sward, and the carefree yet artful combinations of plant form, foliage and texture, it is clear that this is a garden created by a designer working with nature in harmony and balance. The old Tuscan farm was purchased by the Perazzi family in the 1960s, but over the years nature took back the vineyards and olive grove. This fascinated and inspired Perazzi, who studied garden design and landscape architecture at the Polytechnic University of Milan. When he began to garden at Piuca in the 1990s, he experimented by 'indulging its nature with seeds, cuttings and plants . . . giving the start to a space that had its own vocation'. But experiments also require study, and here Perazzi practised observation, for 'to know a place you have to start from a contemplative act; you have to empty your mind and stay listening to the infinite variety that composes it'. His conclusion was that 'taking care of a natural place should mean doing as little as possible . . . spontaneous nature constantly prods creativity'. Much of what Perazzi practises at Piuca is also manifest in his commissions, where he constantly investigates the intriguing paradox of how the garden – a symbol of the domestication and control of nature – can embrace the freedom and wisdom of spontaneous nature and generate harmony by welcoming wild plants, while remaining a work of art.

JANE PERCY, DUCHESS OF NORTHUMBERLAND, WITH WIRTZ INTERNATIONAL

THE ALNWICK GARDEN
Alnwick, Northumberland, England, 2001–

The making of what is arguably Britain's most ambitious new private garden since World War II was the brainchild of Jane Percy, Duchess of Northumberland, who in 1997 commissioned Belgian designers Jacques and Peter Wirtz, the father–son team behind Wirtz International (see p.320), to come up with a plan for a 5-hectare (12½-acre) garden. The sinuous Sage Wealth Management Grand Cascade (as it is now named), with its jets and associated hornbeam bowers, forms the spine of the garden and was one of the first features to be completed in 2001. Above it, to the south, stands the geometrically compartmented Ornamental Garden, which, with its pool and rills, neat hedges, pergolas and 16,000 European plants, has a feel of Islamic meets Dutch Baroque meets medieval herber. To the west of the cascade stands the Cherry Orchard, which boasts 329 specimens of spring-flowering *Prunus* 'Tai-haku'. On the eastern side of the lowest basin are the Bamboo Maze and the Serpent Garden, where eight water sculptures by William Pye nestle in topiary yew coils; and on the western side is the element that most captures the public and journalistic imagination: the Poison Garden. Locked behind black iron gates that are opened only for guided tours are about a hundred intoxicating, narcotic and toxic taxa. At the beginning of her journey, the Duchess's intention of creating new gardens in a historic landscape raised some hackles. History is honoured in the Ornamental and Rose gardens; but, as at Chatsworth (see p.81), Alnwick is a wonderful exemplar of how the old should be complemented by the new, thus keeping the garden dynamic rather than metaphorically pickled in aspic.

ALFONSO PÉREZ-VENTANA

CALA MASTELLA
Ibiza, Spain, 2020

Perched on the top of a cliff on the east coast of the popular Mediterranean island of Ibiza is a 1970s house built from local stone and wood with terraces full of pines and red-berried mastic trees, all enjoying stunning views of the sea. Following modernization by interior design and architecture studio Amaro Sánchez de Moya, the challenge for Madrid-based landscape designer Alfonso Pérez-Ventana was to create a garden that was sustainable while complementing the vibe of the house. His solution was a series of 'garden rooms', from the alfresco pine-shaded dining area overlooking the cove to the moss-ringed flagstones that lead to the pool and the seating areas of white-painted concrete. Pérez-Ventana's choice of plants is determined by the texture they bring to the various areas, and by their ability to withstand wind, sand and salt. Myrtle, roses and bougainvillea provide colour, while other non-native but long-established species, such as date palm, agaves and cacti, provide variation with their angular shapes and height. The spiky agaves contrast with feathery ornamental grasses, while succulents fill the raised beds around the seating area. Foliage in different shades of green dominates in the small beds that are cut out of the rocky ground, and terracotta pots dotted around the garden are filled with more agave. In a nod to the water-filled 'paradise gardens' of the Muslims who ruled southern Spain from 711 until 1492 CE, there is a water trough, an outdoor shower and a bath.

LIANNE POT

PRAIRIE GARDEN
De Wilp, Groningen, The Netherlands, 2009

In the flat agricultural landscape of the northern Netherlands, a colourful and diverse prairie garden comes as a surprise, and indeed almost a relief. Lianne Pot's bold 0.3-hectare (¾-acre) garden blends North American prairie species with plants of European origin that have similar cultural needs. Inspired by her visits to Hermannshof in Germany (see p.258) and a family trip across the American prairie, Pot – a social worker-turned-garden designer and nurserywoman – sought to translate the prairie concept into something that could ornament Dutch domestic spaces. The result is truly immersive; visitors walk along winding paths through a blend of perennials and grasses, but can also get an overview from a mound (a welcome feature that is all too rare in the 'real' American experience). The pragmatism of Pot's own garden sets it apart, as does its openness, with sight lines into the surrounding landscape. Her experience and expertise are available to nursery customers in the form of plant combination modules – based on theme, height or colour – designed for easy adoption as a long-lasting, low-maintenance planting system. Prairies tend to be dominated by late-flowering perennials, which mature to seedheads and thereby provide plenty of winter interest, and these can be spectacular in the hoar frosts that are frequent in the area. However, there is plenty to see earlier in the year, too, notably pasqueflowers (*Pulsatilla vulgaris*) for spring interest and camassias for early summer, showing how ornamental prairies can perform almost all year round.

ANN-MARIE POWELL

WILDLIFE GARDEN
RHS Garden Wisley, Woking, Surrey, England, 2021

The Wildlife Garden at Wisley, by designer Ann-Marie Powell and her team, proves that wildlife gardening is possible throughout the garden – even in dry shade – while also being full of beauty and inspiration. The design, covering about 0.4 hectares (1 acre), is based on a bee's wing and divided into segments, with water an all-embracing theme. There are 'take home' examples for simple habitat creation: log piles; roofs that are one half green, the other half insect habitat; plants for wet, dry and shady growing conditions; a birdwatching hide; and bird feeders. Beaches along the water's edge allow children to get in among the plants to pond dip, and long fingers of vibrant marginal aquatic plants protrude into the water. Much of the bright, bold planting has been chosen because it is attractive to wildlife and creates year-round interest. Almost 200 trees and 120,000 bulbs have been planted in the garden. Paths meander through areas of flowering hedges and past swathes of plants that are attractive to pollinators. At the very heart of the garden stands *The Vessel* by Tom Hare, a sculpture of chestnut and willow filled with pine cones, twigs and organic debris to attract insects, with a door so that it can be cleaned when necessary. It also revolves 360 degrees, so it turns to face the sun throughout the day. In Africa similar structures are used to collect dew from the air; in this practical yet inspirational garden, it collects wildlife.

SARAH PRICE

THE EXCHANGE
Erith, London, England, 2022

This riverside community garden around the restored Old Carnegie Library (1906) in south-east London has quickly become a destination for locals and visiting garden-lovers alike. Designed by Sarah Price (whose notable projects include plantings for the London 2012 Olympic Games, the Art Garden at Manchester's Whitworth art gallery and a captivating iris-filled show garden at RHS Chelsea in 2023), it offers spaces for community gatherings and activities, each with its own distinctive planting palette and, despite the sloping site, all accessible to pushchairs and wheelchairs.

Price – who is known for her light touch with hard landscaping – came on board while the building was undergoing major renovations, so she was able to make sustainability a priority within this compact 700-square-metre (7,500-square-foot) space. The paths linking the 'rooms' are made from recycled aggregate, while the bricks for seating areas were handmade in community workshops led by Local Works Studio, using site waste and clay recovered from local roadworks. Reclaimed corrugated metal panels and black-painted fencing make a recessive backdrop for the richly textured, seasonal planting, some of which, including the elegant *Elaeagnus* 'Quicksilver' and long-flowering *Rosa* × *odorata* 'Mutabilis' in the sloping back garden, was rehomed from a pop-up garden Price had designed for a luxury brand. To address the windswept, sun-baked conditions of the front garden, Price selected a variety of eye-catching Mediterranean plants, including the unusual white *Echium pininana* 'Snow Tower' and coral-flowered *Hesperaloe parviflora* (red yucca). She planted them in sand, a free-draining medium that is finding favour for its ability to promote both drought-tolerance and robustness in plants.

ALLAIN PROVOST

THAMES BARRIER PARK
London, England, 2000

Roughly square, in juxtaposition with the sculptural flood-prevention barriers, this 14-hectare (34½-acre) park – a collaboration between landscape architect Allain Provost (of Paris-based Groupe Signes) and architectural firm Patel Taylor – has transformed a derelict brownfield site on the north bank of the River Thames into an inviting public space. The contaminated soil was first covered with a layer of crushed concrete 1.8 metres (6 feet) deep, to protect the new soil laid on top. The key ornamental element is the 40-metre-long (130-foot) Green Dock, which, echoing Provost's work at Parc André-Citroën in Paris, cuts asymmetrically through the geometric space. Sunken not only to protect it from strong winds but also as a reminder of the area's maritime heritage, the 'dock' is notable for the parallel yew hedges cut into wave-like forms that run its length. Paths pass between them, and the flower beds are filled with a mix of species selected to give year-round interest while encouraging wildlife and thereby increasing biodiversity. Two bridges provide wide prospects over the planting. At the north end is the Fountain Plaza, a stone courtyard featuring thirty-two fountains, and at the south the Pavilion of Remembrance in memory of local people who died in World War II. Elsewhere are expansive lawns, formal groves of trees, a basketball court, and picnic and play areas. The park was so catalytic for the regeneration of the surrounding area that shortly after its completion a neighbouring plot became one of the fastest-selling housing developments in London at the time.

PWP LANDSCAPE ARCHITECTURE WITH SAFDIE ARCHITECTS

JEWEL
Changi Airport, Singapore, 2019

Designed by a team led by Safdie Architects, Jewel is a 3.2-hectare (8-acre) climate-controlled glass dome above retail space that connects directly to Singapore's bus terminal and airport. The gardens within were created by PWP Landscape Architecture (see p.289). The topmost (fifth) floor is the Canopy Park, where *Ficus* trees shade the Hedge Maze, Topiary Walk and Petal Garden. Below, gardens drop down nearly 30 metres (98 feet) to a central gathering space. According to PWP design partner Adam Greenspan, the landscaping emulates a 'forest valley', with terraces like those in a shady plantation. This haven boasts 2,500 trees and 100,000 shrubs, set among tumbling water features. The upper storey features three types of tree: *Agathis borneensis*, native to Malaysia and Indonesia; Australian *A. robusta*; and *Terminalia neotaliala* from Madagascar. Terraced planters faced with Indonesian lava stone hold palms, tree ferns, epiphytes and climbers, while winding paths of stone and wood (some passing through groves of bamboo) immerse visitors in nature. The dominant feature is the spectacular Rain Vortex, which streams through the roof oculus during heavy downpours to create a water sculpture 40 metres (130 feet) tall – currently the world's tallest indoor waterfall. At its peak the flow is 45,460 litres (10,000 gallons) per minute, and the stormwater is recycled throughout the building. According to Moshe Safdie, founding partner of Safdie Architects, 'Jewel weaves together an experience of nature and the marketplace, asserting the idea of the airport as a vibrant, uplifting urban centre, engaging travellers, visitors and residents, and echoing Singapore's reputation as "The City in the Garden".'

PATRICK AND SYLVIE QUIBEL

LE JARDIN PLUME
Auzouville-sur-Ry, near Rouen, Normandy, France, 1996–

Patrick and Sylvie Quibel are plant-nursery owners who have masterminded the creation of their own garden since 1996. Self-taught designers, they now use their wealth of experience and proven skills to design other private gardens. This 2.8-hectare (7-acre) site was previously pasture and orchard, and the Quibels wanted to preserve and work with this legacy. Their masterplan demonstrates the core principles of classical French garden design: symmetry, perspective and the use of axes. But the hard lines of the grid are blurred by abundant, informal planting. Near the house, tall hedges of *Carpinus betulus* (hornbeam) define the boundaries between spaces, and shorter, tightly clipped *Buxus sempervirens* (box) hedging provides an evergreen link and year-round structure across the site. In some places it is clipped straight, while around the Flower and Feather gardens (the latter of which gives its name to the entire plot) it is trimmed freehand so that the top resembles flowing waves. In July the garden as a whole becomes a haze of grass flower heads that appear to float in the summer breezes. The paths vary in width; narrow and brick-paved in some areas, they allow a close-up experience of tall, colourful plants. A clear view across a square reflecting pool through to the Orchard is another key to the design. Set at ground level, the pool matches in its dimensions the small meadow squares between the productive fruit trees, and forms the centre of a gathering space from which to take in this beautiful garden.

RAD+AR

TANATAP FRAME GARDEN
Jakarta, Indonesia, 2024

This large, wedge-shaped structure rises from 2.2 metres (7¼ feet) tall at the rear to a height of 7.5 metres (24½ feet), like a giant, open-fronted stage. Within, an amphitheatre-like seating area winds between the abstract shapes of white or black mosaic-tiled Gaudí-esque planters filled with lush tropical evergreens. This surreal vegetative theme is enhanced by fibreglass structures like vast twisting trunks or perhaps aerial roots that frame the outward view alongside alternating mirrored and glazed panels around the side walls and ceiling; these, in turn, link the installation with the established plants and trees of the adjacent, abandoned public park and the planters below. Created by Indonesian architecture firm RAD+ar (Research Artistic Design + architecture), this project embodies founder Antonius Richard Rusli's distinctive approach to design, which is always rooted in research and embraces the tropical climate of the Indonesian archipelago, where he practises. Viewed from the front, particularly when illuminated at night, the garden appears like a huge 3D television screen with understorey and emergent rainforest plants, reflecting both the park and the region's native vegetation. Beneath its upper level, the partially subterranean ground floor contains a cafe and gallery, its skylights illuminating a smaller tropical garden and a fun element, the 'tease', revealing the activities of oblivious visitors in the garden above. The aim of the project is to enable the local community to make better use of the neglected park and appreciate its value not only to the environment, but also to the surrounding communities.

RAMBOLL STUDIO DREISEITL

BISHAN-ANG MO KIO PARK
Singapore, 2012

This park in the heart of Singapore, constructed in 1988, included an ugly but necessary flood-protection structure: a section of the Kallang River canalized into a straight concrete channel 2.7 kilometres (1¾ miles) long and 24 metres (79 feet) wide. A thoughtful redesign was undertaken from 2009 by urban planner and water artist Herbert Dreiseitl (whose firm, Ramboll Studio Dreiseitl, became part of the global design community of Henning Larsen architects in 2023) to remove the channel and satisfy the city's increasing water management requirements. The canal was transformed into a sinuous, naturalized river and the 62-hectare (153-acre) park a lush, vibrant natural environment in which to escape the densely populated city. One of Singapore's most popular public green spaces, it has open areas, water features, diverse planting, playgrounds, restaurants and Recycle Hill, a lookout point raised from concrete repurposed from the canal. Each element works alone to offer recreational opportunities, while the whole connects users with nature and water. It is an effective example of blue-green infrastructure, whereby 'blue' hydrological elements (canals, floodplains, rivers and so on) are integrated with 'green' vegetation systems. The benefits are the removal of grey infrastructure (the canal), improved air quality, water (including stormwater) and climate regulation, opportunities for recreation and health, and the inspiration nature offers. But the biggest winner has been biodiversity. No wildlife was introduced during the redesign, but flora and fauna have found the park, which now boasts 66 wildflower species, 59 bird species and, in 2014, a (now famous) family of otters.

SARAH RAVEN

PERCH HILL
Robertsbridge, East Sussex, England, 1994–

To visit Perch Hill, the home of gardener, writer and cut-flower trailblazer Sarah Raven, is to be immersed in abundance. Her 0.6-hectare (1½-acre) garden in rural southeastern England is remarkable in its profusion, the trial ground for the colourful annuals, biennials and dahlias with which Raven has made her name. Perch Hill was a run-down farm when she and her husband, writer Adam Nicolson, came to it in the mid-1990s, a collection of decaying outbuildings and heavy clay fields with origins in the 16th century. But Raven saw the potential for indulging what was, then, an unusual passion: a love of growing annual cut flowers, which stemmed from the buckets of zinnias and sunflowers she had encountered in the Mediterranean as a child, and the joy of bringing blooms indoors. Perch Hill was not so much designed as quickly evolved, and a garden of salads, herbs and flowers grown for the house developed into a hive of propagative, experimental activity. Raven soon repurposed a field for stock beds, then converted a barn into a classroom for workshops and fitted out a greenhouse to host lunches. Research trips to Dutch nurseries continue to bring exciting plant varieties for trial in the garden, with such successes as *Salvia viridis* 'Blue Monday', *Cerinthe major* and *Dahlia* 'Akita' making their way into the catalogue of Raven's mail-order business. This is intensive garden-making – it takes a team of five gardeners – but the pay-off is enduring renewal: each year a fresh mix of radiant debutants and dependables; another turn of the kaleidoscope.

**REED HILDERBRAND
WITH SWA GROUP**

JANE GREGORY GARDEN
Buffalo Bayou Park, Houston, Texas,
United States, 2012–15

Whether it's biking, hiking, jogging or other outdoor activities, Houstonians love to get out and about and Buffalo Bayou Park offers them ample opportunity. The park was also a perfect fit for landscape-design studio Reed Hilderbrand to apply its horticultural expertise to a major work of ecological infrastructure. Snaking through Houston, the bayou is crisscrossed by highways but also has robust potential for waterside stroll gardens. That was the goal when Reed Hilderbrand collaborated with SWA Group to design the planting for the 0.8-hectare (2-acre) Jane Gregory Garden (named after a local philanthropist and activist) within the 3.7-kilometre-long (2⅓-mile) park. Flanking the promenade, project leads Doug Reed and Joseph James created a green ribbon bedded in a dense linear meadow of regional wildflowers beneath existing mature live oaks, crape myrtles and camellias. The result is a smart departure from the typical grassy parks of the past, with bonus perks for pollinators and local wildlife as well as resilience to flooding and drought. The experience is a rich and enriching blend of nature framed by the city skyline but within footsteps of the bayou banks. 'You're conscious of the traffic hum, you glimpse the skyline, but you can sit on a bench with lush vegetation around you,' says James. The garden also takes a scenic, inspirational detour into a loblolly pine-surrounded lawn framing Henry Moore's iconic bronze sculpture *Spindle Piece* (1969). No wonder Houston has embraced the Buffalo Bayou project as its 'definitive next-generation park'.

MAT REESE AND THE VON OPEL FAMILY

MALVERLEYS
East End, Hampshire, England, 2010–

Tucked away in a small Hampshire village in the south of England, this 4-hectare (10-acre) privately owned estate possesses one of the finest examples of the new 'English Flower Garden' style. Developed by head gardener Mat Reese for the von Opel family, the garden is laid out as a series of rooms, each with its own atmosphere and planting palette. Having trained at RHS Garden Wisley and the Royal Botanic Gardens Kew, Reese spent six years as part of a small team at Great Dixter, working with gardening geniuses Christopher Lloyd and Fergus Garrett (see p.106). His remit at Malverleys was to create a garden that had a strong connection to the pale stone Victorian mansion but sat comfortably in its landscape. His planting style is inventive and constantly evolving, with an undeniably poetic beauty. Highlights include exuberantly planted long borders, a hot garden, a topiary meadow, a tranquil pond garden, a cloister garden, a magical stumpery and an ornate walled kitchen garden (complete with large ornate fruit cages), a cutting garden and an elegant white garden. On a broad terrace at the back of the house the planting is particularly clever, striking a rare balance between formal and wild, restrained and untamed. An abundance of tried-and-tested perennials, bulbs and annuals sit alongside more experimental selections, with plants spilling over the York stone paving and self-seeders settling into unexpected places. It is easy to feel the joy and fun Reese and his team get from their work, which delights, challenges and informs as only the best can do.

BRUCE JOHN RIDDELL

VAYO MEDITATION GARDEN
Coastal Maine Botanical Gardens, Boothbay, Maine, United States, 2007

This Japanese-inspired garden, with its vistas to the Back River, is deliberately positioned at the boundary between natural forest and the ebbing and flowing water, to enhance the calm atmosphere of this section of Coastal Maine Botanical Gardens. The design is a textbook example of landscape architect Bruce John Riddell's skill in the use of native plants, carefully placed stonework and what he terms 'LandART' (art integrated into the landscape). Tranquillity is enhanced by the subtle use of native flora in many green tints and tones, while the granite stonework and stairs integrate seamlessly into the natural setting. The focal element, placed to unify stone, water and sky, is a large, partially polished basin carved by David Holmes (a sculptor based in Plymouth, Maine) from a huge boulder of Ellsworth Schist found in a blueberry field close to nearby Mount Desert Island. With its mission 'to inspire meaningful connections between people and nature and promote plant conservation through horticulture, education and plant science', this – the largest botanic garden in New England – comprises 132 hectares (325 acres), of which 8 hectares (19 acres) are gardens. The first 52 hectares (128 acres) were purchased in 1996, and Riddell was heavily involved in the early planning. He contributed planting schemes for a number of the garden areas, including the Vayo Meditation Garden, construction of which began in 2005 after a gift from the Vayo family of Sawyer Island.

DEAN RIDDLE

THE ORCHARD
The Catskills, New York, United States, 2012

When Dean Riddle settled in upstate New York after studying horticulture in North Carolina and apprenticing at Hillier Nurseries, he took his cue from the hardscrabble Catskill Mountain terrain to pioneer a tapestry planting style that has been dubbed 'Modern Cottage'. By interweaving loose annuals and blowsy perennials in repeating patterns within a semi-formal rubric, he achieves airiness but also intimacy. That style was exactly what the homeowners requested when Riddle designed the terraced garden beside a house dating from 1906 and draped in climbing hydrangea.

The 3.2-hectare (8-acre) property featured a mature orchard, and Riddle extended that ambiance from the sweeping driveway up to the house with a texturally rich parade of multi-stemmed *Amelanchier* (serviceberry) wading between *Fothergilla* (witch alder), *Clethra* and hydrangeas embedded in ferns, sedges and *Eurybia* (wood aster). For the terrace plantings, the client requested a treatment based on Riddle's own garden, a superabundance of blooms spilling from raised beds. The bounty is corralled by an informal stick fence made of prunings from the surrounding woodland. Working with a ratio of 25 per cent annuals to 75 per cent perennials, Riddle focused on a soothing colour palette of blue, purple, pink and mauve as requested by the client, and wove such vintage favourites as *Nicotiana* (tobacco plant), *Calamintha* (calamint), summer phlox, *Alchemilla mollis* (lady's mantle) and salvias into the tapestry. To add to the romance, fragrance is a leitmotif both night and day. Down three steps is a dining terrace carpeted in creeping thyme, for savouring the mountain view.

FERNANDA RIONDA

CASA ACANTO
San Miguel Chapultepec, Mexico City, Mexico, 2019

Tucked away in San Miguel Chapultepec, a historic neighbourhood of Mexico City, this 1,200-square-metre (13,000-square-foot) garden transforms a 1930s house into a serene refuge from urban life. Offering a modern take on traditional Mexican courtyards, it seamlessly blends historical charm with contemporary design. Its Mexican landscape designer, Fernanda Rionda, executed the project with a masterful blend of beauty and functionality. Renowned for her expertise in naturalistic landscaping, Rionda specializes in creating solutions to environmental challenges, and her approach is evident in this garden's sustainable design features: gravel surfaces, water-efficient plant selections, and a thoughtful layout that encourages exploration while minimizing maintenance. As visitors step into the garden, they are greeted by a harmonious interplay of plants and materials. The absence of a traditional lawn is striking; gravel replaces grass, offering both aesthetic and practical advantages. This deliberate choice ensures excellent drainage during the city's intense summer rains, while promoting the recharge of groundwater. Meandering brick paths weave through lush greenery, inviting visitors to pause and soak in the tranquil atmosphere. Iconic plants, such as *Acanthus mollis* (bear's breeches), evoke a timeless elegance, their repeated forms tying the space to its historical roots. More than just a retreat, this garden serves as a powerful statement on the role of design in urban sustainability. By marrying historical inspiration with innovative solutions, it provides a timeless sanctuary that honours the past while looking to the future.

AMALIA ROBREDO

PRIVATE GARDEN
José Ignacio, Maldonado, Uruguay, 2023

Landscape architect Amalia Robredo envisioned the 2,500-square-meter (27,000-square-foot) beachfront garden for this Grimaldi·Nacht-designed house to be 'as wild as possible,' to make it seem like the house 'landed' on a pristine site. As with all Robredo's work, the plant palette is locally focused, mostly native coastal plants from the dunes and the thorny but spectacular scrub community that is typical of the Uruguay coast – and is also in danger of disappearing because of urban development. Robredo was a pioneer of using the flora of Uruguay's southeast Maldonado coast in domestic gardens, and in recognizing not only its resilience in the face of almost constant wind but also its distinctive visual qualities. Other natives are included from a list of plants that need conservation, enabling the garden to provide a refuge for threatened species. The rocks, placed by Argentinian artist Nicolás Bedel, were carefully selected for their shape and existing lichen flora – the specific inclusion of which is a notable planting design decision in itself. Bedel has tried to develop 'a dialogue between plant shape and that of the rocks', which remind him of whales and seals, providing another link to the coastal location. There is a similar 'local' focus in Robredo's own naturalistic garden, where she is working to preserve Uruguay's native scrubland or monte, a slowly established, delicate ecosystem of trees, shrubs and grasses found on sandy soils. By identifying key native species that also have garden value, she hopes to encourage their appreciation in gardens.

ROOM 4.1.3

GARDEN OF AUSTRALIAN DREAMS
National Museum of Australia, Canberra, Australian Capital Territory, Australia, 2001

One of the most frequent criticisms levelled at the Garden of Australian Dreams – which has been controversial throughout its short history – is that it contains very few plants. And that is true: there are only a couple of trees and a small patch of grass. But contrariness lies at the heart of this competition-winning design, as the garden's acronym, GOAD, deftly hints. Located on Ngambri and Ngunnawal Country, the 0.53-hectare (1⅓-acre) garden forms the centrepiece of the National Museum of Australia, which opened in 2001. The museum's remit covers three interrelated themes: Aboriginal and Torres Strait Islander history and culture; Australia's history and society since 1788; and the interaction of people with the environment. Articulating these to visitors through a focus on land, nation and people, the garden's designers, Richard Weller and Vladimir Sitta (cofounders of landscape architecture studio Room 4.1.3), used giant overlaid maps as the principal organizational and interpretive device. Indigenous linguistic boundaries, for example, contrast with the physical and political delineations of European colonizers, while popular cultural references – the 'Australian Dream' of the title – hint symbolically at complex post-colonial relationships. As befits its setting, the garden is simultaneously a constructed space within the architecture and urban form of the museum; a large sculptural exhibit requiring careful conservation; and an interpretive node that tells its own thematic stories while subtly directing visitors to exhibits displayed more conventionally within the museum. In its impact, the Garden of Australian Dreams remains the most significant polemical garden in Australia.

ROSEBANK

PRIVATE GARDEN
London, England, 2020

Designer Matt Keightley founded his landscape design practice Rosebank Landscaping in 2016 with business partner Cameron Wilson, and the studio has quickly gained international recognition for its award-winning gardens at Royal Horticultural Society shows in the UK and the Shenzhen Flower Show in China. With a focus on refined, sophisticated detailing, Keightley likes to showcase bold architectural choices alongside naturalistic planting. This approach is made to work hard in urban spaces such as this 375-square-metre (4,040-square-foot) garden in northwest London, where function and aesthetic are very much on show in a small space. Keightley uses a geometric form inspired by the clean lines of neoclassical architecture and realized through the division of space into functional zones, balanced with the green structure of topiary. Subtle changes of level define the zones further and give that all-important sense of a journey as you move through the garden. A sharply defined lawn is grounded by four rosemary 'pincushions' that are kept neatly clipped to retain their proportions and form. Rounded pillars of *Carpinus betulus* (hornbeam) 5 metres (16 feet) tall stand sentinel at the change in level, emerging from a row of pleached screening trees. The smooth natural limestone brings character, and a feature wall at the back of the garden provides a focal point. But key to the garden's success are the two gnarled crab apple trees that were retained from the original garden and create a wonderfully characterful dynamic against the formality of the space.

SARA JANE ROTHWELL

PRIVATE GARDEN
London, England, 2019

With a previous career as a designer for film and theatre, Sara Jane Rothwell was drawn to the task of adding drama to tricky garden sites when she set up her garden design studio, London Garden Designer, in 2003. This sloping 610-square-metre (6,500-square-foot) garden in Highgate, north London, is 38 metres (125 feet) long with a daunting 7-metre (23-foot) difference in height from bottom to top. It was an unmanageable and uninviting space that the clients wanted to transform into a place of accessibility and interest for the whole family. Although such a request is technically challenging, Rothwell uses the existing topography to its best advantage, creating terracing to give much-needed vertical interest. A visually restrained use of poured-concrete walls, hardwood timber and Corten steel step risers create crisp horizontals that make the garden feel wider than it is. Rothwell uses mounded naturalistic planting to soften the angles, with repeated *Pinus mugo* (dwarf mountain pine) and *Euphorbia × martini* (Martin's wood spurge) to bounce the eye up the gently curving path to the sunny grassed terrace at the top. The predominance of green harmonizes the landscaping, and two distinct plant palettes – of muted pastels in the spring and fiery reds in the summer – add drama. 'Our designs favour a strong architectural footprint, balanced by naturalistic planting that envelops the space,' explains Rothwell. 'We want our clients to be able to engage with their gardens and to embrace nature, with all its benefits.'

MARGIE RUDDICK

CASA FINISTERA
Cabo San Lucas, Baja California Sur, Mexico, 2001

Tucked into a dramatically sloping mountainside in Cabo San Lucas, Casa Finistera is a 0.8-hectare (2-acre) private residence within Pedregal (a resort community developed by Mexican architect Manuel Diaz Rivera from the 1970s onwards). The sleek, minimalist home, designed by Steven Harris in 2001 for songwriter George David Weiss and his wife, Claire, perches against giant sand-coloured boulders overlooking the Pacific Ocean at the southern tip of the Baja California peninsula. Landscape designer Margie Ruddick, working with Harris, created the ensemble of gardens that borrow from the diverse native flora of this arid, sun-drenched site. Determined to avoid resort-style beds and borders chock-full of tropical plants requiring maintenance and irrigation, she sought out drought-tolerant species whose sculptural forms reflect the challenges of thriving with little water and intense sunlight. At the centre of the casa is a desert courtyard incorporating granite boulders found on the site, and a garden of succulents. *Stenocereus thurberi* (organ pipe cactus), *Ferocactus townsendianus* (Townsend barrel cactus), *Aloe vera*, *Pennisetum* (fountain grass), *Plumeria rubra* (frangipani), *Cylindropuntia cholla* (bald cholla) and *Leucaena leucocephala* (river tamarind) emerge from crevices and gravel beds. Ruddick accompanied the local landscaper on a desert trek to map the distribution of native plants, then listened to the land's fauna to evoke its natural quirkiness. Demonstrating her signature philosophy and commitment to sustainable horticulture, she reflects: 'I planted with grasses, groundcovers and vines that could also be found just up the hill, where a lot of life happens.'

CATHERINE RUSH AND MICHAEL WRIGHT WITH THOMAS GOOCH

SAND GARDEN
Glenluce, Victoria, Australia, 2020–

In the highlands of Central Victoria, on the traditional lands of the Dja Dja Wurrung peoples, landscape architects Catherine Rush and Michael Wright (directors of Melbourne-based Rush Wright Associates) are conducting an experiment to test the resilience of their garden to drought, fire and extreme storms. They want their climate-conscious garden designs to be affordable, to age well and to require little maintenance. The 300-square-metre (3,200-square-foot) Sand Garden, designed in collaboration with landscape architect Thomas Gooch, was begun in 2020 within an established garden in a dry, rocky landscape. Inspiration for it came from mallee heath habitat in Ngarkat Conservation Park, South Australia, and the sand dunes of Wyperfeld National Park in semi-arid northwestern Victoria. A technique whereby deep stone-filled trenches beneath sand are used to retain water for extended periods enables the landscape to adapt to climate extremes. Railway ballast and local soil, rocks and river sand were used to create this low-budget, high-impact garden. Slender, mounded garden beds are interspersed with sand-covered informal paths that widen to a stone fire pit and seating area. Drifts of self-seeding *Xerochrysum bracteatum* (strawflower) are punctuated with the hybrid *Xanthorrhoea* 'Supergrass' (grass tree). *Atriplex nummularia* (Australian saltbush) is planted as a fire-retardant buffer between the garden and a paddock beyond. There is no one 'Australian' garden, but Rush and Wright suggest that this small yet joyful and relaxed plot could provide a model for a new approach in other regions, using a planting palette informed by an understanding of local conditions.

CRISTIANA RUSPA

LA PISTA 500 ROOF GARDEN
Turin, Italy, 2019

Film buffs will recognize Lingotto, the former Fiat factory made famous by the car chase in *The Italian Job* (1969). It was the largest car factory of its time when it was built in 1923, but it closed in 1982 and a new use for the building was sought. In 2019, as part of a masterplan, architect Benedetto Camerana designed a rooftop garden for the Agnelli Foundation (which established the Fiat Foundation). Key to the brief was the stipulation that the rooftop track, La Pista 500, be retained for Fiat to test its electric cars. Camerana worked alongside landscape architect Cristiana Ruspa of Giardino Segreto to create one of the largest roof gardens in Europe at 2.7 hectares (6.5 acres) with planting covering 0.6 hectares (1½ acres). The choice of tough plants was key in Turin's continental climate, which brings very cold winters and extremely hot summers. Ruspa had little depth of soil in which to plant, and the weight limit was restrictive, so the garden mainly comprises perennials and grasses, with a few shrubs, including *Cotinus* and *Corylus*; it was impossible to include trees. Changes have been made to the original planting after problems caused by flooding. The Agnelli Foundation also uses the garden as an outdoor gallery, exhibiting contemporary sculpture, which changes from year to year. The roof-garden cafe is a delightful place to sit and watch the sunset with a glass of wine, while the glass dome known as La Bolla (The Bubble) was designed by architect Renzo Piano and is used by Fiat as a meeting room.

LIBBY RUSSELL

BATCOMBE HOUSE
Shepton Mallet, Somerset, England, 2003–

Creating a new garden around an old property always requires careful thought. Couple that with a location tucked away in a valley grazed by sheep and backed by native woodland in rural southwestern England, and style and sensitivity are also requisite. Landscape designer Libby Russell has allowed herself time to perfect the scene around her 18th-century family home. Starting with little more than two uneven, sloping lawns and an impressive cedar dating back more than 200 years, Russell aimed to connect the 1.2-hectare (3-acre) garden to the other side of the valley with its wildflowers, trees and the contoured striations of sheep-worn paths. Her solution was to split the garden in two. One half is a series of terraces made from local stone that lead up the hill away from the house and contain flowing beds of perennials, fruit trees, a kitchen garden and a meadow. The other half slopes down from the house and features a more open lawn and a contemporary grass amphitheatre that echoes the lines of the valley beyond. The sculpted lawns are bordered by naturalistic displays planted as impactful seasonal swathes of magnolias, hardy geraniums, hostas and euphorbias, among others. The terraces are more managed, with plenty of colour from roses, lavender, foxgloves, valerian and nepeta giving an abundant English country-garden appeal. Russell previously worked with Arabella Lennox-Boyd (see p.165), and it was there that she met fellow landscape architect Emma Mazzullo; they set up their design studio, Mazzullo + Russell, in 2014.

VERO SAGUIER

LA ESTANCIA DE CAFAYATE
Cafayate, Salta, Argentina, 2010

Designing gardens in desertic areas – such as Cafayate in the province of Salta, which receives only 200 millimetres (just under 8 inches) of rain per year (all during the summer months) and where the soil is sandy, very free-draining and slightly salty – is a major challenge that Argentine landscape designer Vero Saguier handles gracefully in her work. She is determined to address this in her designs and to create gardens that are born of their territory. In this project for the communal areas of La Estancia de Cafayate, she drew inspiration from the wild countryside surrounding this 550-hectare (1,360-acre) country club estate. An enthusiastic hiker, she is used to exploring nature and seeing it through her designer's eyes, and she quickly began the process of observing local plant communities and reproducing the plants she found interesting and functional for the site. The beautiful *Sporobolus maximus* took on a prominent role, as well as cacti from the genus *Opuntia* and the towering *Leucostele atacamensis* subsp. *pasacana* (syn. *Trichocereus pasacana*; cardón). *Parkinsonia praecox* (brea), *Neltuma alba* (syn. *Prosopis alba*; algarrobo) and *Schinus molle* (anacahuita), among other trees, became essential for shade and as habitat for birds, small mammals and hundreds of insects, all contributing to a very local soundscape. The garden remains true to the local identity, provides refuge, food and nesting opportunities for much of the area's fauna, contributes to conserving local species, and is an example of sustainability that has been replicated elsewhere in the province.

ANDREW SALTER

PRIVATE GARDEN
near Canterbury, Kent, England, 2014–

Conjuring up the image of a little house on the prairie, Andrew Salter's two-storey black timber 'cabin' (in fact a relocated and converted farm building) is perched on a decking veranda at the centre of a small (70 metres/753 feet square) yet dynamic garden enclosed by a rustic post-and-rail fence beyond which, on two sides, a wildflower meadow transitions gently into picturesque farmland. Salter believes that 'a good garden, an evocative garden, is often achieved by mixing elements that don't ordinarily mingle and combining them in an inspiring way that passes as natural'.

He credits as his inspiration the Long Border at nearby Great Dixter (see p.106), where he volunteered for four years, learning much from head gardener Fergus Garrett. However, there is also more than a hint of Wolfgang Oehme's (see p.207) jewelled tapestry approach about the contrasting yet harmonious planting and the choice of a wide palette of structural plants with flowers an accentuating highlight: brightly coloured gems cast on a verdurous embroidery. Indeed, it is the kaleidoscopic diversity of plant form, foliage texture and colour that gives the garden its structure, the deliberate repetition establishing continuity and forging a coherent whole. While most definitely 'exuberant and uncontrived' (as Christopher Lloyd described his own border at Great Dixter), this is very much Salter's personal interpretation of 'a closely woven tapestry', in which – rather than the linearity of a border – the rectangular garden nods to the Japanese concept of a viewing garden.

ÁLVARO SAMPEDRO

DOGS' GARDEN
La Moraleja, Madrid, Spain, 2018

In a country that has long favoured structural formality and, despite its climate, the irrigated lawn, a new wave of Spanish garden designers is breaking the mould, bringing dynamic, native-led plantings to commercial and domestic settings alike. Among the chief proponents of change is Madrid-born Álvaro Sampedro. His environment-led, water-conscious approach – evident in his gardens for hotels, rooftops and residential estates – seeks to match all-season beauty and rich colour with robust sustainability, employing plants that are naturally adapted to Spain's increasingly hostile, dry summers. And where better to practise artful naturalism than in the homeland of such horticultural staples as germander, euphorbia and creeping thyme – Mediterranean natives enlisted for arid gardens the world over? This 2,400-square-metre (½-acre) private garden in the upmarket Madrid suburb of La Moraleja distils Sampedro's ethos perfectly. A swathe of hardwearing *Teucrium* and *Phillyrea*, clipped yet interwoven, connects the poolside formality with the loose perennial planting below, where the likes of *Achillea* and *Stachys* spill freely over meandering grit paths. In place of turf is the softness of *Stipa* and *Miscanthus* grasses, their shifting colours celebrating, rather than subverting, the changing seasons. La Moraleja's other progressive brushstroke is more subtle: its initial layout was designed by dogs. Wary of the client's spirited canines flattening future plantings, Sampedro chose at the outset to observe the animals' movements around the blank canvas of the property – their route to the garden boundary, to the postman or passerby – and place the paths accordingly. So simple an idea, so reassuring the result.

HARALD SAUER

LUISENPARK
Mannheim, Germany, 2023

A dull expanse of lawn inside the main entrance of the 42-hectare (103-acre) Luisenpark is now an electrifying display of contemporary planting, designed by protean master gardener Harald Sauer to help the city of Mannheim host the German National Garden Show (BUGA) in 2023. His reinvented landscape marks a leap forward in naturalistic design, where visitors wander through a succession of immersive meadow and perennial borders cascading down the slope. Woody shrubs, such as *Cotinus* 'Grace' (smoke bush) and *Rhus typhina* 'Tiger Eyes' (sumac), provide structure, with yew trees as sculptural topiary and Persian silk trees in the distance. Sauer brings immense variation to the borders, combining grassy matrix planting with larger blocks and scattered perennial gems. Supersized perennials, among them *Glycyrrhiza yunnanensis* (Yunnan liquorice), *Datisca cannabina* (Cretan hemp) and *Althaea cannabina* (hemp-leaved hollyhock), heighten the scale, with the elements repeated in subtle variations. It was Luisenpark's gardening director Ellen Oswald who realized that a dramatic redesign was needed in time for the garden show. She put out a call to Sauer, who in 2021 had won the prestigious Karl Foerster Medal for his pivotal role in transforming the gritty Ebertpark in nearby Ludwigshafen to a cutting-edge exemplar of public space design. His ground plan for Luisenpark grew in consultation with Oswald to encompass nearly 1,700 square metres (18,300 square feet) in genre-defying plantings. His brief was to deliver the visual knockout punch for BUGA and create a permanent new face for the park. What worked so well at the big show looks even better now that the party is over.

SCAPE AND STUDIO GANG, WITH THEASTER GATES

TOM LEE PARK
Memphis, Tennessee, United States, 2023

This 12.5-hectare (31-acre) park on the eastern bank of the Mississippi River in Memphis was created collaboratively by landscape architecture and urban design studio Scape and architecture and urban design firm Studio Gang. Celebrated as a model for inclusion and regeneration, it was named to honour the heroism of Tom Lee, a Black river worker who saved dozens of people from a capsized steamboat in 1925. In 2017, a City of Memphis task force working to reinvigorate the industrial riverfront commissioned Studio Gang to develop a masterplan for the transformation of 10 kilometres (6 miles) of underused riverbank into a network of beautiful, natural public spaces that would reconnect Memphis residents with the water. The concept included a vision to improve the existing Tom Lee Park, transforming it into a signature civic space. The park's landscape design was the task of Scape, led by founder and principal Kate Orff, a leading voice in climate adaptation and environmentalism in the field of landscape architecture. Given her expertise, restoring the site's natural ecology was a major goal. The final park design – which was strongly informed by input from the local community – features four distinct zones, each drawing on features of the Mississippi River Basin while also providing areas for recreation, dining, elevated views of the river, gardens for trees and plants, and public art. A permanent installation comprising 32 sculptures created by artist Theaster Gates and named *A Monument to Listening*, honours Lee's courageous act and, along with the park, celebrates his legacy.

MARIO SCHJETNAN WITH VICTOR MARQUEZ

LA MEXICANA PARK
Mexico City, Mexico, 2017

Mario Schjetnan is a renowned landscape architect and pioneer of an ecological approach. The practice he cofounded in 1977, Grupo de Diseño Urbano (GDU), is known for its expertise in large projects that combine environmental rehabilitation with social renewal, often on formerly degraded landscapes. His Natura Garden at Bicentennial Park, San Luis Potosi (2011) is one such defining project on the site of a former oil refinery. With this more recent project, when the extraction of gravel and sand finished at this quarry, the government's plan was to add more housing units to the sprawling metropolis of Mexico City. But residents of the area lobbied for a new green space on the post-industrial site. After a decade of negotiations, agreement was reached to create this 29-hectare (72-acre) park at the heart of an urban community. It was built in just over a year, with Schjetnan and principal architect Victor Marquez collaborating on the design. Environmental management infrastructure is fundamental to the scheme. A 'bio-trench' captures rainwater, filtering it and directing it into a large lake and giant underground cistern that irrigate the plants during periods of drought. Potable water is used only to supply drinking fountains. Above ground, the main walkway reflects the topography of the site. Visitors stroll its length to access separate areas defined by their use: quiet garden spaces or specific sporting provision including a skate park, sports tracks and an amphitheatre. Parkland areas were planted with 2,500 trees and many thousands of smaller plants, mostly pollinators to encourage biodiversity – apt in a landscape park for the 21st century that has the needs of both people and nature at its heart.

CASSIAN SCHMIDT AND URS WALSER

SCHAU- UND SICHTUNGSGARTEN HERMANNSHOF
Weinheim, Baden-Württemberg, Germany, 1983–

Hermannshof is a 1.8-hectare (4½-acre) garden that also functions as a popular public park, offering views over the trees to the surrounding town of Weinheim, the forested hills of the Odenwald and the town's castle. Yet the incredible botanical diversity of the Schau- und Sichtungsgarten always pulls the attention back to what is immediately in front of us. Established as a place for research and trials – its name translates as 'show and viewing garden' – it was adapted from a 19th-century villa garden in 1983 by landscape architect Hans Luz together with its first director, the late Urs Walser, whose planting plans applied and extended a set of principles about creating ornamental plant communities that had been developed at the Weihenstephan trial garden in Munich in the 1950s. From 1998 to 2023, Hermannshof's director was Professor Cassian Schmidt, a visionary plantsman who made the garden into the most exciting place for planting design in Europe. It is composed of around thirty distinct habitats, from light to shade, dry to moist, and fertile to relatively infertile. Natural plant communities are the inspiration, from the dry meadows of central Europe to a range of North American prairie habitats and the monsoon forests of northern Japan. The garden's philosophy is deeply rooted in a German tradition of studying natural plant communities, using this knowledge to inform the creation of what are essentially artificial ecosystems. The 'mixed planting' system that is now used by landscape planners in Germany, and increasingly elsewhere in the world, is one of the outcomes of the research undertaken at Hermannshof.

MARTHA SCHWARTZ IN COLLABORATION WITH 3:0 LANDSCHAFTS-ARCHITEKTUR

VIENNA NORD HEALING GARDENS
Klinik Floridsdorf, Vienna, Austria, 2018

In 1979 Martha Schwartz – who is of the opinion that the inspiration to create attractive spaces can come from anything – created perhaps the first conceptual garden ever, the Bagel Garden, in her own front yard. The narrative in this case was to question the lack of artistry in her profession. Since then she has constantly challenged and pushed the boundaries of design in the urban public realm with a mission to integrate landscape, art and climate adaptation. The healing potential of gardens is well established (Topher Delaney, see p.79, has been making hospital and hospice gardens in the United States since 1989), but Vienna Nord is the first garden to be integrated into the healing concept of an Austrian hospital. And it reveals another ethos of Schwartz's work: that sustainability is dependent on how our environment looks, its longevity proportional to its appeal. Covering 1.3 hectares (just over 3 acres), the tranquil sunken interior gardens and exterior landscapes are aids to patients' mental and physical healing. The masterplan covers three main areas: a vehicle drop-off/emergency services area; a public plaza in front of the hospital, laid out in a pattern of parallel lines; and the landscape behind the building. This flows outwards in a collection of orchards and therapeutic, sensory, contemplation and play gardens connected by looping paths, lawns, wildflower meadows, four citrus-filled conservatories and water features. The whole landscape allows patients to choose what they want to do and their activity level, and encourages them in their journey back to health.

SDARCH WITH ALHADEFF ARCHITECTS

CONSTITUTION GARDEN
Kuwait City, Kuwait, 2012

The difficult growing conditions in Kuwait City, where the temperature regularly exceeds 50°C (122°F), posed a challenge for Italian landscape design firm SdARCH (founded by Alessandro Trivelli and Silvia Calatroni in 1997) when it won a competition to create a public park in the city to celebrate the fiftieth anniversary of the Constitution of Kuwait. The brief was equally challenging: to illustrate the path to democracy. The resulting design, conceived in collaboration with architect Giancarlo Alhadeff, cleverly splits the 0.8-hectare (2-acre) garden into two parts, representing pre-democracy Kuwait (the Old Age) and post-democracy Kuwait (the New Age). The planting in the Old Age section is deliberately chaotic, with trees and shrubs sitting messily in an arid, stony landscape that represents the instability and insecurity of that era. By contrast, the New Age Garden is an organized haven; beds are planted in an orderly, measured fashion with shrubs, grasses and flowering succulents that can withstand the intense heat, including euphorbias, bougainvilleas, lantanas and plumerias. There are precisely 183 olive trees, each representing one of the articles of the Constitution. Simultaneously separating and joining the two gardens is a huge monument that provides a stepping stone to the future. On the Old Age side, the monument is made of brass and titanium, while on the New Age side 183 blocks in relief again reference the Constitution. Water features heavily in the garden in the shape of a large fountain and water jets, cooling the air and reflecting the Islamic idea of the tranquil paradise garden.

SECRET GARDENS

BRACKEN
McKenzies Beach, Malua Bay, New South Wales, Australia, 2023

In 2019 fire swept through this McKenzies Beach property south of Malua Bay, on the traditional lands of the Yuin nation, and then suffered further damage from a fierce hailstorm the following year. The aim of the new 0.8-hectare (2-acre) garden design by Sydney-based practice Secret Gardens, under the creative directorship of Matthew Cantwell, was to complement the local geology and the strongly rectilinear lines of the house, and to marry the building more sustainably with its surroundings. Views through the blackened trunks of beautiful *Corymbia maculata* (spotted gums) to the water were a stark reminder of the fires that have been catastrophic in parts of the south coast of New South Wales, and provided the impetus for the new design to provide enhanced fire protection. This meant pushing planting further from the house and providing useable level, grassed, gravelled or tiled areas close to the dwelling. Stone retaining walls and terraces of weathered Corten steel and locally sourced gravel complement the site's natural character. *Macrozamia communis* (burrawang), *Doryanthes excelsa* (gymea lily), *Westringia fruticosa* (coastal rosemary), *Banksia integrifolia* (coast banksia) and local grass species, including *Poa billardierei* (beach fescue), are supplemented with architecturally striking, exotic agaves. Greater engagement with the landscape is encouraged by meandering paths across the property, which boasts spectacular views through a tracery of tree trunks to the beach and headland across the bay. This is a garden that is respectful to its site and – remarkably for an area that is often windy – exudes tranquillity.

IÑIGO SEGUROLA ARREGUI

LUR
Oiartzun, San Sebastián, Spain, 2012–

In his 'experimental garden' Lur ('earth' in Basque, and also the name of his design company), landscape architect and gardening TV presenter Iñigo Segurola Arregui, along with his partner Juan Iriarte Aguirrezabal, brings to life a vision of an eco-centric yet aesthetically driven landscape. On a 1,125-square-metre (12,100-square-foot) plot inland from San Sebastián in northeastern Spain, the garden merges into the surrounding oak forest, where a spring feeds a series of ponds that connect distinct planting areas. Following the philosophy of Gilles Clément's 'Planetary Garden', Segurola frames nature to let it thrive with minimal intervention, blending respect for ecology with emphatic design. The garden relies heavily on shades of green and textures – of yew, box and bamboo – while restrained colour emphasizes the role of flowers at key moments. Experimentation is an essential part of the garden, since it is here that plants are tested for durability and compatibility before being introduced into Segurola's commercial projects (mainly gardens and parks in the Basque region). Water is important, notably a peaceful pool that reflects a largely yellow herbaceous border behind it. The egg as motif occurs several times, in the shape of small planting beds or the form of clipped shrubs. Slabs of rock, along with the trunks of felled acacia trees and Corten steel, add to a certain elemental look. Above all, however, it is the ability of its creator to do unfamiliar things with familiar plants that gives this garden its incredible freshness.

SEO-AHN TOTAL LANDSCAPE WITH JOH SUNG-YONG URBAN ARCHITECTURE

SEONYUDO PARK
Seoul, South Korea, 2002

Seonyudo Island was once a hill 40 metres (131 feet) high rising out of the Han River in the middle of the South Korean capital, Seoul. It was prized so highly for its beauty that poets and artists climbed to its peak to seek inspiration while admiring the views of the city. Over time, however, as rocks and sand were removed for construction, the hill was reduced to a flat island that, in 1978, became Seoul's water-treatment plant, covered with concrete towers, tanks and pipes. When the facility closed in 2000, a competition was held to reimagine the now industrial site of 11.4 hectares (28 acres) as a public park. The winning design – by South Korean studio Seo-Ahn Total Landscape, working with Joh Sung-yong Urban Architecture – preserves the decaying structures in order to create a landscape palimpsest, whereby the past remains visible through the layer of a green future. Its eight themed 'rooms' include a fern garden, an aromatic garden and a vineyard. The old water tanks are filled with lotus flowers, and ivy climbs over concrete structures. Each filtration tank contains different aquatic plants that act to purify water, since the park aims to teach as well as providing a green place of respite. Walkways connect the various parts of the garden, which is linked to the mainland by a bridge. As the years have passed, the trees and shrubs intended to replace some of the structures have grown so tall and thick that they have created dense green walls.

SHADES OF GREEN
LANDSCAPE ARCHITECTURE

PRIVATE GARDEN
Jenner, California, United States, 2016

High on the north Californian coast, a 1970s pyramid home enjoys spectacular views west down the steep, windswept grassy ridge and out over the Pacific Ocean. But the challenge for Norwegian-born landscape architect Ive Haugeland (who founded her company Shades of Green Landscape Architecture in 2004) was to bring the dwelling into a more functional relationship with the dramatic site, and to this end she has developed a sympathetically integrated garden of flowing, usable spaces that conserve the hillside's natural character. The garden captures and enjoys the magnificent borrowed landscape of sky, partially wooded grassland and ever-changing ocean. Water is a unifying theme; a tranquil infinity pool below the main residence contrasts with the wild ocean. Another element, fire, is introduced in the form of a fire pit on the pool deck, and earth is to be found on the pool house's green roof, which is planted primarily with colourful succulents. A stepped concrete path melds into the hillside, linking residence and pool with pauses along the way for mini-terraces. On the topmost of these 'landings' is a bocce court and a native lawn with a seating area; on the second is a vegetable garden with planters and steps made of Corten steel; and the third is the pool deck, its concrete surface broken up with thin planted strips. The terraces are connected by drifts of drought-tolerant plants, primarily ornamental grasses and coastal perennials with strong colours and textures, all waving in the wind, that fourth element that keeps the garden in constant flux.

PETER SHAW

SUNNYMEADE
Anglesea, Victoria, Australia, 2001–

Since setting up their company, Ocean Road Landscaping, in 1995, Peter Shaw and his wife Simone have created gardens that are sensitive artistic responses to the landscapes along the Great Ocean Road in southern Victoria. Their designs are rooted in a deep understanding of place and a desire for their gardens to belong in it. As design lead, Peter strives for harmony and simplicity, a softness that sits well with the broader landscape. Their own garden, situated on the traditional lands of the Wadawurrung and Eastern Maar Peoples, was based on a concept by landscape architects Sinatra Murphy. The original plan incorporated a meandering entry path, a living screen to obscure the water tanks, and a series of stone walls that define the changing levels and create a courtyard at the front of the house. The firm also suggested planting a *Pistacia chinensis* (Chinese pistachio) tree, affectionately called Charlie, near the front door. Shaw has continued to develop the garden, using tough plants, such as clipped *Westringia* (coastal rosemary), *Correa alba* (white correa) and *Teucrium fruticans* (shrubby germander), that contrast with species of *Poa* (tussock grass), *Lomandra* (mat rushes) and feature plants. An example is the clipped balls of *Westringia fruticosa* 'Smokey' from which slender trunks of *Eucalyptus victrix* (little ghost gum) emerge. Over time the garden has evolved around the magnificent old *Eucalyptus obliqua* (stringybarks), which were retained in the design and are perfect for treehouses. A mounded 140-square-metre (1,500-square-foot) lawn like a spectacular ground-level sculpture, managed with a grass trimmer, has been planted as a foil for their twisted forms.

KIRSTI SHELDON

BANKSIA HOUSE
Kings Beach, Caloundra, Queensland, Australia, 2019–

Owner and landscape architect Kirsti Sheldon of 7b landscapes + interiors conceived Banksia House, on the traditional lands of the Kabi Kabi people, as a holiday home and not a permanent residence, so the intention was to create a relaxing escape from everyday life. She worked closely with architect Dragi Majstorovic to simultaneously develop the design of architecture and landscape and so create a harmonious balance between the two. The structures have a strong connection to sky, natural light and airflow, and a minimal footprint on the 1,500-square-metre (16,150-square-foot) block. Moving between the internal spaces involves immersion in the gardens, and an outdoor bathhouse was influenced by the atmosphere at Pompeii. In this largely suburban setting, Majstorovic designed a massive, fortress-like surrounding wall with cutouts, and Sheldon planted it with *Ficus pumila* (creeping fig) to promote the concept of the house as a ruin over which vegetation would eventually predominate. The design of the pool took advantage of the sloping site, and the addition of a ha-ha negated the need for pool fencing. At one corner of the pool, a *Ficus*-covered tower emerges as a folly, providing a focal point and reinforcing the idea of a ruin. Gabion walls are used to create a change in level. The plant palette, which includes *Banksia robur* (swamp banksia), *B. serrata* (saw banksia) and *B. spinulosa* (hairpin banksia), is 90–95 per cent coastal Australian natives with an adroit layering of texture, and the bottom of the garden, which includes a fire pit, is planted as a native bush.

JILL AND RICHARD SIMPSON

FISHERMANS BAY
Akaroa, South Island, New Zealand, 2005–

On the Banks Peninsula, New Zealand's easternmost point, Jill and Richard Simpson have transformed a 320-hectare (790-acre) farm into a haven of conservation and exemplary gardening. Beef farmers by profession, as well as passionate conservationists, they dedicated 100 hectares (247 acres) to native forest preservation and the protection of two wildlife-rich bays. Above the coastline, a 2-hectare (5-acre) garden faces the Pacific. Despite its breathtaking views and rich volcanic soil, it endures extreme wind and hot summers that make it a challenging location.

But Jill describes herself as an 'obsessive gardener', and although it was a major project to renovate the semi-derelict cottage, the garden was always her focus. What began as a predominantly native garden with conservation firmly in mind has in recent years changed as the climate alters. Many native plants were lost after a recent period of extremely high rainfall, so Jill is constantly developing the garden using a blend of native and non-native species. At its heart is a structure of New Zealand natives, mostly trees that are common locally, which Jill has embellished with plants from 'everywhere', as she puts it. The native trees include *Myoporum laetum* (ngaio); *Pennantia corymbosa* (kaikōmako), with its fragrant flowers; *Melicytus ramiflorus* (mahoe); and *Podocarpus totara*, grown from local seed. *Dacrycarpus dacrydioides* (kahikatea) and *Prumnopitys taxifolia* (matai) were all gathered as seedlings either locally or from the neighbouring Hinewai Reserve. The garden continues to increase in size, and Jill's obsession with trying new plants shows no sign of diminishing.

SLA

AMAGER BAKKE COPENHILL ROOFTOP PARK
Copenhagen, Denmark, 2019

Designed by BIG (Bjarke Ingels Group), this unusual-looking 4.1-hectare (10-acre) waste-to-energy plant has become a landmark in a flat landscape. It was conceived as a key component of Copenhagen's aim to be the world's first carbon-neutral city by 2025, but, as the firm's founder and creative director, Bjarke Ingels, explains, it is also 'a crystal-clear example of "hedonistic sustainability" – that a sustainable city is not only better for the environment [but] also more enjoyable for . . . its citizens'. The green rooftop park by design studio SLA (Stig Andersson Associates) is a year-round recreation hub that simultaneously enhances urban biodiversity. Juxtaposed with the 500-metre-long (1,640 feet) artificial ski slope and set amid a wild 'mountain' landscape are playgrounds, street fitness stations, and hiking and running trails. And, not for the faint-hearted, the climbing wall on the building's facade is the tallest in the world. Once one has wearied oneself, the Rooftop Café at an altitude of 78 metres (256 feet) offers spectacular views across the Øresund to Sweden. The design ethos is nature-based, with planting carefully selected to survive the challenging conditions while providing optimal microclimate and habitats for wildlife. The core planting of 7,000 shrubs and 300 trees was a mix of *Crataegus* (hawthorn), *Hippophae rhamnoides* (seaberry), *Pinus* (pines), *Prunus* (cherries, almonds, etc.), *Quercus* (oaks), *Salix* (willows) and *Sorbus* (mountain ash), with grasses and other native species. The biodiversity is monitored, and in the year following the park's inauguration, species diversity naturally increased to 119 from the 63 species initially planted.

KEN SMITH

ROOF GARDEN
Museum of Modern Art, New York, New York, United States, 2005

One of the most provocative pieces at the Museum of Modern Art isn't accessible or visible to visitors, but is viewable only from above, from a neighbouring skyscraper. It's a roofscape installation on top of an extension designed in 2004 by Japanese architect Yoshio Taniguchi. Six storeys above street level, the 1,600-square-metre (17,200-square-foot) rooftop 'garden' by landscape architect Ken Smith is a decorative viewing garden that explores the relationship between artifice and nature. Influenced by Japanese dry gardens, Smith (who established Ken Smith Workshop in 1993) employs the theory of landscape design in clever and ironic ways. The challenges and limitations imposed by the location render the garden more a museum piece than a garden in the traditional sense. There are no living plants, just simulation, resulting in a playful commentary on inherently imitational gardens. The illusion is composed of artificial boxwood shrubs, sculptural faux boulders and pools of crushed glass to evoke water. Curvilinear forms echo nearby Central Park, referencing its designer Frederick Law Olmsted, and amoebic shapes pay homage to Brazilian landscape architect Roberto Burle Marx. Smith incorporated in the design his interest in military camouflage and its use in landscaping. Here, it's used as a kind of remediation to mask unsightly aspects of the built environment and covertly blend the rooftop into the surrounding urban environment, while also making it stand out. Smith's contemporary addition complements other landscapes at the museum, including the Philip Johnson sculpture garden of 1953, and follows in the footsteps of the original museum building of 1939, which also had a rooftop element that could be seen only from above.

**WILL SOOS AND
SUE POMEROY**

DURNAMUCK GARDEN
Dundonnell, Garve, Ross-shire, Scotland, 2009–

On the southern shore of Little Loch Broom and created by two talented plant artists who met while working at the nearby historic garden of Inverewe, this 0.5-hectare (1¼-acre) garden literally grew, for no plan was ever put on paper. It is a rich mix of herbaceous borders, trees and shrubs, a productive garden, drystone-wall planting and, in the lee of the house, a collection of rarities in pots. But while there is a distinctly South African feel to the planting, the keyword is 'coastal', for – although the climate is mild for the latitude – the warming Gulf Stream also brings high rainfall and ferocious salt-laden winds. The intricate planting around the house features choice treasures in rocky crevices and raised beds, their habitat created for them from local stone. Beyond, flanking a lawn behind the house, informal island beds are planted tapestry-like with a collection of plants that are mostly from Mediterranean climate zones, meaning that they enjoy the warmth but can also withstand wild weather. The right-hand border features a 'Mount' planted with flaming crocosmias and surmounted with a stone bench and fire pit. From here one can enjoy an elevated view of the garden and, beyond it, the meadow that sweeps down to the loch. The colourful blooms and sculptural forms are in perfect proportion to the dramatic frame of mountains and sea; indeed, a key aim is to draw the eye to the plantings and then to the 'borrowed' landscape, uniting them in a theatrical whole.

PHILIPPE DE SPOELBERCH

MARCHE ARBORETUM
Marche-en-Famenne, Wallonia, Belgium, 2023

This visitor centre, which doubles as a research centre, is a green-roofed, limestone-clad building by local firm AW Architectes, designed to fade into the surrounding planting, which in turn blends with the meadows and trees beyond. Its small garden lies at the heart of an ambitious 'museum of plants' created through the vision of Belgian businessman and dendrologist Philippe de Spoelberch. He started collecting trees as he travelled the world on business in the 1970s, filling first his family garden, then his first arboretum, Wespelaar – until he ran out of land. De Spoelberch then acquired 76 hectares (188 acres) for a second arboretum at Marche-en-Famenne in the Wallonia region of eastern Belgium, which he has developed in collaboration with landscape architect Christophe Crock. The culmination of a lifetime's passion, the Marche Arboretum brings together native Belgian species and trees from around the world. Colourful oaks, such as *Quercus imbricaria* (shingle oak) and *Q. coccinea* (scarlet oak), are planted with lime trees and maples from around the world; already striking, they will be even more dramatic as they mature. Unlike the acid soil of Wespelaar, the Marche Arboretum is on limestone, giving the opportunity to grow different plants. The poor soil is a boon to the feathery grasses, seed-grown daisies and ten species of native orchid found in its meadows, which are grazed by sheep and donkeys. Reflecting these surroundings, Crock has used several grasses in planting around the visitor centre, with an intermingled palette of perennials to provide seasonal interest, including *Phlomis russeliana*, *Sanguisorba officinalis* 'Red Thunder', *Rudbeckia fulgida* and *Kalimeris incisa* 'Blue Star'. In shadier areas, the planting takes on a woodland-edge style with ferns, hellebores and *Geranium macrorrhizum* setting the scene for the stretches of woodland beyond.

273

ROBERT STACEWICZ

PRIVATE GARDEN
West Ewell, Surrey, England, 2024

As a child, Robert Stacewicz had contrasting passions – ponds, and cacti and succulents – and the latter theme expanded to include more 'exotics' when he began work on his own garden (his first) in 2020. It started as a sketch on Christmas Eve 2019, with plantings inspired by visits to Indonesia, and materialized as a tranquil space with water features, where he could indulge his passion for plants and encourage as much wildlife as possible. Soil excavated from the lower part of the 110-square-metre (1,180-square-foot) garden was retained behind slim oak sleepers, self-binding gravel allowed the creation of organically shaped paths, and a mix of spent cactus compost, grit and sharp sand filled beds either side of steps. Focusing on plants whose appearance belies their extreme hardiness, Stacewicz filled the garden with species that contribute long flowering seasons, bright colours and bold architecture, such as *Yucca* and *Agave*, bringing a taste of the tropics to a London suburb. Plants arrived from specialist nurseries, friends and mail order. Palms and cycads were high on the list; a large *Cycas revoluta* came from a north London garden centre; speedy purchase of rare palms and *C. panzhihuaensis*, as well as ferns, arrived before post-Brexit customs rules came into force; and a bigeneric hybrid between two palms, *Butia* × *Parajubaea*, was sought as a tough, cold-hardy specimen for this 'exotic'-filled garden. Building on his experiences in this garden that is well adapted to climate change, Stacewicz has now embarked on his second garden, in Britain's reliably milder southwest.

STEFANO MARINAZ LANDSCAPE ARCHITECTURE

CHURCH BARN
Braintree, Essex, England, 2020

When landscape architect Stefano Marinaz first arrived at this barn conversion, he found a large, unsympathetic lawn and patio, and a disproportionately large parking area. The clients' request was merely to screen an unsightly septic tank and reinvigorate a planting bed, but for Marinaz, who has a background in agronomy and a reputation for innovative, sustainable planting, there was far greater potential to change this 700-square-metre (7,500-square-foot) garden. Taking his cue from the surrounding countryside, he created a structure of woody plants and hedges, lush grasses and herbaceous perennials for texture and colour. Informal interconnecting paths divide the garden and lead to three organically shaped open areas, one for sunbathing, another focused on a firepit, and the third somewhere to sit in the sunshine. A long season of interest and low-maintenance regime was created using a wide range of plant groups – bulbs, annuals, grasses, perennials, shrubs and trees – while piles of logs set within the planting create habitat for insects. Marinaz also designed the bespoke furniture for the fire-pit area, which is surrounded by subtle greens and blues in the form of lavender-flowered *Nepeta racemosa* 'Walker's Low' and potted *Salvia × sylvestris* 'Dear Anja', mingling with the paler *Nigella damascena* (love-in-a-mist). The former parking area has been transformed into a stylish courtyard filled with pots, bordered by bespoke rust-coloured, mild-steel estate fencing inspired by the barn's feather-edge cladding. Beyond this tranquil garden stands the borrowed outlook of the ancient village church and lime trees, bringing a sense of permanence and antiquity.

STIMSON

PRIVATE GARDEN
Cape Cod, Massachusetts, United States, 2015

Stephen and Lauren Stimson, partners at design collective STIMSON, always explore and amplify ecological value, and this Cape Cod garden is 'an example of how we work and think,' says Stephen, principal for the project. This 1.6-hectare (4-acre) compound on the coast was divided into two sleek, contemporary dwelling structures – for living and sleeping – but what might have stymied a lesser design team was the deep ravine beside the house. The Stimsons saw it as a unique opportunity rather than a challenge. Not only did they plant the swale with a boisterous, blossom-packed mixture of native performers to add biodiversity, but also they installed a footbridge on slender steel stilts with barely perceptible metal safety cables to create a dramatic event between the guest parking court and the front door. At the house side of the gully, birches wade through ferns to represent 'the wild side' further before the bridge path takes a step down to a series of weathering steel raised beds corralling vegetables, herbs and flowers, celebrating 'the working garden'. 'The wildness is allowed to erupt,' says Stephen, 'but there's always a deliberate tension between cultivated versus wild.' Closer to the water, the Stimsons were given permission to remove undesirable invasive plants from a coastal embankment that has now been restored with native grasses and shrubs. Additionally, by eliminating former tennis courts, just enough lawn was seeded to provide a recreation area for children. The whole constitutes a brilliant balance between cultivated living spaces and a restored ecosystem.

TOM STUART-SMITH

WALLED GARDEN
Knepp Castle, Sussex, England, 2019–

The Knepp Estate is an expansive 1,400 hectares (3,500 acres) of Sussex that its owners, Charlie Burrell and Isabella Tree, shifted in 2002 from an unprofitable arable and dairy enterprise to a wilded landscape where large herds of herbivores run free. The resulting explosion of biodiversity and the success of Isabella's book *Wilding* (2018) has made Knepp a household name, but nestled near the main house is a 19th-century walled garden that has been reimagined by Tom Stuart-Smith in consultation with plant ecologists James Hitchmough and Mick Crawley, and organic gardening expert Jekka McVicar) and is now managed by head gardener Charlie Harpur. In 2019, after the successes achieved in the wider landscape, this 0.5-hectare (1.3-acre) formal garden – dominated as it was by a large, ecologically sterile croquet lawn – seemed out of touch with Knepp's mission. Through radical changes to the topography of the walled garden, natural microclimates can be exploited to support a wider range of species, which are planted primarily into a mineral substrate of three parts crushed concrete to one part sharp sand. This reflects a wider move away from traditional soils for creating diverse plantings, instead using leaner conditions that restrict perennial weeds and the overly competitive perennials that often come to dominate mixed communities. Harpur describes the gardeners at Knepp as equivalent to the keystone species in the wider landscape: 'Our primary role is one of disturbance' – the pulling of weeds and pruning of shrubs akin to the rootling of Tamworth pigs or the grazing of deer. Stuart-Smith, meanwhile, likes to think of this young garden as a 'box of unpredictabilities' that continues to evolve.

STUDIO EGRET WEST

MAYFIELD PARK
Manchester, England, 2022

The transformation of 2.6 hectares (6½ acres) of derelict land next to Manchester Piccadilly railway station into a biodiverse green space created the city's first new urban park in more than a century. If the industrial history and surviving architectural heritage provided inspiration, a key objective was the creation of natural habitat to increase biodiversity, integrated with spaces for active recreation, all arranged along the 'new' River Medlock. In response, design firm Studio Egret West (founded in 2004 by Christophe Egret and David West) included an expansive public lawn that is perfect for recreational sports, play and picnicking, complete with amphitheatre-style seating; meandering riverside walkways; and a large exploratory play area with play tower and slide. The naturalistic planting of 140 semi-mature trees and 120,000 plants and shrubs is artful and resilient, creating a collection of planted habitats that not only encourage wildlife but also build a journey through distinctive spaces. Rain gardens of moisture-tolerant plants absorb surface run-off, while the wildscaped river edge and meadows allow temporary flooding. Since the park's debut, the river – now released from a culvert – has played a major role in attracting wildlife back to the area. Scattered throughout are such biodiversity-encouraging features as nesting boxes and tunnels, shelters for hibernating animals, rock riprap and stone riffles. With its mix of blue and green infrastructure, repurposed materials salvaged from the site, river system restoration and flood mitigation, Mayfield Park has many parallels with Singapore's Bishan-Ang Mo Kio Park (see p.236).

STUDIO GPT

AGRO-ORNAMENTAL PARK I.LAND
Bergamo, Italy, 2012

This 1.8-hectare (4½-acre) park around i.land, a research and development centre for cement company Italcementi in northern Italy, connects a contemporary building and landscape with ancient crops and agricultural traditions. The project was intended to demonstrate the company's commitment to sustainability and local heritage by evoking the agricultural history of its site, and the landscaping by agronomists Maurizio Vegini and Lucia Nusiner of Studio GPT takes up this theme of old and new. The expanses of glass and white concrete are softened with sustainable, naturalistic, meadow-like landscaping and planting of *Anemone × hybrida* 'Honorine Jobert' (white Japanese anemones), *Oenothera lindheimeri* (gaura), *Nassella tenuissima* (syn. *Stipa tenuissima*; Mexican feather grass) and *Miscanthus sinensis* 'Morning Light', while a white sculpture by architect Richard Meier shimmers in the water among marginal aquatic plants. Elsewhere, the focus is on heritage crops and ornamentals. Once common but now rare heirloom varieties of apple and pear, a grove of local raspberries and examples of local maize – a plant Nusiner studied in depth at University of Milan – are a reminder of the area's agricultural and culinary heritage, and simple, repeating waves of *Carpinus betulus* (hornbeam) hedging, providing foliage of bright green in the spring and rich yellow in the autumn, and *Populus nigra* 'Italica' (Lombardy poplar) acknowledge the local trees. A simple meadow of wildflowers, once typical of the local countryside but now rarely seen in this heavily built-up area, is a sea of poppies, buttercups and cornflowers in the spring.

ANDY STURGEON

BATTERSEA POWER STATION ROOF GARDENS
London, England, 2022

When this immense decommissioned mid-century power station was sold in 2012, the aim of its new owners was to convert the crumbling landmark into a mixed-use destination with apartments, retail, leisure and office space. Unifying the spaces with 0.8 hectares (2 acres) of roof garden was truly visionary. With twenty-five years of rooftop design experience, it was Andy Sturgeon – brought in by landscape architects LDA Design (responsible for landscaping the first three phases of the 42-acre Battersea Power Station masterplan) – who had the insight to make it happen. Each rooftop was given an elemental theme. The central Boiler House, with its glass roof and tall chimneys, was a natural for 'air', using cloudlike trees. The flowing beds of ornamental grasses on Switch House West symbolize rippling 'water', and plumes of *Cotinus coggygria* (smoke bush) with coal-dark gravel mulch represent 'fire' on Switch House East. As well as dealing with the weight problems inherent in old roofs, Sturgeon explains, the challenge was to create a park-like ambiance above ground: 'something that felt like a garden, rather than a series of containers that compose the typical rooftop composition'. The park concept was also a practical solution, since this exposed bend in the River Thames receives ferocious winds. Sturgeon planted trees that are tolerant of the shallow soil: pine trees at each end of the central roof, flanking a birch forest, as well as hornbeam and hawthorn. Native species, as he points out, 'never go out of fashion'. The planting beneath them is more Mediterranean, a tapestry of colour and texture. The result is a unified garden spanning all seasons, and a relic restored beyond anyone's fondest dreams.

SURFACEDESIGN

EXPEDIA HQ
Seattle, Washington, United States, 2019–21

Convincing travel technology company Expedia to build a landscape that beckoned its employees outside was as easy as producing a Stanford University study that found productivity and cognitive abilities increased dramatically when people get out of the cubicle and into nature. What proved more of a challenge was converting an infill site that was formerly two disused piers along Seattle's Puget Sound into a space offering numerous reasons for employees at Expedia's global headquarters to venture outside. With a nod towards Expedia's focus, Surfacedesign began by incorporating transportation themes into the 16-hectare (40-acre) campus: recycling railway tracks into kerbing and using shimmering stone and water features to echo the sparkle of Elliott Bay as seen by incoming jets to the airport. The selection of plants takes its cues from the surrounding landscape, creating an arrival experience wooded in fir trees that echo the forest of the Pacific Northwest. To coax employees out, there's a cricket oval beside meadows, a meeting room hidden beneath a green roof, and numerous opportunities for 'walking meetings' weaving through grassland and mini meadows within footsteps of the office buildings. A grove of katsura (*Cercidiphyllum japonicum*) fills the autumn air with the fragrance of candyfloss just before its leaves drop, and boulders and fallen trees serve as benches. Soil remediation and stormwater wetlands feed into a green infrastructure system that promotes long-term ecological resilience. Meanwhile, the campus's public component is provided with bike and pedestrian trails along the water. In this landscape, everyone is plugged in outside.

SWA

PANYU CENTRAL PARK
Guangzhou, Guangdong Province, China, 2020

Founded in the year 214 BCE, Panyu is at the heart of the Pearl River Delta. A decade later Emperor Zhao Tuo made it the capital of his Nanyue kingdom, and it subsequently became an important terminus of the Silk Road. Today it is a 530-square-kilometre (200-square-mile) urban district of Guangzhou city, and the 4.7-hectare (11½-acre) Panyu Central Park is one of twenty-eight new or refurbished green spaces intended to give the district a resilient, nature-based, multifunctional green infrastructure. With Panyu Square to the north and views of the river to the south, this park in the heart of the district is enjoyed by residents of this dense urban community and visitors alike. The landscape design by SWA, a community-orientated studio founded in 2005 by managing principal Ying-yu Hung and co-CEO Gerdo Aquino, has at its centre a large tree-flanked, central lawn enlivened with bleachers, allowing people to be active or simply sit and enjoy nature. In the northeastern corner stands the civic centre, in front of which the landscaping of artful sward-covered landforms, reflecting pool and clean-lined paths nods to Charles Jencks and Maggie Keswick Jencks's Garden of Cosmic Speculation in Scotland. The pavilion's sculptural architecture makes it a gathering point, while a bike trail, children's playground, jogging route, fitness facility and therapy garden allow varied activities. An extensive network of paths featuring sculptures and seating nooks links the park to the adjoining preserved forest and integrated throughout is a series of 'rain gardens' that facilitate stormwater harvest.

TAA DESIGN

THE RED ROOF
Quang Ngai, Vietnam, 2019

Like many Vietnamese architectural practices, award-winning firm TAA Design (established by Nguyen Van Thien and Nguyen Huu Hau) regularly incorporates planting into its projects, be they high-rise buildings or public spaces. For this home designed for a couple in their fifties, the studio came up with an unusual 'green roof' as a response to changing times. Increased urbanization has altered landscape and lifestyle in this village, but traditions have been maintained in this home with a footprint of just 80 square metres (860 square feet), so that a plot that would once have allowed for vegetable beds in the back garden is now taken up by the house and the garden is located on the roof. The approach has brought unexpected benefits. Soil and foliage act as an insulating layer, increasing humidity and cooling the house below. In a climate where hot-season temperatures reach 40°C (104°F), it is consistently around 8°C (14°F) cooler indoors, making the productive vegetable garden a more effective form of insulation than a modern corrugated roof, while also reducing heat radiation. Another advantage is that the regular supply of fresh vegetables is shared with neighbouring families, enhancing the sense of community. The stepped design maximizes the use of space and allows easy access to the vegetable beds, the tilework of paths and beds on the roof reflect traditional roofing materials, and trailing squash plants provide natural shading above an internal courtyard. This imaginative use of a roof not only provides access to fresh food, but also allows the traditional agricultural lifestyle to be preserved and to develop in parallel with continuing urbanization.

PATRICE TARAVELLA WITH KOOS BEKKER AND KAREN ROOS

BABYLONSTOREN
Franschhoek, Western Cape, South Africa, 2007

In 1692 at the foot of Simonsberg in the Franschhoek wine valley, about 50 kilometres (30 miles) east of Cape Town, Pieter van der Byl founded Babylonische Tooren – named after the conical hill on the estate, which was thought to resemble the shape of the Tower of Babel mentioned in the Bible. Today it is one of the oldest Cape Dutch farms, and the owners since 2007 are Koos Bekker and Karen Roos (also of The Newt in Somerset, England), who have developed the 200-hectare (495-acre) estate into a working farm, winery, boutique spa hotel and productive garden. To lay out the last of these, Roos commissioned Italo-French architect and garden designer Patrice Taravella of Prieuré Notre Dame d'Orsan and The Newt fame. Within the rectangular plot of 4 hectares (9 acres), Taravella arranged fifteen axially aligned 'clusters' that fulfil a range of cultivation and biodiversity-enriching uses. His design has strong echoes of the disciplined, alluring French potager ideal, but also draws inspiration from German astronomer and explorer of South Africa, Peter Kolb's plan of 1725 for the Company's Garden in Cape Town (founded in 1652 as a source of fresh produce to revictual the sailing ships of the Dutch East India Company; it survives now as a public park). Applying his mantra that a garden should be both beautiful and useful, Taravella created an artful, architectonic structure with rustic wood bowers and tunnels, pergolas and plant supports, espaliers and allées, raised beds, rills and pools. These elements are as much a visual feast as are the serried ranks of more than 300 different fruits and vegetables, which are destined to become an edible feast in the hotel kitchen.

TAYLOR CULLITY LETHLEAN WITH PAUL THOMPSON

AUSTRALIAN GARDEN
Cranbourne Gardens, Victoria, Australia, 2006, 2012

To descend into the Australian Garden at Cranbourne is to enter a beguiling showcase of Australian flora. Unashamedly linking science and art, this 25-hectare (62-acre) botanic garden lies some 50 kilometres (30 miles) south of its city parent, Melbourne Gardens, within a generous remnant heathland of 350 hectares (865 acres). The endangered heathland provides a vital buffer against one of the fastest-growing areas of the city, while enhancing the central garden's jewel-like quality. Opened in two stages (2006 and 2012), the Australian Garden was crafted by landscape architect Taylor Cullity Lethlean around a river's symbolic journey from a central desert, ever quickening in pace through rocky outcrops, to a serene riverine estuary. As the visitor approaches this landscape through the elevated entrance, a sand garden streaked with sparse vegetation dominates the immediate view, physically secluded and evoking the psychological apprehension many viewers associate with Australia's Red Centre. The nascent stream is suggested by sculptural white rocks, which soon metamorphose into the jagged stone bed of the tree-fringed watercourse. Flanking beds showcase Australian flora, while branching paths, leading towards the garden's midpoint, offer a diverse range of experiences. These paths highlight the extraordinary floristic range and the creative way horticulturist Paul Thompson integrated it into temperate-zone garden landscapes. Among the thousands of species represented, painterly drifts of *Anigozanthos* (kangaroo paw), incised-trunked *Eucalyptus haemastoma* (scribbly gum) and bizarre forms of *Brachychiton rupestris* (Queensland bottle tree) all command attention.

CHRISTINE TEN EYCK

THE CAPRI GARDEN
Marfa, Texas, United States, 2010

When she was asked to transform a car park beside a decommissioned military hangar into a 0.8-hectare (2-acre) welcoming community space complete with outdoor restaurant and bar, Christine Ten Eyck didn't flinch: 'Parking lots are my favourite projects – it's always fun to transform asphalt.' Known for her site-appropriate solutions in arid climates, she encourages her clients to own their geography and connect with the local conditions. At Marfa, Ten Eyck used stains on the asphalt as a clue to 'the memory' of where water naturally flowed during the summer monsoons, creating a rain-harvesting arroyo (dry gully) that flows into an adjacent creek. She surrounded seating areas with gabion walls of local stone to mediate the fierce winds that can make outdoor gathering challenging, and a grapevine-draped mesh arbour provides shade for the restaurant. As a focal point, a long, cast-concrete rain-harvesting trough was constructed alongside the converted building, letting rainwater spill from the roof scupper and overflow directly into the arroyo, recirculating in dry seasons. Ten Eyck sourced plants native to the Trans-Pecos Mountain Region, mixing *Bouteloua curtipendula* (sideoats grama), *B. gracilis* (blue grama) and *Muhlenbergia emersleyi* (bull grass) with *Fallugia paradoxa* (Apache plume), *Salvia farinacea* (mealy sage) and *S. greggii* (autumn sage) to form a grassland matrix. Architectural yuccas, agaves and *Fouquieria splendens* (ocotillo) punctuate regionally native trees, such as elderberry, red oak, honey mesquite, desert willow and live oak. And people come to the venue. The newly created community space hosts weddings, parties and other events, immersing all in the local flora.

TERREMOTO

A QUINCY JONES VS. TERREMOTO
Holmby Hills, Los Angeles, California, United States, 2020–22

When Terremoto was asked to reimagine the landscape at this house, designed in 1969–73 by A. Quincy Jones, one of the great California Mid-century Modern architects, it was the firm's focus on native and water-wise plants and ecology that appealed to the owner and her interior designer, Studio Shamshiri. For Terremoto, a young and innovative Los Angeles- and San Francisco-based landscape architecture design studio established in 2013, the opportunity to work on a historic property was especially appealing. Jones's original design work to the house was intact, as was that of the property's more recent landscape designer, Kinya Hira, director of the Portland Japanese Garden from 1964 to 1969, who had been hired to create a Japanese garden for the owner in 2006. Recognizing the enduring value of these earlier designs, the team at Terremoto, led by Kara Holekamp, focused on retaining as much as they could while bringing a native Californian twist to the planting. They were asked to expand the views and create a sense of spaciousness, which they accomplished by relocating the perimeter fence, thus accessing more of the garden and opening up new vistas. Jones's large-scale cobble-set circular pavers that wind through the garden and into the house itself were enhanced with new paths. While deferring to the earlier designers, Terremoto left its mark with regionally appropriate and resilient plantings that knit the different styles together seamlessly. Mediterranean and Australian plants combine with traditional Japanese species to create a naturalistic landscape; the overall effect is of a dynamic natural world for wildlife, plants and people.

THE LANDSCAPE STUDIO

OLLIE HOUSE
Ngare Ndare, Meru County, Kenya, 2020

The design of the 28-hectare (69-acre) landscape garden surrounding this private house in central Kenya had to reflect and respond to its location, next to the Lewa Wildlife Conservancy. Meru County has a naturally semi-arid climate and increasingly suffers from extended drought, so its ecosystem remains delicate. The solution for design firm The Landscape Studio (founded in Nairobi in 2014, and currently based in Europe) was to concentrate the planting close to the house in small, dense squares of mixed-height grasses, such as blush-pink-flowering *Melinis repens* (Natal grass) and tall *Hyparrhenia rufa* (jaraguá), alongside border flowers. The squares are cut into the property's three courtyards, which link the two main buildings while also protecting the structure from strong winds associated with El Niño, which blow during the summer months. The planting gradually thins out as it approaches the boundary with the savannah, blending into the natural landscape with sage-green shrubs and native grasses. That colour palette contrasts with the local Isiolo stone, which was used to create the smooth tiled floors of the courtyards, the rough pathways that link the spaces, and the gravel for the vegetable garden, which – in an echo of the kitchen gardens of English estates – is surrounded by walls to protect the crops from extreme weather. The rust-red bark of the native *Vachellia seyal* (red acacia) trees that dot the landscape provides the inspiration for the colour of the many large handmade ceramic pots that are scattered near the house, filled with drought-resistant agaves.

THOMAS PHIFER AND PARTNERS WITH PWP LANDSCAPE ARCHITECTURE

GLENSTONE WATER COURT
Potomac, Maryland, United States, 2018

This 1,675-square-metre (18,000-square-foot) water garden is at the heart of Glenstone, a complex celebrating post-war art, architecture and nature on a campus of approximately 120 hectares (almost 300 acres). Anchoring the Pavilions, the largest of the two museum buildings, the Water Court and its entrance sequence are a collaboration between building architect Thomas Phifer and Partners and PWP Landscape Architecture (see p.233 and p.308). Under partner in charge and lead designer Adam Greenspan, PWP has been working on the entire site since 2003, transforming a former subdivision into rolling meadows and native woodlands. The psychological preparation for the Water Court begins with a winding walk through swaying meadows towards nine minimalist cubes that make up the above-ground portion of the Pavilions. Inside the building, steps immediately descend to the dramatic Water Court, and the solid white volumes of the galleries rise from the flourishing aquatic garden, where the water accentuates the play of natural light through large windows. The innovative structure enables more than 4,000 plants, including irises, rushes and waterlilies, to be planted in a modular grid at the depth each species requires. The plants have moved and reseeded over time, although their distribution is controlled to some extent by the depth of water in the modules. In a large central area the water is 1.2 metres (4 feet) deep, and here only the low-growing waterlilies thrive. The expanse of waterlilies lying almost flat on the surface subtly suggests a reflecting pool; in the winter, when they disappear, it becomes one.

ALEXANDRE THOMAS

JARDIN AGAPANTHE
Grigneuseville, Normandy, France, 1980s–

Tucked away in a little village north of Rouen in Normandy, this 0.9-hectare (2¼-acre) garden is the life's work of landscape architect, designer, singer, composer and artefact-collector Alexandre Thomas. Begun when he was a mere fifteen years old, it has a 'secret garden' quality with numerous exceptionally atmospheric spaces, cleverly divided by hedging, walls and terraces. In fact, the garden comprises two parts: the original, oldest section, set around Thomas's parents' house; and the second, which he opened to the public in 2010, surrounding his own house across the road. A strong structure underlies the whole, but the garden is constantly evolving, since Thomas uses it as a place of experimentation for his professional work designing gardens for private clients around the world. Signposts guide visitors along labyrinthine pathways through a profusion of trees, shrubs, perennials, grasses and bulbs, each layer rich in colour, texture and form. Open spaces segue into more enclosed areas, and throughout are carefully considered compositions of garden furniture, sculpture and other artefacts, providing resting spots or intrigue. Streams, fountains and ponds bring the gentle sound of water. The garden has a dreamy, magical quality, and it's impressive how much is worked into a relatively small space. In design terms, this is not an easy garden to define; some parts are timeless and classic, while others are surprisingly exotic and fantastical. Thomas's distinctive aesthetic, inventiveness and sense of playfulness make it a genuinely original labour of love.

JO THOMPSON

COOL GARDEN
RHS Rosemoor, near Torrington, Devon, England, 2019

RHS Garden Rosemoor, the most southerly of the Royal Horticultural Society's five flagship gardens, covers 26.3 hectares (65 acres) and typically attracts some 240,000 visitors a year. Within it, the Cool Garden opened in 2019, named for its colour palette of white and misty blues highlighted with other pastel shades. The area has some of the highest rainfall in the United Kingdom, which inspired designer Jo Thompson – winner of several medals at the RHS Chelsea Flower Show – to make water the animating spirit of her design. Surrounded by tall yew hedges, this enclosed space evokes the natural progress of water from sky to stream, pond and river. From the terrace at its highest point to the teardrop-shaped pond at its lowest, visitors are lured in by seductive rills of granite setts that intertwine with clear channels flowing along the natural contours of the site, crisscrossed by bridges and flanked by billowing borders. Thompson also replaced old asphalt paths with porous resin-bound surfacing to prevent wasteful water run-off. She planted to give interest throughout the year (Rosemoor opens daily), and the local clay soil is mulched annually. Blue summer flowers, with scent and forage for pollinators, include *Salvia* 'Blue Spire' (syn. *Perovskia* 'Blue Spire'), *Amsonia* 'Blue Ice' and *Geranium* Rozanne ('Gerwat'). Fastigiate silver birches provide winter presence, as do evergreen *Phillyrea angustifolia* 'French Fries', *Hebe* and *Pittosporum*, punctuated with upright grasses, such as *Panicum virgatum* 'Northwind'. The Cool Garden is popular with visitors all year round as a sensuous haven of colour, texture, scent and sound.

THUPDI AND TSINGHUA UNIVERSITY, BEIJING WITH VALENTIEN + VALENTIEN

QUARRY GARDEN
Chenshan Botanical Garden, Shanghai, China, 2010

Completed to coincide with EXPO 2010 and located about 30 kilometres (18½ miles) from central Shanghai, this 200-hectare (494-acre) park – one of the city's largest – is also China's largest municipal botanic garden. It was masterplanned by international landscape architecture office Valentien + Valentien. A wide landformed ring up to 14 metres (46 feet) high surrounds the inner 94-hectare (232-acre) garden like a bowl. This is an artistic, informal sculptured landscape with echoes in its layout of the great Chinese scholar gardens, with sinuous waterways and planted lakes that define more than thirty-five themed gardens. The ring symbolizes the world, and the dominating spatial themes within the inner area are mountain, water and sky. Here, too, is the Quarry Garden, an innovative restoration project led by Tsinghua University and the state-owned design institution THUPDI. The design repurposed two east–west quarries dug into Chen Mountain, pagoda-capped and 70 metres (230 feet) high. Covering 4.3 hectares (10½ acres), it comprises three zones: to the west the Lake Area and Platform Area, which renewed the quarry landscape through cut-and-fill to form the Mirror Lake and the Flower-seeing Platform (or mound); three stone- and Corten steel-faced recessed terraces rising to a secret garden at the high point; and the Deep Pool. The sunken quarry lake covers about 1 hectare (2½ acres) and has a dramatic, rocky cliff backdrop; no intervention was made here except to add the cascade and a route that permits visitors to experience the quarry from various dramatic positions.

FRANCISCO TOLEDO WITH ALEJANDRO DE ÁVILA BLOMBERG AND LUIS ZÁRATE

OAXACA ETHNOBOTANICAL GARDEN
Oaxaca City, Mexico, 1998

Nestled behind the high walls of the 16th-century Santo Domingo monastery complex, Oaxaca's Ethnobotanical Garden is a remarkable testament to the grassroots campaign that led to its foundation. The army had commandeered the monastery in the late 19th century and used the garden as a rubbish dump. In the 1990s plans emerged to develop a large car park there, but local action, spearheaded by such influential artists as Francisco Toledo and Luis Zárate, successfully lobbied to establish a garden of about 1 hectare (just under 2½ acres), which celebrated the rich ethnobotanical heritage of Oaxaca. In establishing the garden, Toledo was joined by botanist and anthropologist Alejandro de Ávila Blomberg, who became its founding director. The state of Oaxaca is one of the most floristically rich and ethnically diverse in Mexico, and is home to many Indigenous peoples who have preserved traditional knowledge. This cultural heritage is celebrated in the garden with zigzag paths, railings and walls – devised mainly by Zárate – echoing the geometric designs of the Zapotec culture. The planting reflects ancient agricultural practices, such as the 'three sisters' (beans, squash and maize), as well as a range of wild species. A striking feature is the high fence of cardon cactus set behind a reflective pool and enclosing a grove of prickly pear cactus – a plant that is strongly associated with the red dye cochineal, which underpinned Oaxaca's historic wealth.

JULIE TOLL

BLACK SAND COVE
Nevis, St Kitts & Nevis, 2007

Drawn to this property on the Caribbean island of Nevis by its rugged coastal setting and secluded site, Linda Burkett wanted her 0.4-hectare (1-acre) garden to reflect the beauty of its location and the wildness of the surrounding native vegetation, and was drawn to designer Julie Toll by her planting approach. Toll was one of the earliest UK landscape designers to adopt a 'new' wilder prairie style of naturalistic planting with perennials, chosen to suit the conditions of each garden. Her sandy coastal show garden at the RHS Chelsea Flower Show in 1993 was beautifully planted with native species suited to its setting, won a Gold Medal and was judged Best in Show, but some complained that it was merely planted with 'weeds'. Burkett, however – a long-term resident of a home on the edge of the North American prairie – decided she had found the ideal designer for her Nevis garden. The natural landscape of the driest part of Nevis defines the ground plan of this space, which sits on heavy clay soil and is subject to salt-laden winds and flash floods. Toll's design divides it into different spaces with organically shaped mounded planting areas. The 'lawn' of native grasses is mown infrequently, and takes on different hues through the year. Toll and Burkett worked and experimented together with local plants over a number of years. Native agaves and aloes add architectural presence, thrive on minimal watering and attract wildlife – all essential elements for Toll and her client.

TOPOPHYLA

YSIDRO
Montecito, California, United States, 2022

When Nahal Sohbati and Eric Arneson of TOPOPHYLA (the studio they established in 2019) arrived for their initial consultation at this private garden, they found a common but underwhelming 0.7-hectare (1¾-acre) lawn. 'Unless you fertilize and irrigate intensively, lawns don't do well here,' Arneson explains, referring to the region's low rainfall and the unsustainable fertilization and irrigation practices that are generally suggested. The team had a better idea that played to the studio's strengths in designing in function, aesthetics and ecology. The property was endowed with glorious mature oaks, and a plan emerged to preserve them as a leitmotif while crafting a riveting, species-rich stroll garden that would provide a thrilling outdoor experience. The palette of drought-tolerant plants to choose from in USDA Zone 11 (one of the warmer hardiness zones defined by the US Department of Agriculture) is vast, even while focusing exclusively on those that can endure lean conditions. In this rarity-rich broadloom 'there's something to trigger curiosity every few steps,' says Arneson. From *Aloe* to *Anigozanthos* (kangaroo paw), from palms to *Muhlenbergia* (muhly grass), the garden weaves textures with such stalwart choices as *Salvia clevelandii* (Cleveland sage), gaura and numerous succulents and ornamental grasses. The plantings stitch together various destinations, including several patios, as well as forming paths that culminate in recreation spaces. Importantly, they work with Landlorde, a maintenance contractor that keeps the scene trimmed and tidy without pouring on water or food. The resplendent result is infinitely more compelling – not to mention lower-maintenance – than the former lawn.

TURENSCAPE

JINHUA MEI GARDEN
Jinhua, Zhejiang Province, China, 2013

Faced with a challenging site and climate, landscape architect Kongjian Yu (who founded Turenscape in 1998) created a matrix of inviting spaces for this public garden inspired by China's cultural history. Socially and culturally, the objectives were to facilitate pleasant outdoor use in a subtropical monsoon climate (hot and rainy) and to celebrate mei (*meihua*), or plum blossom (*Prunus mume*), arguably China's most revered flower and especially beloved in this city. Mei is not to be displayed but rather hidden, requiring devotees to undertake a quest or encounter it unexpectedly. The practical objectives of this 13-hectare (32-acre) park on the west bank of the polluted River Wuyi, paralleling its course, were to transform a swamp of urban debris into a terraced valley garden 6 metres (20 feet) deep. At its base a wetland park cleans eutrophic (nutrient-rich, oxygen-depleted) water and restores habitat, thus increasing biodiversity. The constructed wetland is an exploratory, educational space threaded with boardwalks. A windmill pumps river water into a creek, where four ecological weirs slow the flow and five vegetative biofilters cleanse the water before it enters a three-by-three square of boxes at the north end, each 24 metres (79 feet) square, 4.5 metres (15 feet) tall and joined by covered walkways. The black walls are covered with *Parthenocissus tricuspidata* (Boston ivy) and – inspired by the traditional scholar gardens of China – pierced with viewing windows. Three are water gardens filled with *Nelumbo nucifera* (lotus), which in Chinese culture symbolizes purity, spiritual growth and resilience; the other six conceal cultivars of the elusive mei.

SAYUKI UENO

UENO FARM
Asahikawa, Hokkaido, Japan, 2001

Deep in the interior of the indomitable, snow-strewn Japanese island of Hokkaido, a whimsical fantasy reigns. In 2000, aged twenty-six and working in a shop, farmers' daughter Sayuki Ueno perceived an absence of meaning, and her trajectory was forever altered by a subway advertisement for foreign internships. Responding largely to her mother's unexplored love of English gardens, Ueno moved to a small village near Winchester, southern England, and at Bramdean House was introduced to the magic trick of successional, perennial flower gardening: 'Everything was fresh and beautiful, and every month was different, *but nobody changed the plants*.' This precious insight was spirited home and, with a section of the family rice farm sundered for experiment, Hokkaido disclosed itself a region entirely dissimilar to Hampshire. In the absence of local nurseries, Ueno imported seed from Europe, and, when foxgloves and mulleins first germinated on her bedroom windowsill, a meaningful and even propitious existence became palpable. Two curious, dedicated decades later Ueno has become a pioneering authority on cold-tolerant non-natives (the region can endure temperatures below -20°C/ -4°F, and 95 per cent of her carefully trialled perennials overwinter), her colourful floral combinations have engulfed the 1.2-hectare (3-acre) former family farm entirely, and every year she welcomes more than 70,000 paying visitors. Fundamental to her vision is the encouragement of children, offering them the horticultural enchantment she knew only from hearsay, and a spired, fairy-tale brick-and-cedar 'Gnome House' ('the gnomes work at night') has become the centrepiece of the garden's most iconic and colourful scene.

UNTERMYER GARDENS CONSERVANCY

WALLED GARDEN, UNTERMYER PARK
Yonkers, New York, United States, 2011

Once called the finest garden in the world, Untermyer Park, now a 17.5-hectare (43-acre) city park in Yonkers, New York, is the remnant of Greystone, the former grand estate of lawyer and civic leader Samuel Untermyer. Untermyer was passionate about horticulture, and in 1916 he hired Beaux Arts-trained landscape designer William Welles Bosworth to create his garden. After years of neglect and deterioration following Untermyer's death in 1940, the park and its crown jewel, the 1-hectare (2.5-acre) Walled Garden, were rescued by the formation of the Untermyer Gardens Conservancy by architect Stephen F. Byrns in 2011. Renowned horticulturist Marco Polo Stufano (best known for his directorship at the acclaimed Bronx garden Wave Hill) was recruited, and work began on rebuilding the Mughal-inspired Walled Garden, which forms the monumental entrance to Untermyer. Divided into quadrants by canals, the design is based on the traditional idea of the Garden of Eden. This enclosed garden was the biggest part of the renovation. A Classical-influenced amphitheatre, a pair of marble sphinx-topped Ionic columns, the colonnaded 'Temple of the Sky' and a ziggurat-shaped pool lined with a mosaic of Medusa have been magnificently restored. Thanks to the Conservancy and head gardener Timothy Tilghman's efforts, in partnership with the Yonkers Parks Department, the Walled Garden is once again lush with contemporary plantings that change with the seasons. Pots of bright tropical annuals echo the papyrus and lotus depicted in the newly replaced tilework, and two existing weeping beeches are complemented by additional colourful perennials, shrubs and specimen trees.

URQUHART & HUNT

GIARDINI PISTOLA
Fasano, Puglia, Italy, 2021

The brief to design a one-of-a-kind public garden on 4 hectares (nearly 10 acres) of sloping terrain in Puglia, southern Italy, was both exciting and challenging for British landscape design studio Urquhart & Hunt. The sloping site – 8 metres (26 feet) higher at the top than the bottom – had been landscaped as three terraces, and the client's wishlist included a large events space, an amphitheatre, a water feature and a series of experiences that would surprise and intrigue visitors. The team undertook immersive research into the local flora, fauna, climate and traditional vernacular. The region has been affected by the destructive pathogen *Xylella fastidiosa*, so the designers were determined to devise a plant palette that did not include any host species. This meant leaving out such favourites of Italian gardens as lavender, oleander and olive, and introducing more unusual plants, such as the exotic-looking × *Chitalpa tashkentensis* Summer Bells ('Minsum'). Drawing on their experience of creating sustainable, biodiverse schemes, the team devised six distinctive terraces with paths of permeable local gravel, taking visitors on a journey of scent, season and habitat. Each draws the visitor along its east/west access, rather than up the centre, through a maze of clipped Italian buckthorn on the first terrace, through shoulder-high perennials and *Stipa* grasses on another, under a tunnel of kiwis and gourds and, in the centre of the garden, along a playful rill, where mastic trees (*Pistacia lentiscus*) in a line suggest the evergreen form of olive trees.

URQUIJO-KASTNER

WATERMILL GARDEN
Rascafría, Madrid, Spain, 2010

Set at an altitude of 1,600 metres (5,250 feet) in the Sierra de Guadarrama, north of Madrid, this garden around a former watermill is the work of studio Urquijo-Kastner, founded in 2001 by husband-and-wife team Miguel Urquijo and Renate Kastner. Their approach to the project sets out to challenge traditional Spanish garden design, although it continues to employ an important traditional management technique: the clipping of shrubs. Surrounded by the wild environment of a national park, the 500-square-metre (5,380-square-foot) space contains clipped evergreen foliage – of *Taxus baccata* (yew) and *Erica × darleyensis* (heather) – that reflects the wind-sculpted forms found naturally in this mountainous region. The use of yew and heather, birch trees and low stone walls gives the garden a Nordic feel, making it both unexpected and innovative for Spain. The clipping of the yew and heather to evoke the shapes of naturally windswept plants is also a nod to the Japanese garden tradition, to which this practice is central. A few flowering perennials – irises, *Dianthus gratianopolitanus* (cheddar pink) and the silvery, creeping *Stachys byzantina* (lamb's ears) – are arranged in flowing, organic shapes and add a contrast of colour and texture early in the year. With its simplicity and focus on natural forms, the garden appeals to those who value a controlled look, yet it presents a completely new way of achieving this: through the use of organic, flowing shapes inspired by nature rather than geometry.

DRIES VAN NOTEN WITH ERIK DHONT

RINGENHOF
Lier, Antwerp, Belgium, 1997

Taking its inspiration from the classic English gardens of Sissinghurst, Great Dixter (see p.106) and Hidcote, the 0.4-hectare (1-acre) Victorian Rose Garden shown here, which belongs to Belgian fashion designer Dries Van Noten and his partner Patrick Vangheluwe, is divided into quadrants, each with a different atmosphere. Flowering in the early summer, it is crammed with roses squeezed into beds with scented plants, such as lavender, while creeping *Helichrysum* spills from the huge stone urns that line the paths and climbing roses 'Blossomtime' and 'Aloha' twist over delicate iron arches. The rose garden is just one of a series of enclosures in the 22.3-hectare (55-acre) park that makes up Van Noten's property in the Belgian countryside near Antwerp. Van Noten and acclaimed landscape architect Erik Dhont (see p.82) divided the huge garden into sections. Formal lawns surround the restored neoclassical house, while a large lake is set in deliberately overgrown woodland. Van Noten planned his many flower gardens so that there is colour throughout the year, starting with cyclamen in January. Delphiniums, magnolias, peonies and dahlias each have their own garden, and the property has fifty different types of hydrangea. Espaliered fruit trees hug old walls, while in another section Dhont designed a zigzag avenue of yew hedges to provide privacy. A more recent addition is the grass border created by Piet Oudolf. Although Van Noten hated gardening as a child, the horticultural passion he cultivated as an adult has always informed his fashion designs, which often feature roses, flowers and leaf prints.

VIS À VIS ONTWERPERS

WILDE WEELDE WERELD
Bloemenpark Appeltern, Appeltern,
Gelderland, The Netherlands, 2013–

Ben van Ooyen, sometime DJ, now garden designer and creator, began building demonstration gardens around his home in 1988, to show a range of designs to potential clients. When landscape suppliers and nurseries learned of his projects, they began offering materials, so that there are now around 200 inspirational gardens on the site, and counting. Although many of them are designed by Van Ooyen, he also invites designers to create their own. One such garden, the 0.5-hectare (just over 1-acre) Wilde Weelde Wereld (Wild Wealth World), a contemporary interpretation by designers Emiel Versluis and Margo van Beem of Vis à Vis Ontwerpers, introduces the idea and principles of eco-logical gardening. It also demonstrates how the garden environment can be enriched for humans while optimizing its potential for wildlife using native plants and lesser-known garden varieties. The aim is to inspire visitors to realize the potential within their own gardens, neighbourhoods and schools, while helping them to understand how the garden works. On one wooded bank, a tree has been dissected from root to leaf. Hard landscaping materials are environmentally friendly, up-cycled, recycled or from sustainable sources. There are also plenty of garden activities on show, including a swimming pond and spiral mound – all useful ideas for the home gardener. The space is constantly evolving, and projects are undertaken to monitor how wild plants thrive in a garden situation. As the plantings become established, the wildlife value increases. A volunteer group called the Wild Weelders helps with the maintenance of this garden for communities, wildlife and the planet.

VLADIMIR DJUROVIC
LANDSCAPE ARCHITECTURE

AGA KHAN PARK
Toronto, Ontario, Canada, 2015

The brief to Lebanese landscape architect Vladimir Djurovic and his eponymous firm (founded 1995) was to design a contemporary Islamic garden that would resonate in the present and provide a contemplative space to encourage reflection and engagement in a multi-ethnic population. It also had to link two architecturally imposing contemporary buildings on a 7-hectare (17-acre) site on the outskirts of Toronto, beside a busy highway intersection. Djurovic designed a geometric formal garden between the two buildings using a restrained vocabulary of white granite paving and gravel for the ground plane with five dramatic raised reflecting pools in black granite. Inspired by the clarity of the traditional Persian garden (*chahar bagh*), the space is divided into quadrants around the central pool. Eight rows of native serviceberries (*Amelanchier*) define the space further, their airy woodland texture and green underplanting contrasting arrestingly with the pure volumes of the hard materials. The trees are a contemporary nod to the orchards (*bustan*) that frequently accompanied Islamic gardens. Djurovic is deliberate in his choice of plants and materials, always keeping the five senses in mind. Thus, the serviceberry provides four seasons of interest, and thyme and a bank of *Salvia yangii* (syn. *Perovskia atriplicifolia*; Russian sage) introduce scent, texture and colour. The pools are positioned to reflect both sky and architecture, but are also important for the subtle, refreshing sound of murmuring water. Emerald cedars enclose the formal enclave, and the rest of the park unfolds in a series of pathways, meandering through a tree-covered community park.

ANOUK VOGEL

GARDENS OF THE JAMEEL ARTS CENTRE
Dubai, United Arab Emirates, 2018

The Jameel Arts Centre, on the Jaddaf waterfront in Dubai, was established to exhibit contemporary art in this fast-changing city, and its architecture and seven courtyard gardens reflect this purpose. Each garden was designed by the Swiss-born, Amsterdam-based landscape architect Anouk Vogel to feed natural light into the galleries while showcasing a range of unique desert environments. The courtyard at the front of the gallery greets the visitor and sets the tone for the experience. An array of drought-resistant plants, including cacti, agave and numerous palms, are planted in an open corridor clad with white aluminium panels. The plants sit in a 'soil' of pink terrazzo chips, while a white terrazzo path guides the visitor through the space. Inside the gallery, the other courtyard gardens – filled with sculptural plants – reflect the legacy of naturalist adventurers and the odysseys of seeds and species that have travelled the world both intentionally and by chance. Each garden represents a different desert biome, and is named after a country, region or species – Namib, Socotra, Chihuahuan, Australian, Silk Floss, Arabian and Spiny Woodlands – and feature sculptural plants native to desert ecosystems. The 149 included species range from common plants, such as *Kumara plicatilis* (fan aloe) and *Cereus marmoratus* (marble cactus), to rarer examples, including *Dracaena cinnabari* (dragon's blood tree) and *Alluaudia procera* (Madagascar ocotillo), melding the gardens' atmosphere of reflection and contemplation with a strong sense of geography and history. A further courtyard has been designated the Artist's Garden, for creative interpretation via an annual commission.

JO WAKELIN

PRIVATE GARDEN
Central Otago, South Island, New Zealand, 2016

Jo Wakelin's own garden in Central Otago, New Zealand, feels boundless, merging seamlessly with the towering mountains that frame the landscape. Although it is modest in size, at 2,000 square metres (21,500 square feet), Wakelin speaks of its strong connection to the land, the *tūrangawaewae* in Maori, every element reflecting the muted, natural hues of its surroundings. The greens, greys and fawns of the plants blend effortlessly with the bleached grass and grey rock of the local pasturelands. History is referenced, too, with one low mound of stones that echoes the shape of the surrounding borders and mimics 'the early goldminers' tailings, piled rock by rock during the gold rush in the 1860s', as Wakelin explains. Embracing the harshness of this arid climate, where rainfall is scarce and the soil a nutrient-poor glacial outwash, she does not irrigate or fertilize, but relies on resilient climate-appropriate species. She has divided the space in two: one half dedicated to regionally native plants, such as *Sophora microphylla* (small-leaved kōwhai), which would once have covered the surrounding hills, and the dramatic *Pseudopanax ferox* (known as horoeka or toothed lancewood); the other to more colourful, non-native species including many European and American dry-habitat plants. Inspired by Beth Chatto's gravel garden in Essex, southeast England, Wakelin uses a mineral gravel mulch to conserve moisture, letting the natural rhythm of the seasons shape the garden's character. It stands as both an expression of her personal love for the land and a reflection of its rugged beauty.

PETER WALKER IN COLLABORATION WITH MICHAEL ARAD AND DAN EUSER

9/11 MEMORIAL
New York, New York, United States, 2011

The horrific attacks of 11 September 2001 on New York City shook the world and transformed Manhattan's iconic skyline. As part of the efforts to memorialize the many lives lost, Peter Walker of PWP Landscape Architecture (see p.233) worked with architect Michael Arad to design a site that would serve as a public park and a space for contemplation, solace and remembrance. The focus is provided by two beautiful waterfall pools of 4,000 square metres (43,000 square feet), 9 metres (30 feet) deep, designed by artist and landscape architect Dan Euser, filling the voids left by the fallen twin towers of the World Trade Center. The names of the victims are carved into the bronze sides. Inspired by minimalist art, the work of Modernist landscape architect Dan Kiley, site-specific land art and traditional Japanese gardens, Walker's design brings tranquillity by maintaining a simple, flat plane, to complement the memorial without competing with it. Using his signature axis lines to attain shifting sight lines, Walker used minimal materials and a simple plant palette. Stone monoliths throughout the 3.2-hectare (8-acre) plaza create calm. More than 400 locally sourced swamp white oaks (*Quercus bicolor*), a hardy and long-lived species, were planted in dense rows. The uniform trees are aligned in a slightly irregular grid, organized so that from one perspective they appear in formal allées, while from another they resemble a forest. This memorial grove surrounds the Callery pear (*Pyrus calleryana*) known as the 'Survivor Tree', which incredibly withstood the destruction and is now preserved as a symbol of resilience.

SOPHIE WALKER

ROUND DELL
Borde Hill, Haywards Heath, West Sussex, England, 2018

When Sophie Walker – garden designer and art historian – read Frances Hodgson Burnett's *The Secret Garden* (1909) as a child, she dreamed of creating a garden expressing a similar sense of wonder at nature's magic. That experience served as inspiration for Walker's resplendent foliage garden at RHS Hampton Court Palace Flower Show in 2013. Filled with dramatic, oversized plants that dwarfed visitors (especially small ones), it boasted a unique layout of converging paths. That concept was the seed for the Round Dell at Borde Hill, a country estate comprising 14 hectares (35 acres) of formal gardens within a 154-hectare (380-acre) park. The project brings the 'found space' of a former quarry into the prevailing vision of other cultivated areas within the gardens. For close encounters to make the heart race, some of the paths are defined by concrete raised beds that culminate in a point, like a ship's prow. On one path, a waterfall adds drama. With the help of plant-collectors Bleddyn and Sue Wynn-Jones of Crûg Farm Plants, Walker included newly discovered species with an emphasis on greenery. 'Something happens when you see green in all its shades; it forces you to zoom into detail and becomes a restful monochrome,' she explains. Gingers, *Rodgersia*, *Persicaria*, bananas, *Gunnera*, *Fatsia*, bamboos and oddities of all sorts are part of the Wonderland amassed in these action-packed beds. 'It's lyrical,' Walker says, remembering the impact of her original *Secret Garden* experience. 'It's something like walking into the actual book.'

ALICE WATERS

EDIBLE SCHOOLYARD PROJECT
Berkeley, California, United States, 1995

It all started with a vacant plot and a vision. Originally trained as a Montessori teacher, Alice Waters found her niche as a chef in 1971, pioneering the farm-to-table movement. Nearly twenty-five years later, she heard from the principal of nearby Dr Martin Luther King, Jr Middle School, who had the dream of converting a vacant car park into an edible garden. Waters agreed to help, but only if an 'all or nothing' approach was accepted, with vegetable and fruit beds, flowers, an open kitchen, a cafeteria, outdoor classrooms, and outreach to support all aspects of the school curriculum and community. That original garden now supports 1,000 students and a network of connections. 'If they grow it, they'll eat it,' says Waters of her goal to expose an impressionable audience to fresh produce, and essentially the students grow their own food. Although the 0.4-hectare (1-acre) garden is hard-working, the design is beautiful, with sixteen beds devoted to vegetables, herbs, flowers, espaliered fruit trees and berry bushes, and a circular iron ramada for gathering. An arched tunnel shoulders grapevines, seeds sprout in a small greenhouse, soil is built in four compost piles, supplies are stored in a tool shed, and an outdoor kitchen receives the harvest while also recycling grey water into the beds. Delicious, nutritious food is not the only goal; as Waters explains, it 'also supports the curriculum in history, geography, math, science, and even music lessons'. Currently more than 6,500 schools in seventy-five countries have been inspired by the Edible Schoolyard programme.

WATSON PELLACINI

GARDEN IN THE AIR
Cape Town, South Africa, 2017

Perched high on the slopes of Table Mountain with spectacular panoramas up to its peak and down over Cape Town, the house of architect-owner Greg Truen of SAOTA melds with its natural setting so subtly that it is hard to see where the garden ends and wild nature begins. Truen is passionate in his appreciation of the local flora, so it was key that the garden embrace a rich mosaic of species from the Cape Floral Region. The response by its designer, landscape studio Watson Pellacini (founded in 2016 by established landscapists Franchesca Watson and Fabio Pellacini), is detailed, embracing and intuitive, simultaneously calming and invigorating, with sophisticated, glamorous planting that comes so close to the architecture as to blur inside and out. Similarly, the hard landscaping, such as swimming pool, flagstone terraces and courtyards, seems to merge into the greenery, anchoring house and garden into their setting. Watson and Pellacini are interested in gardens' potential and ability to connect humans and nature, and strongly believe that they are good for wellness both psychological and physical.

Applying the philosophy that to be truly sustainable, a garden must be right first time, Watson Pellacini and SOATA have blended architecture, art and beauty with sound ethical principles and ecologically informed solutions to deliver the requisite lifestyle. 'We saw the garden as little slabs of landscape that we could surround the spaces with,' says Truen. 'The result is a building that feels like it's been dropped on to the mountain.'

WEISS/MANFREDI AND REED HILDERBRAND

LONGWOOD GARDENS WEST CONSERVATORY
Kennett Square, Pennsylvania, United States, 2024

For a century, glasshouses have been a hallmark of Longwood Gardens, the majestic Pennsylvania landscape of Pierre S. du Pont (1870–1954). But technology has grown apace and creating a befitting 0.3-hectare (¾-acre) state-of-the-art West Conservatory as part of the extensive Longwood Reimagined project took vision and expertise. Fittingly, Marion Weiss and Michael Manfredi, principal architects at Weiss/Manfredi, were called in for the transformation fifteen years ago and took their cue from the quintessential Brandywine Valley setting and the century-old London plane grove on site. The arching trunks and branches of those trees were translated into the repeating columns and beams of the newly designed greenhouse. For the roof, 'pleated origami' was the inspiration. The structure is also environmentally responsible with underground collection tanks capturing and storing rainfall, operable glass panels for ventilation, 'earth tubes' for cooling and warming the air, and climate-activated shades. Heating and cooling are further augmented by a geothermal system. Meanwhile, landscape architects Reed Hilderbrand, with Kristin Frederickson as principal, brought together plants from Mediterranean eco-regions while – given du Pont's love of fountains – water features were a natural for the conservatory's motif. Framed in a reflective 'lake' of water, the theme is echoed indoors by water rills and jets between planted beds of grevillea and agave, and an acacia allée. Above, hanging baskets are staggered for a chandelier effect while custom steel structures shoulder flowering vines. Truly a work of art, the West Conservatory is poetry, design and horticulture in unison.

WEST 8

MÁXIMAPARK
Utrecht, The Netherlands, 2013–

The creation of diverse, high-quality urban parks creates communities, providing a public space for all through participation and connection. One such facility, the multiphase 300-hectare (740-acre) Máximapark in a modern residential area of western Utrecht, spans decades of continuous growth and iterative development, with the shared message of bringing the surrounding neighbourhoods together through ecology. The design concept of Adriaan Geuze – founder of West 8, one of Europe's leading, forward-thinking urban-design practices – for Máximapark rests on four spatial pillars: 'Het Lint', the 'Binnenhof', the 'Parkpergola' and the 'Vikingrijn'. These compelling, innovative design elements multi-task, simultaneously creating a strong sense of place, dividing the space, and increasing habitat and biodiversity. Het Lint (The Ribbon) is a wide, car-free connecting path that meanders through the woods, waterways, playing fields and meadows of the entire site, while the iconic Parkpergola (900 metres/ nearly 3,000 feet long, 6 metres/20 feet high) enables ecological connections to originate on an infrastructural scale. The concrete and 'growcrete' honeycomb frame encourages seasonal climbing plants, such as wisteria, Virginia creeper and ivy to grow up it, and provides shelter and nesting sites through custom-made bat boxes, insect hotels and planters. It also functions as the entrance to the 50-hectare (124-acre) Binnenhof, or courtyard, which forms the park's green core. The Vikingrijn, formerly part of the River Rhine, has been excavated on the location it had in Roman times. Characterful bridges encourage access and engagement, restoring people's relationship with this aquatic land.

CLEVE WEST

HORATIO'S GARDEN
Salisbury District Hospital, Wiltshire, England, 2012

This, the first of eight Horatio's Gardens, commemorates schoolboy Horatio Chapple, who volunteered at the Duke of Cornwall Spinal Treatment Centre and had the idea to create a garden here. Tragically Horatio was killed at just seventeen by a polar bear in Svalbard in 2011, while on an expedition, but his parents – determined that his vision should become reality – established a charity in his name. The charity commissions gardens for the therapeutic benefit of spinal injury patients, their families and carers, assigning high-profile designers to each project. Cleve West was the first, designing this garden in Salisbury: 'When I started, I didn't fully appreciate what Horatio's Garden was going to bring to people in terms of hope and sustenance and realigning their lives to cope with life-changing injuries.' The 1,672-square-metre (18,000-square-foot) garden has a calm tranquillity. A summerhouse offers privacy and a space for quiet reflection; a rill runs alongside an archway of apple trees and introduces the murmur of water, while a glasshouse and horticultural therapy area host gardening activities for patients. The wider garden features mixed planting of aromatic herbs, perennials, grasses, shrubs and trees – aesthetically pleasing, wildlife-friendly and stimulating to the senses. Through it all winds a wheelchair-accessible path 2 metres (6½ feet) wide, and two stone walls shaped 'like spines, broken by an intersecting path before coming together in a continuous wall – a metaphor for every patient's recovery journey', bring a succession of prospects over the borrowed landscape beyond, leading to a large, open gathering space.

XANTHE WHITE

MAMAKU
Grey Lynn, Auckland, North Island, New Zealand, 2016

With echoes of Topher Delaney's anthropological approach (see p.79), award-winning New Zealand designer Xanthe White believes that design is the art of making connections between people and place. She also holds that sustainability can be achieved passively by creating functional living areas, planting the remaining spaces diversely, then allowing the plants to grow as nature intended. This ethos is on display at Mamaku, an immersive 1,000-square-metre (10,760-square-foot) garden with simple spaces heightened by the split level of the site, which gives two differing perspectives. One looks down over the garden, a prospect that highlights the architectonic plant forms and in particular the mamaku or black tree fern (*Sphaeropteris medullaris*) after which the garden is named; the other is experienced from under the canopy, as it were 'inside' the garden, with the verdant tints and forms of the understorey planting, looking up through the silhouetted canopy of fronds. The effect is delightful and the subtle hand of the designer almost invisible as native species blend in an alluring fusion, and here too the art of horticulture is again on show – or rather not. Deliberately subtle, low-key cultivation permits nature to define and fill the spaces by means of the plants growing to their natural forms and shapes. Nature is mostly in control, but assisted gently so as to present her best, most artful face. This is also beautifully evident when the garden is seen from within the house with its large sliding glass doors, which open to bring the jungle inside.

MADE WIJAYA

VILLA BEBEK
Ubud, Bali, Indonesia, 1983

A controversial and flamboyant character, Made Wijaya (1953–2016) was born Michael White in Australia, arrived in Bali in 1973 and immediately fell under the spell of the island and its people. These locally inspired thatched buildings, which were originally designed for a friend from whom he later bought them back, are in what Wijaya called Bali Baronial Style, traditionally arranged and defining courtyard spaces into which the living spaces, pools, swimming pool and gardens are integrated. This was also his laboratory, where he experimented with plantings. The garden is suburban and relatively small at 0.3 hectares (less than ¾ acre), but the naturalistic-looking flora brings a wild ambiance, a tamed but fecund nature in perfect harmony with its setting. Look more closely, however, and it is evident that the plantings are as carefully orchestrated as the positioning of the collection of traditional sculptures and contemporary works. Wijaya titled himself the world's 'last poetic gardener', and his design style has been described as having 'the tropical Cotswolds look'. Certainly his work – his portfolio extended to more than 600 tropical gardens globally, but with a focus on Southeast Asia and particularly Bali – weaves a magical, artful, near-rustic European sensibility into the riotously flamboyant, architectonic, diversely green and brightly flowered tropical flora. But this is to miss Wijaya's love and deep understanding of Balinese architecture and culture, both of which are integrated subtly and delightfully into this garden.

KEITH WILEY

WILDSIDE
Buckland Monachorum, Devon, England, 2003

Keith Wiley's own garden is testament to a remarkable combination of artistry and ecological principles. Nestled in the slopes of Dartmoor, in the southwest of England, this 1.6-hectare (4-acre) landscape showcases a wide range of plants thriving in carefully sculpted micro-habitats. Wiley's first task was to rent a mini-digger and 'play God' by developing miniature hills, ridges and valleys on what was a flat field, resulting in a unique experience as the topography frames the visitor's journey as well as providing varied growing environments. Through meticulous land-shaping and plant selection, Wiley has created a garden that evokes the rolling hills of Devon while also offering a sense of a miniature world within a larger one. Much of the garden's aesthetic is rooted in Wiley's extensive travels and observations of wild plant communities, and he emphasizes the importance of learning from nature and applying those principles to planting design. The result is a harmonious blend of plants that mimic the distribution patterns found in natural habitats. Wildside offers a constantly changing display of colour and texture with, crucially, repetition of key species for maximum impact. In the spring, the garden is a profusion of bulbs and woodland perennials at ground level. As the year progresses, the scale of vision needed to appreciate the planting expands, encompassing perennials and grasses. This repetition creates visual rhythm and unity, while the variations in elevation within the garden offer both grand vistas and intimate corners.

KIM WILKIE FOR THE 10TH DUKE OF BUCCLEUCH

ORPHEUS
Boughton House, Kettering, Northamptonshire, England, 2009

It is unusual to find a formal 18th-century, French Baroque-inspired garden that was not subsequently remodelled in the naturalistic style. Boughton House is one: geometrically formal yet arcadian, it was laid out by Ralph, 1st Duke of Montagu, who, as English ambassador to France in the late 1660s, presumably had Versailles in mind. The parterres are now gone, but canals and pools, avenues and vistas survive, as do sculptural landforms by Charles Bridgeman (1690-1738), whose transitional landscapes marked the beginnings of a shift from formal to naturalesque. Ralph's descendant John Scott, 9th Duke of Buccleuch, began the restoration in 2003, and it has been continued by the 10th Duke, Richard Scott, who wished to add a contemporary yet complementary feature to emphasize the garden's continuing evolution. Kim Wilkie, an acclaimed conceptual landscape architect, was commissioned to create a new feature. His *Orpheus* is named after the illustrious musician of Greek myth who descended into Hades to try to reclaim his dead wife, Eurydice. It is the inverse negative space to the positive of the restored grassed pyramidal (Olympian?) Mount, and both are sculptural forms with serene lines. Separated from the Mount by a canal, the inverted grass pyramid descends 7 metres (23 feet) below the level of the restored terraces. It is invisible until one comes upon its 60-metre square sides that open up to reveal a grass path, which spirals down to a square, still pool that, like an inverted oculus, reflects the sky. From here the visitor – unlike poor Orpheus – has the chance to return to the upper world without loss. The sculpture in front of the landform represents The Golden Ratio.

KURT WILKINSON

YALAMURRA
Yattalunga, Adelaide, South Australia, Australia, 2012–

An unprecedented spectacle borne of necessity and rigour, Yalamurra is a garden like no other. Kurt Wilkinson, then a skilled 'formalist' specializing in hedging and topiary, endured six years marooned among dead and dying plants surrounding a newly purchased home on a hot, dry hilltop location nearly 50 kilometres (30 miles) from Adelaide. The primary culprit was *Phytophthora*, a water mould that attacks a wide range of plants, and Wilkinson – suddenly a desperate novice – resolved to find material that could thrive in this truculent location and make it sing. 'This was going to be my one chance,' he says, 'so everything was on the line.' With a forcibly limited palette he has crafted a psychotropic tornado of a garden over 1.2 hectares (3 acres), ever-changing and on the move: 'I want to see 700 gardens a year,' he says. Star performers include *Cupressus sempervirens* 'Glauca' (Mediterranean cypress), *Alyogyne huegelii* (blue hibiscus), *Centaurea gymnocarpa* (Capraian cornflower), *Melaleuca nesophila* (showy honey-myrtle) and *Aeonium arboreum* 'Atropurpureum' (purple houseleek). Countering death with creativity rather than expense, Wilkinson has learned to spurn the blithe temptation of nurseries and rather to plug gaps tirelessly with his cast of dependables, striking cuttings directly into the ground then editing fervently. He is an ardent photographer and works in the Adelaide area as a designer. Yalamurra has informed his work: 'Now when I design a garden, I've got some loose ideas. I go to the nursery, I plant, then I edit. It comes from love, and it has to be art.'

WIRTZ INTERNATIONAL

VAN MOL GARDEN
near Brussels, Belgium, 2013

The brief for renowned Belgian landscape architect Martin Wirtz was to create a 'masculine' garden to complement a strikingly Modernist family home. The family also wanted the design to incorporate the stables and fields of their beloved horses. Wirtz's solution is a garden without flowers, a sculpted landscape of green lawns that mimic the rolling hills of the rural setting. He brings the landscape into the garden in a manner reminiscent of the 'borrowed landscapes' of such large 18th-century English country estates as Rousham Hall, Oxfordshire, with uninterrupted vistas of formal lawns giving way to the green hills beyond. A long drive lined with precisely clipped box hedges twists and turns until it delivers visitors to the house and opens to reveal the vista. Wirtz planted a grove of nearly mature *Metasequoia* (dawn redwoods) on the lawn to provide a primordial contrast with the manicured lawns; amid the trees, he placed a sculpture of four horses and their riders. The real horses are kept safely separate from the lawn by a ha-ha – a ditch used in many stately homes to provide a barrier without breaking the view – that neatly cuts the garden in two. A large waterlily pond adds to the tranquillity of the sculpted landscape, in which shades of green combine to create calm. In keeping with the founding principle of Wirtz International (the firm started by Martin's late father, Jacques, and continued by Martin and his brother Peter; see p.227), the garden is effective all year round.

TOM DE WITTE

PRIVATE GARDEN
Aardenburg, Zeeland, The Netherlands, 2004–14

Elegance can arise in the most unlikely setting. In 2004 Dutch garden designer Tom de Witte moved into a new town house in Zeeland in the southwestern corner of The Netherlands, eager to make a first real garden of his own. The sloping slice of backyard – 75 metres (246 feet) long but only 4 metres (13 feet) wide – presented him with an opportunity to reconfigure the space and enhance it with naturalistic planting. He had introduced himself at sixteen to the legendary Piet Oudolf (see p.101 and p.216) at his garden in Hummelo, to learn from the master, and this found its way into his home design experiments. He did the work himself over ten years, structuring the garden into six distinct rooms to choreograph the experience. It begins as you step off the deck into the first garden room, between a shaggy *Acer griseum* (paperbark maple) and a mound of *Hakonechloa macra* (Japanese forest grass). Walk forward and your gaze is drawn upwards by drifts of ivy and roses on trellised brick walls. From there, you head into a rectilinear maze of manicured beech hedging with the crackle of shale under your feet. The next, wilder space is different again, with low, feathery grasses and ruby-red *Astrantia*, *Allium* and *Aquilegia*. The final sections dip into a shady enclave overhung by giant trees from the cemetery next door. The long view back up the garden offers a Zen moment of contemplation. From blowsy and wild to minimalist and clipped, De Witte squeezes the essence of the Dutch Wave into a multipart creative runway.

ADAM WOODRUFF WITH MATTHEW CUNNINGHAM

PRIVATE GARDEN
Marblehead, Massachusetts, United States, 2020

Standing in the far corner of Adam Woodruff's sumptuous matrix meadow, one can see the patterns at play. From this viewpoint, his own garden reveals itself as a floral tapestry laid out in three diagonal bands of perennials and grasses, repeated across the space with seasonal precision and covering just 260 square metres (2,800 square feet). A naturalistic planting designer of cool sophistication, Woodruff (who is principal at his eponymous garden and landscape design consultancy established in 1994) has interwoven hard and soft elements in this backyard refuge overlooking the harbour on Marblehead Bay, a collaboration with landscape architect Matthew Cunningham. The underlying hardscape provides the structure, with lengths of recycled granite forming walkways that cross the garden. Four shrubby *Cotinus coggygria* 'Royal Purple' frame the brick patio, set out with low-slung teak furniture and a minimalist zinc table. For years, Woodruff has surveyed the leading currents of planting design in Europe and the UK. He sees this garden as an experiment, inspired by the work of such innovative planting designers as Bettina Jaugstetter (see p.146) in Germany. He planted his artful, stylized meadow in the quiet of the COVID-19 pandemic, using around thirty-five species to create a layered matrix of tall structural plants, seasonal theme plants and groundcover. Late spring kicks off with a wave of blue *Salvia* (ornamental sages) interplanted with tangerine *Geum* and purple *Allium*. Cool-season grasses form a base layer through which emergents including *Echinacea* and *Stachys* rise in the summer, edged with fragrant bursts of *Origanum* and *Calamintha*.

OKSANA YAZYKOVA

ZHYVA NYVA
Zhytomyr, Ukraine, 2022

In the midst of the Russian invasion of Ukraine in 2022, landscape designer Oksana Yazykova created Zhyva Nyva (Living Field), a nature-inspired, eco-friendly garden in the country's Zhytomyr region. Seeking solace from the devastation of war, Yazykova transformed a 2,000-square-metre (21,500-square-foot) plot on her family's organic farm into a therapeutic oasis. She was inspired by childhood memories of her grandmother's home, and sought to blend nostalgia with references to farming. The garden features grasses to evoke such grain crops as wheat and rye, complemented by flowers; while dahlias and peonies were the flowers of her youth, she used more contemporary perennials here, such as cultivars of *Salvia*, *Allium* and *Achillea*, and some annuals, including *Amaranthus*. The space is intentionally kept low-key and slightly untamed. The farm includes old buildings that she has preserved rather than demolished, adding historical depth to the project. A wooden, slate-clad house makes a useful focal point. A mature apricot tree once stood at the entrance to the garden, but it died in 2024; rather than removing it, Yazykova left it *in situ* as a poignant symbol of life's impermanence and renewal. The garden remains a place of refuge where visitors can escape the noise of the city, and relax and reconnect with nature. Yazykova also envisions the project – part personal sanctuary, part monument – as contributing to a movement to use gardens as therapeutic places, with the idea of demonstrating that such spaces can be more powerful than any antidepressant.

HIROMITSU YOSHIYA AND TAKASHI KAWAI

THE ROSE GARDEN AT NAKANOJO GARDENS
Nakanojo, Agatsuma, Japan, 2018

Surrounded by mountains north of Tokyo, the Nakanojo Gardens have little in common with the austere Buddhist-inspired gardens of Japan's ancient capital, Kyoto. Instead, this 12-hectare (30-acre) park has its roots in Western ideas of the garden; it is less a place of meditation than a site in which to wander, chat and enjoy. Comprising seven gardens, Nakanojo is set in an extensive area of meadows and fields. It is an ongoing project, with one of its feature areas, Ohfujidana, a vast wisteria trellis, still maturing to its full beauty and overseen by Konami Tsukamoto, one of Japan's leading wisteria specialists. The popular Rose Garden (illustrated) was developed by landscape designer Hiromitsu Yoshiya and planted by horticulturist and rose breeder Takashi Kawai. Seven contrasting rooms are planted with over 400 rose cultivars selected to provide interest for much of the year, and including a modern Japanese rose garden with traditional golden motifs. The Spiral Garden, designed by horticulturist Keiko Yoshiya, is notable for raised walls of lava rock that delineate planting beds for perennials and grasses. Spirals of wheat – and seasonal mass plantings of, for example, red poppies or mauve *Ageratum* – encompass the garden and add contrast. The Natural Garden is filled with vibrant flowers and tall grasses, while the plants in the Knot Garden are arranged in complex entwined patterns. The Community Garden invites locals to plant their own flowers on small plots, placing particular importance on horticultural awareness for children. Finally, Furusato no Noyama is an area directly inspired by the flora of Nakanojo and created by the garden's former director Tomoyoshi Fukuda.

Z'SCAPE

HYLLA ALPINE GARDEN
Hylla Vintage Hotel, Lijiang, Yunnan Province, China, 2022

Widely explored by plant-hunters, Yunnan Province is a globally significant floral biodiversity hotspot. This garden, described by Z'scape's founders, Zhou Liangjun and Zhou Ting, as a 'place of comfort, solitude and peace', celebrates both these floral riches and the culture of the Indigenous Naxi people. At an altitude of 2,560 metres (8,500 feet) and enjoying views of Jade Dragon Snow Mountain, the garden graces the 6-hectare (15-acre) Hylla Vintage Hotel complex, which has breathed new life into an abandoned Naxi village. It comprises three main areas. The Alpine Lawn is a large event space dominated by the Xupai tree, a centuries-old oak that would have had protective significance for the original villagers and is now approached by a snaking boardwalk. The juxtaposed Wilderness Garden has restored 90 per cent of the native plant communities and created a diverse alpine habitat with a particularly lovely perennial meadow. The Amphitheatre, an elegant, sward-covered piece of land art with terraced bleachers, functions as an exhibition space, a gathering place for local people and a stage for traditional festivals.

Unifying elements throughout are the walls and water features built of local limestone by artisans from the area. The pools and rills evoke the traditional 'three well' system that made use of meltwater from the mountain: an upper well for drinking water, a middle well for cleaning fruit and vegetables, and a lower well for laundry, with the outflow irrigating the surrounding fields. Here, the system provides stormwater mitigation, a reservoir for irrigation and habitat for wildlife.

INDEX

3:0 Landschafts-Architektur 259
7b landscapes + interiors 267
9/11 Memorial 308

A
A Quincy Jones vs. Terremoto 287
ABB Factory 146
African Ancestors Memorial Garden 138
Aga Khan Centre, London 175
Aga Khan Park, Canada 304–5
Agence APS 12
Agnelli Foundation 249
Agro-Ornamental Park i.Land 279
Aguirrezabal, Juan Iriarte 262
Alexander-Sinclair, James 13
Alhadeff Architects 260
Alice Springs Desert Park 220
Allis, Bill and Jane 163
The Alnwick Garden 227
Alphabet City Landscape 17
Amager Bakke Copenhill Rooftop Park 269
Amaro Sánchez de Moya 228
Amazon Horticulture 14
AMELD 15
Andersson, Julia 158–9
Ando, Tadao 16
Andreyeva, Anna 17
Angelou, Maya 138
Annenberg, Walter and Leonore 209
Aquino, Gerdo 282
Arad, Michael 308
Ardissone, Lucía 54
Areal Landscape Architecture 18
Argentina
  La Estancia de Cafayate 251
  YPF Service Station 54
Arijiju 40
Arneson, Eric 296
Arregui, Iñigo Segurola 262
Arrernte people 220
Arroyo Residence 178
Art Institute of Chicago 83
Arterra Landscape Architects 19
Arundel Castle, The Collector Earl's Garden 27
Assemble 20
Assogna, Stefano 21
Australia
  Alice Springs Desert Park 220
  Australian Garden 285
  Banksia House 267
  Barwitian Garden 48–9
  Bracken 261
  Chelsea Australian Garden at Olinda 149
  Fire and Beauty 10, 189
  Garden of Australian Dreams 244
  Guilfoyle's Volcano 162
  Karkalla 51
  Musk Cottage 93
  Nevell Garden 201
  private gardens 75, 150
  Sand Garden 248
  Stone Hill 185
  Stonefields 26
  Sunnymeade 266
  Walama | Ballast Point Park 186
  Woodleigh School Senior Campus 72
  Yalamurra 319
Austria
  Garden of the Giant 57
  Vienna Nord Healing Gardens 259
Autonomous Province of Bolzano/ Bozen – South Tyrol 22
AW Architectes 273
Azaren 214–15

B
Baan Botanica 32
Babylonstoren 284
Bahía Azul 116
Baird, Mara 59
Baldwin, Alistair W. 23
Balenciaga store frontage 96
Baljon 24–5
Baljon, Lodewijk 25
Ball, Jonathan 117
Bangay, Paul 26
Banksia House 267
Bannerman, Julian and Isabel 27
Barbican Centre 901
Barfoot, Stuart 28
Bargmann, Julie 87
Barragan, Luis 154
Bart & Pieter 29
Barwitian Garden 48–9
Basson, James 30
Batcombe House 250
Batten, Conrad 15
Battersea Power Station Roof Gardens 280
Beazley, Elisabeth 8
Bedel, Nicolás 243
Beech Gardens 90–1
Beem, Margo van 303
Bekker, Koos 284
Belgium
  Bonemhoeve 82
  Marche Arboretum 272–3
  The Panoramic Garden 29
  private garden 39
  Ringenhof 302
  Tuin Oostveld 109
  Van Mol Garden 320
Benech, Louis 31
Bensley, Bill 32
Berg, Peter 33
Bergé, Pierre 68
Berger, Patrick 9
Berger Partnership 34
Bhagwat, Aniket 35
Bhagwat, Prabhakar 35
BIG (Bjarke Ingels Group) 269
Birrabirragal people 75
Birtle, Mark 23
Bishan-Ang Mo Kio Park 236, 278
Black Sand Cove 295
Blake, Jimi 36, 37
Blake, June 37
Blanc, Patrick 38
Blanchard, Hortense 100
Blanckaert, Piet 39
Blom, Jinny 40
Blomberg, Alejandro de Ávila 294
Blondie's Treehouse 105
Blue Stick Garden (Le Jardin de Bâtons Bleus) 69
Bluegreen 41
Boëdec, Gaël 42
Boekel, Arjan 43
Boekel Tuin & Landschap 43
Boeri, Stefano 44
Boeri Studio 44
Bonemhoeve 82
Bonnard, Pierre 83
Bosco Verticale 44
Boswall, Marian 45
Bosworth, William Welles 299
Botanica 46
Botswana Innovation Hub 115
Boulud, Daniel 105
Bouroullec, Ronan and Erwan 216
The Bower 163
Bowman, Mary 123
Boyce, Hallie 210
Bracken 261
Bradley-Hole, Christopher 47
Brady, Sheila 207
Brazil
  GMC Garden 126
  Instituto Inhotim 213
  Ramp House Garden 92
Bridgeman, Charles 318
Bridgewater, RHS Garden 127
Bristow, Ralph 48–9
Broad, Myles 93
Brockbank, Jane 50
Brockhoff, Fiona 51
Brookes, John 134
Brooklyn Grange 52
Brooklyn Museum Garden 156
Brooklyn Navy Yard Farm 52
Brooks, Miranda 53
Buccleuch, 10th Duke of 318
Buffalo Bayou Park 238
Bugg, Hugo 127
Bulla 54
Bunurong people 72
Burkett, Linda 295
Burle Marx, Roberto 92, 154, 213, 270
Burnett, Frances Hodgson 309
Burnett, James 209
Burrell, Charlie 277
Bury Court 47
Byl, Pieter van der 284
Byrns, Stephen F. 299

C
Caisson Gardens 137
CaixaForum Vertical Garden 38
Cala Mastella 228
Calatroni, Silvia 260
Calder, Alexander 148
Calistoga Residence 64
Calvo, Macarena 55
Cambo Gardens 104
Cambo Heritage Trust 104
Camerana, Benedetto 249
Campbell-Preston, Rosemary 70
Canada
  Aga Khan Park 304–5
  Blue Stick Garden (Le Jardin de Bâtons Bleus) 69
  Mountain & Trees, Waves & Pebbles 114
  Riley Park 46
  Toronto Music Garden 152
Cancela, Helder 56
Cantwell, Matthew 261
Cao, Andy 57
Cao Perrot 57
The Capri Garden 286
Caruncho, Fernando 58
Casa Acanto 242
Casa Finisterra 247
CCxA 69
Cells of Life 147
Central Garden at the Getty Center 140
Chamberlin, Powell and Bon 91
Changi Airport Garden 233
Chanticleer gardeners 59
The Chapel 50
Chapple, Horatio 314
Chatsworth House 81, 227
Chatto, Beth 9, 120, 134, 145, 307
Chelsea Australian Garden at Olinda 149
Chenshan Botanical Garden 292–3
Chihuly, Dale 60
Chihuly Garden & Glass 60
Chihuly Studio 60
Chile
  Bahía Azul 116
  Palmar de Panquehue 55
  Punta Pite 190
Chin, Calvin 79
China
  Hylla Alpine Garden 325
  Jinhua Mei Garden 297
  Panyu Central Park 282
  Quarry Garden 292–3
Choupis, Emmanuel 107
Church, Stuart 68
Church Barn 275
Church House 84
Cistercian Abbey and Chapel 133
Cistus 135
CJ Corp 219
Clément, Gilles 9, 61, 193, 262
Cleveland Public Library 166
Clorofilla Kindergarten 11, 184
CMG Landscape Architecture 62
Coastal Garden 222–3
Coastal Maine Botanical Gardens 240
Cobb, Henry N. 138

Cobe 63
Cochran, Andrea 64
Cohabitatio landscapes 88
Coke, John 47
The Collector Earl's Garden, Arundel Castle 27
Coloco 61
Colwell Shelor 65
Compton, Tania 66–7
Connelly, Maryanne 136
Conran, Jasper 68
Conran, Terence 8, 11
Constitution Garden 260
Cool Garden, RHS Rosemoor 291
Cooper, Anthony Ashley 79
Core City Park 87
Cormier, Claude 69
Corner, James 101
Coulson, Kate 70
Coward, Tom 71
Cox, Madison 68, 175
Cox, Sam 72
CPG Consultants 73
Craftworks 50
Craig Reynolds Landscape Architects 74
Cranbourne Gardens 285
Crawley, Mick 277
Crock, Christophe 373
Croes, Pieter 29
Cumberlidge, Will 15
Cunningham, Matthew 322
Cushman, Connor 52

D
Dandenong Ranges Botanic Garden 149
Dangar, William 75
Dangar Barin Smith 75
Darby, Andrew 148
Dariotis, Eleftherios 76
Das Reservat 167
David Austen Roses 23
DDS Projects 77
De Theetuin 157
Deborah Nevins & Associates 78
Delaney 10, 79, 315
Delomez, Dominique and Benoît 80
Denmark
　Amager Bakke Copenhill Rooftop Park 269
　The Opera Park 63
Determann, Ron 14
Devonshire, 12th Duke and Duchess of 81
Dhont, Erik 82, 302
Diblik, Roy 9, 83
Dickey, Page 84
Didier, Emmanuel 85
Didier Design Studio 85
Diller Scofidio + Renfro 101
Dillon, Helen 86
The Dillon Garden 86
D.I.R.T. Studio 87
Dja Dja Wurrung people 185, 248
Djurovic, Vladimir 304–5

Dogs' Garden 253
Donahue, Marcia 59
Dot Dash 105
Doxiadis+ 88
Doxiadis, Thomas 88
Doyle, James 144
Dreiseitl, Herbert 236
Dronet, Monique and Thierry 89
du Pont, Pierre 10, 312
Dunnett, Nigel 10, 46, 90–1
Duprat, Isabel 92
Durnamuck, Dundonnell 271
Dyck, Anthony van 27

E
Ebner, Manfred 22
Eckbo, Garrett 218
Eckersley, Rick 93
Eckersley Garden Architecture 93
Eden Project 117
Edible Schoolyard Project 310
Egret, Christophe 278
Eischeid, Austin 94
Elephant Park 110
Elgueta, Cristóbal 55
Elizabeth II, Queen 141
Elks-Smith, Helen 95
Elysian Landscapes 96
Empty River 155
Endemic School Grounds 77
Enea, Enzo 97
Enea Landscape Architecture 97
Enea Tree Museum 97
England
　The Alnwick Garden 227
　Batcombe House 250
　Battersea Power Station Roof Gardens 280
　Beech Gardens 90–1
　Bury Court 47
　Caisson Gardens 137
　The Chapel 50
　Chatsworth House 81, 227
　Church Barn 275
　Coastal Garden 222–3
　The Collector Earl's Garden 27
　Cool Garden, RHS Rosemoor 291
　Eden Project 117
　Elephant Park 110
　The Exchange 231
　Experimental Station 98–9
　Garden of Childhood Memories 177
　The Garden of Tranquility 175
　Granby Winter Garden 20
　Grasslands Garden, Horniman Museum and Gardens 132
　Gravetye Manor 26, 71
　Great Dixter 10, 26, 71, 106, 239, 252, 302
　Hailstone Barn 13
　Hilldrop 169
　Horatio's Garden 314
　The Kitchen Garden, RHS Garden Bridgewater 127

　Knepp Castle Walled Garden 277
　Malverleys 239
　Mayfield Park 278
　the Orozco Garden 212
　Orpheus 318
　Perch Hill 237
　Plaz Metaxu 102
　private gardens 15, 45, 95, 143, 170, 181, 183, 245, 246, 252, 274
　Re-Green North Kensington 121
　Round Dell 309
　Sculpture by the Lakes 122
　Thames Barrier Park 232
　U.S. Embassy London Gardens 210
　Walled Garden 151
　Wildlife Garden, RHS Garden Wisley 10, 230
　Wildside 317
　Wynyard Hall Rose Garden 23
Erik Dhont Landscape Architects 82
Erlam, Emily 98–9
Erskine family 104
Eskenasy, Alex 144
Estudio Emmer 54
Estudio Ome 100
Euser, Dan 308
Everett, Thomas H. 207
Evoke International Design 46
The Exchange 231
Expedia HQ 281
Experimental Station 98–9

F
Fabbrica 111
Falcon Ridge 120
Farm Fields 136
Farrar Pond Garden 188
Federal Twist 112
Fernandes, Errol Reuben 132
Feuillet, Raoul-Auger 31
Field Operations 101
Filippi, Clara 67
Filippi, Olivier 10, 12, 67, 70, 107, 195
Fire and Beauty 10, 189
Fishermans Bay 268
Flanner, Ben 52
Fleurquin, Ignacio 54
Folcarelli, Mikel 125
Fomenko, Yury 192
Fondazione André Heller 130
Forbes, Alasdair 102
Ford, Gordon 72
Forest Garden 100
Forrest, Andrea and Peter 103
Förster, Susanne 33
Forsyth, Elliott 104
Fox, Kohn Pedersen 105
France
　Jardin Agapanthe 290
　Jardin des Migrations 12
　Jardin du Tiers-Paysage 61
　Jardin Intérieur à Ciel Ouvert 80
　Le Grand Launay 42
　Le Jardin de Berchigranges 89

　Le Jardin Plume 125, 234
　Le Terrain 205
　Les Jardins de L'Imaginaire 124
　Les Jardins d'Étretat 119
　Luberon Garden 70
　Museum Park Louvre-Lens 191
　private gardens 30, 193, 197, 206
　Water Theatre Grove 31
Frederickson, Kristin 312
French, Morag 17
Friedman, Tom 41
Friedrich, Caspar David 167
Frinke, Michael 145
Fukuda, Tomoyoshi 324
Fuller, Richard Buckminster 117
Future Green Studio 105

G
Gadigal people 75, 186
Garden in the Air 311
Garden of Australian Dreams 244
Garden of Childhood Memories 177
Garden of the Giant 57
Garden Mizuniwa 153
Garden of Rohuna 221
Garden in the Round 134
The Garden of Tranquility 175
Gardens by the Bay 113
Gardens of the Jameel Arts Centre 306
Gardner, Isabella Stewart 187
Garrett, Fergus 10, 106, 111, 239, 252
Gates, Theaster 256
Gay, Jennifer 107
Gehry, Frank 62, 165, 216
George King Architects 121
Germany
　ABB Factory 146
　Hortus 145
　Landschaftspark Duisburg-Nord 9, 164
　Luisenpark 254–5
　Oudolf Garden 216
　private garden 33
　Ruin Garden 167
　Schau- und Sichtungsgarten Hermannshof 8–9, 229, 258
　Vitra Campus 10
Gerritsen, Henk 8, 43, 118
Getty Center, Central Garden at the 140
Geuze, Adriaan 313
GGN 83, 108
Ghost Wash 65
Ghyselen, Chris 109
Giardini Pistola 300
Giardino di Piuca 226
Giardino Segreto 249
Gillespies 110
Giubbilei, Luciano 111
Glen, Stuart 115
Glenstone Water Court 289
GMC Garden 126
The Goat Garden 76

327

Golden, James 112
Gomes, João Paulo 56
Gooch, Thomas 248
Gormley, Antony 165
Granby Winter Garden 20
Grant, Andrew 113
Grant Associates 113
Grantham, Martin 14
Grasslands Garden 132
Gravetye Manor 26, 71
Great Dixter 10, 26, 71, 106, 239, 252, 302
Greece
　The Goat Garden 76
　Ilias Estate 66–7
　Kiradikea 107
　landscapes of Cohabitatio 88
　Stavros Niarchos Foundation Cultural Center 78
Green Over Grey 114
GREENinc 115
Greenspan, Adam 233, 289
Grimaldi.Nacht 243
Grimm, Juan 116
Grimshaw, Sir Nicholas 117
Grintjes, Jelle 118
Grivko, Alexandre 119
Groningen City Garden 24–5
Ground Studio Landscape Architecture 120
Groupe Signes 232
Grow to Know 121
Grupo de Diseño Urbano (GDU) 257
Gudgeon, Simon and Monique 122
Guichard, Hubert 12
Guilfoyle, William 162
Guilfoyle's Volcano 162
Gustafson, Kathryn 123, 124
Gustafson Porter + Bowman 113, 123
Gwynne, John 125

H
Hadid, Zaha 216
Hailstone Barn 13
Hall, Sir John 23
Hanazaki 126
Hanazaki, Alex 126
Hannon, Dylan 14
Hare, Tom 230
Haring, Keith 130
Harpur, Charlie 277
Harris, Charlotte 127
Harris, Cyril 102
Harris, Lawren 114
Harris, Steven 247
Harris Bugg Studio 127
Hartlage, Richard 60
Haugeland, Ive 265
Haverkamp, Bart 29
Hayashi, Mitsushige 224
Hayden-Smith, Tayshan 121
Haynes-Roberts 136
Heatherwick Studio 128–9
Heller, André 57, 130

Heller, Margot 212
Henning Larsen 236
Hers-Schaffner, Karin 46
Hicks, David 26
Hidden Hideaway 74
The High Line 9, 62, 101, 164, 167, 198
Hilderbrand, Reed 238
Hill of the Buddha 16
Hilldrop 169
Hinkley, Daniel J. 9, 131
Hira, Kinya 287
Hitchmough, James 10, 81, 132, 277
Hobhouse, Penelope 131
Hocker 133
Hocker, David 133
Hoerr, Douglas 134
Hoerr Schaudt 134
Hofu City Crematorium 182
Hogan, Sean 135
Holekamp, Kara 287
Hollander, Edmund 136
Hollander Design 136
Höller, Carsten 216
Holmes, David 240
Honey, Amanda 137
Honey, Phil 137
Hood, Walter J. 138
Hood Design Studio 138
Horatio's Garden 314
Horniman Museum and Gardens 132
Hortus 145
Howard, Susan 202
Howard, Thomas 27
Hull, Miller 34
Hung, Ying-yu 282
Hunting Brook Gardens 36
Husby, Chad 14
Hwang, Jihae 139
Hylla Alpine Garden 325

I
Il Nature 119
Ilias Estate 66–7
In the Line of Fire 79
India
　Rao Jodha Desert Rock Park 160
　Udaan 35
Indian Ecological Restoration Alliance 160
Indonesia
　Tanatap Frame Garden 235
　Villa Bebek 316
Ingels, Bjarke 269
Instituto Inhotim 213
International African American Museum 138
Irish, Mary 208–9
Irwin, Robert 140
Isabella Stewart Gardner Museum 187
Ishigami, Junya 153
Ishihara, Kazuyuki 141
Italcementi 279
Italy
　Agro-Ornamental Park i.Land 279

　Bosco Verticale 44
　Clorofilla Kindergarten 11, 184
　Fabbrica 111
　Giardini Pistola 300
　Giardino di Piuca 226
　La Pellegrina 28
　La Pista 500 Roof Garden 249
　Podere Casanuova di Sicelle 21
　private gardens 225
　Trauttmansdorff Castle 22
Izumi, Yukiyo 142

J
Jack, Sheila 143
Jaffe, Norman 161
James, Joseph 238
James Doyle Design Associates 144
Jane Gregory Garden 238
Janke, Peter 145
Jansen, Coen 8
Japan
　Empty River 155
　Garden Mizuniwa 153
　Hill of the Buddha 16
　Mihara Garden 141
　The Rose Garden at Nakanojo Gardens 324
　Tashiro-no-Mori 142
　Tokachi Millennium Forest: the Meadow Garden 224
　Ueno Farm 298
　Yu-Kyu-En 182
Jardin Agapanthe 290
Jardin des Métis/Redford Gardens 69
Jardin des Migrations 12
Jardin du Tiers-Paysage 61
Jardin Intérieur à Ciel Ouvert 80
Jardin Seco 195
Jardins de Luxembourg 18
Jarman, Derek 9, 99
Jaugstetter, Bettina 146, 216, 322
Jekyll, Gertrude 8, 69
Jencks, Charles 147, 165, 282
Jencks, Maggie Keswick 11, 165, 282
Jensen, Jens 134
Jewel 233
Jianguo, Sui 41
Jinhua Mei Garden 297
Jodry, Jean-François 9
Joh Sung-Yong Urban Architecture 263
Johannsohn, Sally 148
Johnson, Philip 149, 270
Jones, A. Quincy 209, 287
Jones, Inigo 27
Jones, Jane 150
Jones, Robert 131
Joseph, Colm 151
Julie Moir Messervy Design Studio 152
Jungles, Raymond 154
Junya Ishigami + Associates 153
Jupiter Artland 147

K
Kabi Kabi people 267
Kafka, Philip 87
Karkalla 51
Kass, Deborah 156
Kastner, Renate 301
Katran, Sergey 119
Kawai, Takashi 324
Keane, Marc Peter 155
Keightley, Matt 245
Ken Smith Workshop 270
Kenya
　Arijiju 40
　Ollie House 288
Khoo Teck Puat Hospital 73
Kiley, Dan 308
Kim, Jungyoon 219
Kim, Mikyoung 188
Kingwood Center Gardens 94
Kiradikea 107
Kirby, Simon 173
The Kitchen Garden, RHS Garden Bridgewater 127
Klausing, Brook 156
Kligerman, Thomas 136
Klinta Trädgård 158–9
Kloet, Jacqueline van der 157
Knepp Castle 277
Knidel, Jean-Louis 12
Kolb, Peter 284
Korn, Peter 158–9
Kramer, Hans 194
Kremali, Terpsithea 88
Krishen, Pradip 160
Ku, Andrea 20
Kuwait, Constitution Garden 260

L
La Estancia de Cafayate 251
La Mexicana Park 257
La Pellegrina 28
La Pista 500 Roof Garden 249
LaGuardia, Christopher 161
LaGuardia Design Group 161
Laidlaw, Andrew 162
Lake Flato Architects 85
Lamprecht, Barbara 218
Land Morphology 60
The Landscape Studio 288
Landschaftspark Duisburg-Nord 9, 164
Langendoen, Annemieke 25
Larry Weaner Landscape Associates 163
Latz, Peter 164
Latz + Partner 9, 164
LDA Design 280
Le Grand Launay 42
Le Jardin de Berchigranges 89
Le Jardin Plume 125, 234
Le Nôtre, André 31
Le Pavillon 105
Le Terrain 205
Lee, Tom 256
Lee Kuan Yew 113

Léger, Fernand 130
Lennox-Boyd, Arabella 165, 250
Leopold, Rob 8, 118
Les Jardins de L'Imaginaire 124
Les Jardins d'Étretat 119
Leslie, Shannon 34
Lethlean, Taylor Cullity 285
Lichtenstein, Roy 130
Lift Studio 41
Lin, Maya 166
Lin, Tan 166
Lincke, Tanja 167
Linden, Ton ter 8, 43, 118, 168
Little, John 9, 169
Little Island 128–9
Lloyd, Christopher 9, 10, 26, 106, 239, 252
Longstaffe-Gowan, Todd 170
Longwood Gardens West Conservatory 10, 312
Louis Sullivan Arch 83
Louis XIV 31
Luberon Garden 70
Luisenpark 254–5
Lur 262
Lutsko, Ron 171
Lutyens, Edwin 106
Luxembourg, Jardins de Luxembourg 18
Luz, Hans 258

M
Maas, Winy 198
Mabberley, Sue and Ian 172
McCoy, Michael 185
McGregor Coxall 186
McHarg, Ian 9
Mack Landscaping 87
MacKensie, Lincoln 87
McKim, Mead & White 156
McKinney, David 204
McMackin, Rebecca 156
McVicar, Jekka 277
Maggie's Dundee 11, 165
Magoon, Nancy and Bob 41
Magoon Sculpture Garden 41
Maher, T.J. 173
Maia, Margarida 9, 174
Majstorovic, Dragi 267
Maki, Fumihiko 175
Maki and Associates 175
Malverleys 239
Mamaku 315
Manfredi, Michael 312
Manoylo, Victoria 176
Marche Arboretum 272–3
Maria, Ula 177
Marie Antoinette 119
Marnanie 26
Marquez, Victor 257
Marriot, Michael 23
Martha Schwartz Partners 259
Martino, Steve 10, 178
Martos, Fernando 179
Masedo, Juan 180
Masía Eolo 154

Massey, Tom 181
Masuno, Shunmyō 182
Maurières, Arnaud 214–15
Máximapark 313
Mayfield Park 278
Maynard, Arne 183
Mazzucchelli, Cristina 11, 184
Mazzullo, Emma 250
Mazzullo + Russell 250
Meacock, Anthony Engi 20
Meier, Richard 279
Melbourne Gardens 162
Messervy, Julie Moir 152
Meta Rooftop 62
Mexico
   Casa Acanto 242
   Casa Finistera 247
   Forest Garden 100
   La Mexicana Park 257
   Oaxaca Ethnobotanical Garden 96, 294
   Michael Van Valkenburgh Associates 187
Mihara Garden 141
Mikyoung Kim Design 188
Miró, Joan 148
Mitchell, Bill and Diane 10, 189
MNLA 128–9
Moller, Teresa 190
Monet, Claude 119, 162
The Monk's Garden 187
Montagu, Ralph, 1st Duke of 318
Montiel, Rozana 100
Moore, Henry 238
Moreu, Belén 195
Moritaki 103
Morley, Jonathan 34
Morocco
   Anima 130
   Azaren 214–15
   Garden of Rohuna 221
   Villa Mabrouka 68
Morrison, Darrel 9
Morrison, Toni 138
Mosbach, Catherine 191
Mosbach Paysagistes 191
Mountain & Trees, Waves & Pebbles 114
Mountain and Water 219
Moving Seeds 139
MOX Landscape Architecture 192
MuCEM (Museum of Civilizations of Europe and the Mediterranea) 12
Muller, Camille 193
Muller, Ton 194
Municipality of Amsterdam 194
Muñoz y Moreu 195
Muñoz-Rojas, Clara 195
Mure, Véronique 12
Murphy, Dominick 196
Murphy + Sheanon 196
Murray, Sam 52
Mus, Jean 197
Museum of Modern Art 270
Museum Park Louvre-Lens 191
Musk Cottage 93

MVRDV 198
MXarchitecture 107

N
Nakanojo Gardens 324
Nant-y-Bedd 172
National Museum of Australia 244
Native Plant Garden at New York Botanical Garden 207
Naxi people 325
NBBJ 14
Negri, Lisa 199
Nehring, Pedro 213
Neil Dusheiko Architects 143
Nelson, Jay 62
Nelson Byrd Woltz 175, 200
The Netherlands
   De Theetuin 157
   Groningen City Garden 24–5
   Máximapark 313
   Orlyplein Sloterdijk 194
   Prairie Garden 229
   private gardens 118, 168, 321
   Rooftop Garden 43
   Wilde Weelde Wereld 303
Neutra, Richard 218
Nevell, Claudia 201
Nevell Garden 201
Nevins, Deborah 78
New York Botanical Garden 207
New Zealand
   Fishermans Bay 268
   Mamaku 315
   Moritaki 103
   private garden 307
   Te Henui Cemetery Garden 211
   Welton House 217
Nichol, Shannon 108
Nicolson, Adam 237
Noble, Bill 202
Nordfjell, Ulf 203
Norris, Kelly D. 10, 204
North Wind 83
Noten, Dries van 302
Nucera, Marc 205
Nusiner, Lucia 279
Nuttall, Duncan 15

O
Oaxaca Ethnobotanical Garden 96, 294
Ocean Road Landscaping 266
Oceanfront Garden 161
Oehme, van Sweden 163, 207
Oehme, Wolfgang 8, 9, 207, 252
OJB Landscape Architecture 208–9
Old Rose Garden, Great Dixter 10, 106
OLIN 210
Olin, Laurie 166
Oliveira do Hospital, Quinta do Lameiro Longo 56
Oliver, Sue 211
Ollie House 288
Olmsted, Frederick Law 270

O'Neill, Alejandro 206
O'Neill, Kevin 26
Ooyen, Ben van 303
The Opera Park 63
The Orchard 241
Orff, Kate 256
Orlyplein Sloterdijk 194
Orozco, Gabriel 212
the Orozco Garden 212
Orpheus 318
Orsini, Luiz Carlos 213
Ossart, Eric 214–15
Oswald, Ellen 255
Othoniel, Jean-Michel 31
Oudolf, Anja 8
Oudolf, Piet 8, 43, 94, 99, 112, 118, 174, 321
   Bury Court 47
   The High Line 101, 167
   Lurie Garden 10, 157
   Millennium Park 83
   Oudolf Garden 10, 216
   Ringenhof 302

P
Page, Russell 26, 225
Palmar de Panquehue 55
Palmer, Ross and Wendy 217
Pamela Burton & Company 218
Panama, Masía Eolo 154
Pangalou, Helli 78
The Panoramic Garden 29
Panyu Central Park 282
Park, Yoonjin 219
PARKKIM 219
Parks and Wildlife Commission of the Northern Territory 220
Parque Central 123
Pasti, Umberto 221
Patel Taylor 232
Patthana 173
Paul, Anthony 222–3
Paxton, Joseph 81
Paz, Bernardo 213
Peabody Essex Museum 200
Pearson, Dan 8, 10, 11, 81, 224
Pejrone, Paolo 225
Pellacini, Fabio 311
Penn State University 85
Perazzi, Antonio 226
Perch Hill 237
Percy, Jane, Duchess of Northumberland 227
Pérez-Ventana, Alfonso 228
Perrot, Xavier 57
Phyto Studio 85
Piano, Renzo 187, 216, 249
Picasso, Pablo 130
Plakias, Anastasia Cole 52
Planting Strategies 17
Plaz Metaxu 102
Podere Casanuova di Sicelle 21
Poiraud, Patrick 114
Pollinator and Bird Garden, Penn State University 85

Polshek, James 156
Pomeroy, Sue 271
Porter, Neil 123
Portugal
  private garden 174
  Quinta do Lameiro Longo 56
Pot, Lianne 229
Powell, Ann-Marie 9–10, 230
Prairie Garden 229
Price, Sarah 231
Prince Concepts 87
Provost, Allain 9, 232
Punta Pite 190
PWP Landscape Architecture 233, 289, 308
Pye, William 227

Q
Quarry Garden 292–3
Quibel, Patrick and Sylvie 234
Quinn, Justin 144
Quinta do Lameiro Longo 56

R
RAD+ar 235
Rafiuddin, Ishtiaq 87
Ramboll Studio Dreiseitl 236
Ramp House Garden 92
Rao Jodha Desert Rock Park 160
Raven, Sarah 237
RDR 54
Re-Green North Kensington 121
Reading a Garden 166
The Red Roof 283
Reed, Doug 238
Reed Hilderbrand 312
Reese, Mat 239
Reford, Elsie 69
Rengthong, Jirachai 32
Renzo Piano Building Workshop 78
Republic of Ireland
  the Dillon Garden 86
  Hunting Brook Gardens 36
  Patthana 173
  private garden 37
  Sheilstown Garden 196
Reyle, Anselm 167
Reynolds, Craig 74
RHS Garden Bridgewater 127
RHS Garden Wisley 10, 230
RHS Rosemoor 291
Ricci, Ana García 54
Riddell, Bruce John 240
Riddle, Dean 241
Rijs, Jacob van 198
Riley Park 46
Rilke, Rainer Maria 102
Ringenhof 302
Rionda, Fernanda 242
Ritchie, Ian 124
Rivera, Manuel Diaz 247
Robinson, William 26, 71
Robredo, Amalia 243

Rodin, Auguste 130
Roof Garden, Museum of Modern Art 270
Rooftop Garden, Rotterdam 43
Room 4.1.3 244
Roos, Karen 284
The Rose Garden at Nakanojo Gardens 324
Rosebank Landscaping 245
Rosemoor, RHS 291
Rosengarten family 59
Rothwell, Sara Jane 246
Round Dell 309
Rousseau, Henri 106
Royal Oaks Residence 218
Ruddick, Margie 247
Ruin Garden, Berlin 167
The Ruin Garden at Chanticleer 59
Rush, Catherine 248
Rush Wright Associates 248
Rusli, Antonius Richard 235
Ruspa, Cristiana 249
Russell, Libby 250
Russia, private gardens 17, 192
Ruys, Mien 8, 168

S
Sackville-West, Vita 26
Safdie, Moshe 233
Safdie Architects 233
Sager McFadden, Mary 218
Saguier, Vero 251
St Kitts & Nevis 295
Saint Laurent, Yves 68
Sakonnet Garden 125
Salter, Andrew 252
Sam Cox Landscape 72
Sampedro, Álvaro 253
SANAA 153, 191
Sand Garden 248
Sanderson, Parker 135
Sanzone, Sheri 41
SAOTA 311
Saperia, Phillip 112
Sauer, Harald 254–5
Saviñón, Susana Rojas 100
Scape, Tom Lee Park 256
Scape Design 30
Schaffner, Otto 46
Schalit, Jean 42
Schau- und Sichtungsgarten Hermannshof 8–9, 229, 258
Schell, Bosco 84
Schjetnan, Mario 257
Schmidt, Cassian 8–9, 258
Schuth, Mirjam 33
Schwartz, Martha 10, 69, 259
Scotland
  Cambo Gardens 104
  Cells of Life 147
  Durnamuck, Dundonnell 271
  Maggie's Dundee 11, 165
Sculpture by the Lakes 122
SdARCH 260
Secret Gardens, Bracken 261

Seo-Ahn Total Landscape 263
Seonyudo Park 263
Seoul Botanic Park 139
Seoullo 7017 Skygarden 198
Shades of Green Landscape Architecture 264–5
Shaw, Peter 266
Shaw, Wesley 132
Sheanon, Colum 196
Sheilstown Garden 196
Sheldon, Kirsti 267
Shelor, Michele 65
Shintani, Midori 224
Shively, Evan 62
Simpson, Jill and Richard 268
Sinatra Murphy 266
Singapore
  Bishan-Ang Mo Kio Park 236, 278
  Gardens by the Bay 113
  Jewel 233
  Khoo Teck Puat Hospital 73
Site Workshop 14
Sitta, Vladimir 244
SLA 269
Smid, Gijsbert 82
Smit, Sir Tim 117
Smith, Ken 270
Smith Allen 62
Sohbati, Nahal 296
Soos, Will 271
South Africa
  Babylonstoren 284
  Endemic School Grounds 77
  Garden in the Air 311
South Korea
  Mountain and Water 219
  Moving Seeds 139
  Seonyudo Park 263
  Seoullo 7017 Skygarden 198
South London Gallery 212
Spain
  CaixaForum Vertical Garden 38
  Cala Mastella 228
  Dogs' Garden 253
  Jardin Seco 195
  Lur 262
  Parque Central 123
  private gardens 58, 179, 180
  Watermill Garden 301
The Spheres 14
Spoelberch, Philippe de 272–3
Stacewicz, Robert 274
Stacke, Gareth 52
Stavros Niarchos Foundation Cultural Center 78
Steenkamp, Danie 77
Stefano Boeri Architetti 44
Stefano Marinaz Landscape Architecture 275
Stickley, Kate 19
STIMSON 276
Stimson, Stephen and Lauren 276
Stone Hill 185
Stonefields 26
Stones, Ellis 72

Stuart-Smith, Tom 10, 81, 143, 175, 277
Stubbergaard, Dan 63
Studio Egret West 278
Studio Gang 256
Studio GPT 279
Studio Shamshiri 287
Stufano, Marco Polo 299
Sturgeon, Andy 280
Summerhome Garden 199
Sunnylands Center & Gardens 208–9
Sunnymeade 266
Surfacedesign 281
SWA Group 238, 282
Swann, David 51
Swarovski Crystal Worlds 57
Sweden
  Klinta Trädgård 158–9
  private garden 203
Sweden, James van 8, 9, 196, 207
Switzerland, Enea Tree Museum 97

T
TAA Design 283
Tabak, Gert 168
Takano Landscape Planning 224
Tallamy, Douglas 84
Tanatap Frame Garden 235
Taniguchi, Yoshio 270
Taravella, Patrice 284
Tashiro-no-Mori 142
Tasmania, private garden 148
Te Henui Cemetery Garden 211
Ten Eyck, Christine 286
Terra Design Studio 94
Terremoto 287
Thailand, Baan Botanica 32
Thames Barrier Park 232
Thébault, Madame 119
Thomas, Alexandre 290
Thomas, Bill 59
Thomas, Graham Stuart 131
Thomas Phifer and Partners 289
Thompson, Jo 291
Thompson, Paul 285
Thoreau, Henry David 188
Three Oaks 10, 204
THUPDI 292–3
Tilghman, Timothy 299
Tokachi Millennium Forest: the Meadow Garden 224
Toledo, Francisco 294
Toll, Julie 295
Tom Lee Park 256
TOPOPHYLA 296
Toronto Music Garden 152
Townshend Landscape Architects 175
Trainor, Bernard 120
Tranter, John 186
Trauttmansdorff Castle 22
Tree, Isabella 277
Trivelli, Alessandro 260
Truen, Greg 311
Tsinghua University, Beijing, Quarry Garden 292–3

Tsukamoto, Konami 324
Tuin Oostveld 109
Turenscape 297

U
Udaan 35
Ueno, Sayuki 298
Ueno Farm 298
Ukraine
　private garden 176
　Zhyva Nyva 323
Undecorated 87
United Arab Emirates, Gardens of the Jameel Arts Centre 306
United States
　9/11 Memorial 308
　A Quincy Jones vs. Terremoto 287
　African Ancestors Memorial Garden 138
　Arroyo Residence 178
　Balenciaga store frontage 96
　The Bower 163
　Brooklyn Museum Garden 156
　Brooklyn Navy Yard Farm 52
　Calistoga Residence 64
　The Capri Garden 286
　Central Garden at the Getty Center 140
　Chihuly Garden & Glass 60
　Church House 84
　Cistercian Abbey and Chapel 133
　Core City Park 87
　Edible Schoolyard Project 310
　Expedia HQ 281
　Falcon Ridge 120
　Farm Fields 136
　Farrar Pond Garden 188
　Federal Twist 112
　Garden in the Round 134
　Ghost Wash 65
　Glenstone Water Court 289
　Hidden Hideaway 74
　The High Line 9, 62, 101, 164, 167, 198
　In the Line of Fire 79
　Jane Gregory Garden 238
　Kingwood Center Gardens 94
　Le Pavillon 105
　Little Island 128–9
　Longwood Gardens West Conservatory 10, 312
　Louis Sullivan Arch 83
　Magoon Sculpture Garden 41
　Meta Rooftop 62
　The Monk's Garden 187
　Museum of Modern Art Roof Garden 270
　Native Plant Garden at New York Botanical Garden 207
　Oceanfront Garden 161
　The Orchard 241
　Peabody Essex Museum 200
　Pollinator and Bird Garden 85
　private gardens 19, 53, 108, 144, 171, 202, 264–5, 276, 322

Reading a Garden 166
Royal Oaks Residence 218
The Ruin Garden at Chanticleer 59
Sakonnet Garden 125
The Spheres 14
Summerhome Garden 199
Sunnylands Center & Gardens 208–9
Three Oaks 10, 204
Tom Lee Park 256
Vayo Meditation Garden 240
Von Schlegell Garden 135
Walled Garden, Untermyer Park 299
Whidbey Island Residence 34
Windcliff 131
Ysidro, Montecito 296
Untermyer, Samuel 299
Untermyer Gardens Conservancy 299
Untermyer Park, Walled Park 299
Urquhart & Hunt 300
Urquijo, Miguel 301
Urquijo-Kastner 301
Uruguay, private garden 243
U.S. Embassy London Gardens 210

V
Valentien + Valentien 292–3
Van Mol Garden 320
Vangheluwe, Patrick 302
Vayo Meditation Garden 240
Vegini, Maurizio 279
Versailles 31, 318
Versluis, Emiel 303
Vésian, Nicole de 205
Vienna Nord Healing Gardens 259
Vietnam, The Red Roof 283
Viguier, Jean-Paul 9
Villa Bebek 316
Villa Mabrouka 68
Vis à Vis Ontwerpers 303
Vitra Campus 10, 216
Vladimir Djurovic Landscape Architecture 175, 304–5
Vogel, Anouk 306
von Opel family 239
Von Schlegell Garden 135
Vries, Nathalie de 198
Vugteveen, Ryan 41

W
Wadandi Noongar people 189
Wakelin, Jo 307
Walama | Ballast Point Park 186
Wales, Nant-y-Bedd 172
Walker, Peter 308
Walker, Sophie 309
Walled Garden, Knepp Castle 277
Walled Garden, Suffolk 151
Walled Garden, Untermyer Park 299
Walling, Edna 72
Walser, Urs 258
Wangal people 186
Water Theatre Grove, Versailles 31
Watermill Garden 301

Waters, Alice 310
Watson, Franchesca 311
Watson Pellacini 311
Weaner, Larry 9, 163
Weinfeld, Isay 105
Weinmaster, Mike 114
Weiss, George David and Claire 247
Weiss, Marion 312
Weiss/Manfredi 312
Weller, Richard 244
Welton House 217
West 8 313
West, Claudia 85
West, Cleve 314
West, David 278
Whidbey Island Residence 34
White, Michael 316
White, Xanthe 315
Wijaya, Made 316
Wilde Weelde Wereld 303
Wildlife Garden, RHS Garden Wisley 230
Wildside 317
Wiley, Keith 317
Wilkie, Kim 318
Wilkinson, Kurt 319
WilkinsonEyre 113
Williams, Kevin Philip 199
Wilson, Nicky and Robert 147
Windcliff 131
Wintour, Anna 53
Wirtz, Jacques and Peter 227, 320
Wirtz, Martin 320
Wirtz International 227, 320
Wisley, RHS Garden 10, 230
Witte, Tom de 321
Woodleigh School Senior Campus 72
Woodruff, Adam 322
Woods, Christopher 59
Wright, Michael 248
Wynn-Jones, Bleddyn and Sue 309
Wynyard Hall, Rose Garden 23

Y
Yalamurra 319
Yazykova, Oksana 323
Yo-Yo Ma 152
Yoshida, Hiro 103
Yoshitani, Keiko 324
Yoshiya, Hiromitsu 324
YPF Service Station 54
Ysidro, Montecito 296
Yu, Kongjian 297
Yu-Kyu-En 182
Yuin nation 261

Z
Zárate, Luis 294
Zhao Tuo 282
Zhou Liangjun 325
Zhou Ting 325
Zhyva Nyva 323
Z'scape 325
Zuckerberg, Mark 62

GARDEN DIRECTORY

This directory provides a list of public gardens featured in this book – gardens that can be visited throughout the year, or by prior arrangement, or on regular open days. Please check individual garden websites for opening hours and visiting information. Many of the gardens illustrated are private and not open to the public, and any garden not listed in the directory can be assumed to fall into this category. Other gardens offer restricted visitor access through organizations such as the national garden scheme in the United Kingdom (www.ngs.org.uk), the garden conservancy in the United States (www.gardenconservancy.org) and the My Open Garden scheme in Australia (www.Myopengarden.com.au).

Garden opening times may vary across the year and access may be limited during restoration work. It is advisable to check the times and dates of opening in advance of making travel arrangements.

ARGENTINA
YPF Service Station, Buenos Aires

AUSTRALIA
Alice Springs Desert Park, Mparntwe | Alice Springs, Northern Territory
Australian Garden, Cranbourne Gardens, Victoria
Chelsea Australian Garden at Olinda, Dandenong Ranges Botanic Garden, Olinda, Victoria
Garden of Australian Dreams, National Museum of Australia, Canberra, Australian Capital Territory
Guilfoyle's Volcano, Melbourne Gardens, Melbourne, Victoria
Walama | Ballast Point Park, Birchgrove, Sydney, New South Wales
Woodleigh School Senior Campus, Langwarrin South, Victoria

AUSTRIA
Garden of the Giant, Swarovski Kristallwelten, Wattens
Vienna Nord Healing Gardens, Klinik Floridsdorf, Vienna

BELGIUM
Marche Arboretum, Marche-en-Famenne

BRAZIL
Instituto Inhotim, Brumadinho

CANADA
Aga Khan Park, Toronto, Ontario
Blue Stick Garden (Le Jardin De Bâtons Bleus), Jardins De Métis/Reford Gardens, Métis-Sur-Mer, Québec
Mountain & Trees, Waves & Pebbles, Guildford, Surrey, British Columbia
Toronto Music Garden, Queen's Quay West, Toronto

CHILE
Punta Pite, Near Santiago

CHINA
Hylla Alpine Garden, Hylla Vintage Hotel, Lijiang, Yunnan Province
Jinhua Mei Garden, Jinhua, Zhejiang Province
Panyu Central Park, Guangzhou, Guangdong Province
Quarry Garden, Chenshan Botanical Garden, Shanghai

DENMARK
Amager Bakke Copenhill Rooftop Park, Copenhagen
The Opera Park, Copenhagen

DUBAI
Gardens of the Jameel Arts Centre

FRANCE
Jardin Agapanthe, Grigneuseville
Jardin des Migrations, Mucem, Marseilles
Jardin Du Tiers-Paysage, Saint-Nazaire
Les Jardins D'étretat, Étretat, Normandy
Les Jardins De L'imaginaire, Terrasson-Lavilledieu
Museum Park Louvre-Lens, Lens
Water Theatre Grove, Versailles

GERMANY
Oudolf Garden, Vitra Campus, Weil Am Rhein
Landschaftspark Duisburg-Nord, Duisburg-Meiderich
Luisenpark, Mannheim
Schau- und Sichtungsgarten Hermannshof, Weinheim

GREECE
Stavros Niarchos Foundation Cultural Center, Athens

INDIA
Rao Jodha Desert Rock Park, Jodhpur, Rajasthan

INDONESIA
Tanatap Frame Garden, Jakarta

ITALY
Agro-Ornamental Park I.Land, Bergamo
Bosco Verticale, Porta Nuova, Milan
Clorofilla Kindergarten, Milan
Giardini Pistola, Puglia
La Pellegrina, Viterbo
La Pista 500 Roof Garden, Turin
The Gardens of Trauttmansdorff Castle, Merano

JAPAN
Hill of the Buddha, Makomanai Takino Cemetery, Sapporo
Garden Mizuniwa, Tochigi
Mihara Garden, Mihara, Nagasaki City
Tokachi Millennium Forest: The Meadow Garden, Kamikawa District, Hokkaido
Ueno Farm, Asahikawa, Hokkaido
The Rose Garden at Nakanojo Gardens, Nakanojo, Agatsuma

KUWAIT
Constitution Garden, Kuwait City

LUXEMBOURG
Jardins de Luxembourg, Luxembourg City

MEXICO
La Mexicana Park, Mexico City
Oaxaca Ethnobotanical Garden, Oaxaca City

MOROCCO
Anima, Ourika Valley

NETHERLANDS
Groningen City Garden, Groningen,
Máximapark, Utrecht
Orlyplein Sloterdijk, Amsterdam
Rooftop Garden, Rotterdam
Wilde Weelde Wereld, Bloemenpark Appeltern, Appeltern

NEW ZEALAND
Te Henui Cemetery Garden, New Plymouth, Taranaki, North Island

SINGAPORE
Bishan-Ang Mo Kio Park
Gardens by the Bay, Marina Bay
Jewel, Changi Airport Garden
Khoo Teck Puat Hospital, Yishun

SOUTH AFRICA
Endemic School Grounds, Green School, Paarl
Babylonstoren, Franschhoek

SOUTH KOREA
Mountain And Water, CJ Blossom Park, Gwanggyo
Moving Seeds, Seoul Botanic Park, Seoul
Seonyudo Park, Seoul
Seoullo 7017 Skygarden, Seoul

SPAIN
Caixaforum Vertical Garden, Madrid
Parque Central, Valencia

SWITZERLAND
Enea Tree Museum, Rapperswil-Jona, Zurich

UK
Beech Gardens, Barbican Centre, London
Cambo Gardens, St Andrews
Cells of Life, Jupiter Artland, near Edinburgh
Chatsworth House, Bakewell, Derbyshire
Cool Garden, RHS Rosemoor, Near Torrington, Devon
Eden Project, Bodelva, Cornwall
Elephant Park, Elephant and Castle, London
Granby Winter Garden, Granby, Liverpool
Grasslands Garden, Horniman Museum and Gardens, London
Horatio's Garden, Salisbury, Wiltshire
Maggie's Dundee, Ninewells Hospital, Dundee
Mayfield Park, Manchester
Old Rose Garden, Great Dixter, Northiam, East Sussex
Orpheus, Boughton House, Kettering, Northamptonshire
Re-Green North Kensington, London
Round Dell, Borde Hill, Haywards Heath, West Sussex
Sculpture by the Lakes, Pallington Lakes, Dorchester
The Alnwick Garden, Alnwick, Northumberland
The Collector Earl's Garden, Arundel Castle, Arundel, West Sussex

The Exchange, Erith, London
The Garden of Tranquility, Aga Khan Centre, London
The Kitchen Garden, RHS Garden Bridgewater, Salford, Greater Manchester
The Orozco Garden, South London Gallery, London
The Rose Garden at Wynyard Hall, Stockton-On-Tees, County Durham
U.S. Embassy London Gardens, London
Walled Garden Knepp Castle, Sussex
Wildlife Garden, RHS Garden Wisley, Woking, Surrey

UNITED STATES

9/11 Memorial, New York
African Ancestors Memorial Garden, International African American Museum, Charleston, South Carolina
Brooklyn Museum Garden, Brooklyn, New York,
Brooklyn Navy Yard Farm, New York
Central Garden at the Getty Center, Los Angeles, California
Chihuly Garden & Glass, Seattle, Washington
Didier Design Studio with Phyto Studio and Lake Flato Architects
Edible Schoolyard Project, Berkeley, California
Glenstone Water Court, Potomac, Maryland
Jane Gregory Garden, Buffalo Bayou Park, Houston, Texas
Kingwood Center Gardens, Mansfield, Ohio
Little Island, New York
Longwood Gardens West Conservatory, Kennett Square, Pennsylvania
Louis Sullivan Arch, Chicago, Illinois
Meta Rooftop, Menlo Park, California
Native Plant Garden at New York Botanical Garden, New York
Peabody Essex Museum, Salem, Massachusetts
Pollinator and Bird Garden, The Arboretum at Penn State, State College, Pennsylvania
Reading a Garden, Cleveland Public Library, Cleveland, Ohio
Roof Garden, Museum of Modern Art, New York
Store Frontage for Balenciaga, West Hollywood, California
Summerhome Garden, Denver, Colorado
Sunnylands Center & Gardens, Rancho Mirage, California
The Bower, Shermans Dale, Pennsylvania
The Capri Garden, Marfa, Texas
The High Line, New York,
The Monk's Garden, Isabella Stewart Gardner Museum, Boston, Massachusetts
The Ruin Garden at Chanticleer, Wayne, Pennsylvania
Tom Lee Park, Memphis, Tennessee
Untermyer Gardens Conservancy, Walled Garden, Untermyer Park, Yonkers, New York
Vayo Meditation Garden, Coastal Maine Botanical Gardens, Boothbay, Maine

FURTHER READING

Aitken, Richard. *The Garden of Ideas: Four Centuries of Australian Style*. Melbourne: Melbourne University Press, 2010.

Foster, Clare and Andrew Montgomery. *Pastoral Gardens*. London: Montgomery Press, 2024.

Gardens Illustrated Editors, with an introduction by Stephanie Mahon. *The New Beautiful: Inspiring Gardens for a Resilient Future*. New York: Rizzoli, 2025.

Kingsbury, Noel and Claire Takacs. *Wild: The Naturalistic Garden*. London: Phaidon Press, 2022.

Musgrave, Toby. *Green Escapes: The Guide to Secret Urban Gardens*. London: Phaidon Press, 2018.

Musgrave, Toby. *The Garden: Elements and Styles*. London: Phaidon Press, 2020.

Oudolf, Piet and Noel Kingsbury. *Planting: A New Perspective* (Revised Edition). Portland: Timber Press, 2013.

Oudolf, Piet, with an introduction by Cassian Schmidt. *Piet Oudolf at Work*. London: Phaidon Press, 2023.

Phaidon Editors, with an introduction by Madison Cox. *The Gardener's Garden*. London: Phaidon Press, 2014; Classic Format, 2017.

Phaidon Editors, with an introduction by Matthew Biggs. *Garden: Exploring the Horticultural World*. London: Phaidon Press, 2023.

Richardson, Tim (ed.) and Phaidon Editors. *The Garden Book, Revised and Updated Edition*. London: Phaidon Press, 2021.

Richardson, Tim. *The New English Garden*. London: Frances Lincoln, 2013.

Stuart-Smith, Sue. *The Well-Gardened Mind: Rediscovering Nature in the Modern World*. Glasgow: Williams Collins, 2020.

Takacs, Claire with Giacomo Guzzon. *Visionary: Gardens and Landscapes for our Future*. Melbourne: Hardie Grant, 2024.

Taylor, Patrick, ed. *The Oxford Companion to the Garden*. Oxford: Oxford University Press, 2006.

Walker, Sophie. *The Japanese Garden*. London: Phaidon Press, 2017.

WRITER CREDITS

RICHARD AITKEN is an historian, curator and author based in Melbourne, Australia. pp.26, 49, 220, 244, 285

REBECCA ALLAN is a painter, garden designer, and founder of Painterly Gardens, based in New York. pp.39, 53, 82, 109, 247

MATTHEW BIGGS is a gardener, author and broadcaster based in Hertfordshire, UK. pp.38, 40, 63, 77, 96, 119, 121, 147, 182, 211, 217, 230, 235, 274, 275, 279, 283, 303

JONNY BRUCE is a gardener, writer and planting consultant based in the Cotswolds, UK where he is establishing a business growing organic perennials called The Field Nursery. pp.30, 86, 67, 100, 106, 112, 145, 159, 194, 277, 294

RUTH CHIVERS is a writer and garden designer based in Gloucestershire, UK. pp.9, 27, 64, 91, 92, 116, 126, 171, 234, 257, 295

MATT COLLINS is a garden writer and head gardener at the Garden Museum in London. pp.71, 237, 253

ANITA CROY is a London-based writer who loves visiting gardens wherever she is in the world. pp.18, 115, 192, 193, 198, 213, 219, 225, 228, 260, 263, 273, 288, 306, 320, 324, 302

SORREL EVERTON is a garden writer and editor based in Bristol, UK. pp.15, 36, 95, 110, 120, 129, 143, 151, 181, 245, 246, 250

JOANNA FORTNUM is a retired editor and active gardener based in Cheltenham, UK. pp.32, 107, 209, 291

CLARE FOSTER is a writer and gardens editor of *House & Garden* magazine. She is based in Berkshire, UK. p.170

HANNAH GARDNER is a horticultural consultant, garden designer, and freelance writer based in the UK and working throughout Europe. pp.76, 122, 313

ANNIE GATTI is an award-winning Irish writer and editor, based in Somerset, UK. pp.29, 37, 50, 127, 173, 196, 203, 212, 231, 300

JENNIFER GAY Jennifer Gay is a gardener, landscape architect and writer based in Greece. pp.61, 215

ANNIE GUILFOYLE is a garden designer and international lecturer based in West Sussex, UK. She is cofounder of Garden Masterclass. pp.28, 45, 83, 94, 99, 103, 111, 137, 162, 184, 249, 268

LOUISA JONES is an author of numerous books on French and Mediterranean gardens. She has lived in southern France for fifty years. pp.12, 88, 205

NOEL KINGSBURY is a garden designer, author and cofounder, Garden Masterclass, UK and Portugal. pp.13, 17, 25, 35, 56, 89, 102, 135, 142, 146, 157, 160, 169, 174, 176, 179, 206, 229, 243, 258, 262, 301, 307, 317, 323

MARIANNE LOISON is an agronomist, journalist, photographer and editor of *L'Art des Jardins* in France. pp.42, 80, 197

SUSAN LOWRY AND NANCY BERNER are garden writers based in the Hudson Valley of New York. pp.287, 289, 305

TOVAH MARTIN is an author, photographer, lecturer, garden writer and goatherd based in the United States. pp.20, 34, 41, 60, 65, 74, 78, 108, 125, 131, 133, 134, 136, 138, 144, 155, 161, 177, 188, 199, 202, 204, 210, 218, 238, 241, 276, 280, 281, 286, 296, 309, 310, 312

COLLEEN MORRIS is a garden historian, heritage specialist, writer and curator based in New South Wales, Australia. pp.51, 72, 75, 149, 150, 185, 186, 189, 201, 248, 261, 266, 267

DR TOBY MUSGRAVE is an author, plants and gardens historian, and designer based in Denmark. pp.14, 16, 21, 22, 44, 58, 62, 68, 69, 73, 79, 81, 101, 117, 118, 123, 124, 130, 132, 139, 140, 141, 154, 165, 172, 175, 178, 180, 191, 195, 200, 207, 221, 223, 226, 227, 232, 233, 236, 240, 252, 259, 265, 269, 271, 276, 282, 284, 293, 296, 311, 314, 315, 316, 318, 325

KRISTINE PAULUS is a writer, librarian at the New York Botanical Garden, and president of the Council on Botanical and Horticultural Libraries, United States. pp.23, 31, 47, 52, 57, 59, 84, 87, 97, 105, 113, 114, 156, 163, 166, 256, 270, 299, 308

GEORGINA REID is a writer, editor and designer based in Sydney, Australia. She is also founding editor of the online magazine *Wonderground*. p.93

JULIET ROBERTS is a garden writer and former editor of *Gardens Illustrated*, now based in France. pp.104, 148, 183, 187, 190, 224, 239, 290

AMALIA ROBREDO is a landscape designer, plant hunter, university teacher and writer based in José Ignacio, Uruguay. pp.54, 55, 242, 251

ANDREW SALTER is a gardener and writer based in Kent, UK. pp.43, 70, 153, 167, 299, 319

TONY SPENCER is the Canadian writer, photographer and planting designer behind The New Perennialist. pp.33, 46, 85, 152, 164, 168, 216, 254–55, 321, 322

ACKNOWLEDGEMENTS

A project of this size requires the commitment and expertise of many people. Special thanks are due to the following for their knowledge, passion, and advice in the selection of the works for inclusion, as well as to Annie Guilfoyle for writing the introduction:

RICHARD AITKEN
Historian, curator and author, Melbourne, Australia. He has published widely on domestic life, particularly gardening, home-making and collecting.

ANNIE GUILFOYLE
Garden designer, international lecturer and writer based in West Sussex, UK. She is cofounder of Garden Masterclass.

NOEL KINGSBURY
Garden designer, author and cofounder, Garden Masterclass, UK and Portugal.

STEPHANIE MAHON
Garden writer, podcast host and editor of *Gardens Illustrated*. She is based in the Wye Valley, UK.

MICHAEL MCCOY
TV host, writer, broadcaster, educator and garden designer in Australia. He is the author of three books on garden design, and his television show, Dream Gardens, has been broadcast worldwide.

BILL NOBLE
Garden designer and author who gardens in New England, United States.

KRISTINE PAULUS
Collection Development Librarian, LuEsther T. Mertz Library, New York Botanical Garden, United States.

PAUL B. REDMAN
President and Chief Executive Officer, Longwood Gardens, Pennsylvania, United States.

We would also like to extend our thanks to Richard Bloom, Marion Brenner, Tania Compton, Joanna Fortnum, Clare Foster, Annaick Guitteny, Jason Ingram, Victoria Manoylo, Toby Musgrave, Clive Nichols, Amalia Robredo, Bennet Smith, Claire Takacs, Sachi Tanabe and Elizabeth White.

Additional thanks are due to Jennifer Veall for her picture research, to Rosanna Fairhead for copyediting the texts, to Hilary Brown for proofreading, and to Caitlin Arnell Argles, Vanessa Bird, João Mota, and Baptiste Roque-Genest for their invaluable assistance. Finally, we would like to thank all the designers, garden owners, photographers, and garden organisations who have given us permission to include their work and images.

PICTURE CREDITS

Every reasonable effort has been made to identify owners of copyright and clear all necessary permissions. Errors and omissions will be corrected in subsequent editions.

365 Focus Photography/Shutterstock: 147; Mohamed Abd El-Maguid, Nelson Garrido: 260; © Aga Khan Museum/Aga Khan Park, Janet Kimber: 304–5; Henry Alcock-White: 46; Tamara Alvarez: 74; Mark Andrews/Alamy Stock Photo: 292–3; ANIMA/Albina Bauer: 130; Courtesy Arterra Landscape Architects/Michele Lee Willson Photography: 19; Courtesy Stefano Assogna: 21; Photo: Caitlin Atkinson: 65, 218; Photo: Caitlin Atkinson. Courtesy Ten Eyck Landscape Architects: 286; Audrey Walker Images/Alamy Stock Photo: 20; Photo: Iwan Baan: 289; Babylonstoren: 284; Photo: Christopher Baker: 188; Courtesy Battersea Power Station and Willerby Landscapes Ltd. Photo: Rachel Warne: 280; Photo: Heidi Bertish: 311; Courtesy Jinny Blom/Photograph by Andrew Montgomery: 40; Richard Bloom: 47, 66–7, 76, 81, 95, 119, 123, 132, 151, 183, 231, 253, 276, 277; Brett Boardman: 186; Arjan Boekel – Boekel Tuin en Landschap: 43; Marion Brenner: 62, 64, 171, 178, 208–9, 264–5, 281; Brooklyn Grange, Brooklyn Navy Yard Farm: 52; Allen Brown/Alamy Stock Photo: 14; Jonathan Buckley: 237; Built Work Photography: 34; Macarena Calvo, Cristóbal Elgueta: 55; Matthew Cantwell – Secret Gardens. Photo: Nicholas Watt: 261; GAP Photos/Matteo Carassale – Nursery/Kindergarten Clorofilla. Design: Cristina Mazzucchelli: 184; Photographer: Max Carballo: 242; Photo: Rob Cardillo: 85; Rob Cardillo/Courtesy of Gardens Illustrated: 322; Caruncho Studio. Garden and architecture in San Sebastián de los Reyes, Madrid, Spain. © Maru Serrano: 58; Courtesy Chanticleer/Photo by Lisa Roper: 59; Photo: Charles Mayer Photography: 276; Courtesy Gilles Clément: 61; Courtesy of Coastal Maine Botanical Gardens: 240; Cobe: 63; © Sahar Coston-Hardy/Esto: 138; CPG Consultants: 73; Courtesy Dan Pearson Studio/Photograph by Kiichi Noro/Tokachi Millennium Forest: 224; Photo: David Dawson: 170; Courtesy DDS Projects. Photo: Daniela Zondag: 77; Dreamstime/Nicolas De Corte: 213; Maayke de Ridder: 321; Courtesy Benoît and Dominique Delomez: 80; Roy Diblik: 83; Luke Donovan: 121; Doxiadis+/Photo Cathy Cunliffe: 88; Photo courtesy DREISEITLconsulting: 236; Photo: Stephen Dunn. Courtesy of Raymond Jungles, Inc.: 154; Courtesy Austin Eischeid: 94; © Enea Landscape Architecture. Photographer: Martin Rütschi: 97; © EPV/Thomas Garnier: 31; Courtesy Emily Erlam: © Peter Marlow/Magnum Photos: 98–9; Courtesy Estudio Bulla. Photo: Ivan Breyter: 54; Courtesy Estudio Ome. Photo: Diego Padilla: 100; Photo: James Ewing: 238; Photo: Renzo Delpino Fabre: 116; Lucas Fladzinski: 79; Scott Frances/OTTO (designed by Steven Harris Architects): 247; Ed Francissen/Dreamstime.com: 117; Courtesy Future Green Studio. Photo: Thomas Schauer: 105; Photo © Jean-Pierre Gabriel: 39, 82, 272–3, 302, 320; Garden of Australian Dreams, National Museum of Australia. Photo: Richard Poulton: 244; Photo: Rory Gardiner: 306; Shilpa Gavane/M/s. Prabhakar B. Bhagwat: 35; Courtesy GDU Mario Schjetnan. Photo Fernando Barragán: 257; GGN: 108; GAP Photos/Suzie Gibbons – Design: Allain Provost group: 232; Courtesy Luciano Giubbilei/Photograph by Andrew Montgomery: 111; Photo: John Gollings: 285; © Enrique Gomez Tamez | Dreamstime.com: 294; Helder Gomes: 56; Green over Grey – Living Walls & Design Inc. www.greenovergrey.com: 114; Photo: Simon Griffiths. Courtesy Paul Bangay Studio: 26; Annaick Guitteny: 42, 122; © Kathryn Gustafson: 124; Photograph by Giacomo Guzzon: 110; Photo by Dimitar Harizanov. Courtesy: Stefano Boeri Architetti: 44; Copyright Tom Harris, courtesy Studio Gang: 256; Photo: Millicent Harvey: 133; Marnie Hawson: 267; Joachim Hegmann: 254–5; Photograph by Manuel Heslop: 243; Photo: Holi Photography: 325; Hollander Design: 136; Photo: Chloe Humphreys: 190; © Tim Hursley: 233; Jason Ingram: 36, 45, 137, 172, 203, 230, 250, 291, 300; Photo: John Jacomo: 299; Photo: Jason Dewey Photography: 41; Photo: Stephen Jerrome: 57; © Andrea Jones/Garden Exposures: 32, 86, 210; Jane Dove Juneau: 211; Marc Peter Keane: 155; Brandon Klein/Alamy Stock Photo: 308; Jacqueline van der Kloet: 157; Pedro Kok: 92; Courtesy Pradip Krishen: 160; Photo: Kyungsub Shin: 219; © Maya Lin Studio, courtesy Pace Gallery. Photography: Rose Marie Cromwell: 166; Jason Liske: 120; Pernille Loof/Trunk Archive: 78; Photo: Anoek Luyten: 29; Courtesy LWLA. Photo: Mark Weaner: 163; Maggie's: 165; © MMGI/Marianne Majerus: 18, 30, 33, 50, 106, 109, 145, 174, 196, 246, 309; Photographer: Tom Mannion: 96; Stefano Politi Markovina/Alamy Stock Photo. © ARS, NY and DACS, London 2025: 60; Courtesy of Martha Schwartz Partners. Photo: Rudolph Steiner: 259; Andres Garcia Martin/Shutterstock: 128–9; Hilke Maunder/Alamy Stock Photo: 12; © 2005 Peter Mauss/Esto: 270; Courtesy Rebecca McMackin and Brook Klausing. Photo: Douglas Lyle Thompson: 156; Photo: Tabata Minao: 182; Photographer – Andrew Montgomery. villamabrouka.com: 68; © Catherine Mosbach/Mosbach Paysagistes: 191; Courtesy MOX/Photo by Ivan Boyko: 192; Muñoz Y Moreu Jardines: 195; © MVRDV: 198; Courtesy Nakanojo Gardens: 324; Nathan Schroder Photography: 144; Eva Nemeth: 70; Claudia Nevell: 201; Ngoc Minh Ngo: 53, 84, 221, 312; Juliet Nicholas: 103, 217; © Clive Nichols: 23, 71, 107, 173, 205, 222–3, 225, 245, 274, 279, 314; Courtesy of Nikissimo Inc.: 153; Bill Noble: 202; Courtesy Kelly D. Norris: 204; Photograph by Yuri Palmin: 17; Alberto Paredes/Alamy Stock Photo: 38; Courtesy Peabody Essex Museum: 200; Yovenn Peignet: 290; Philippe Perdereau: 197; Alfonso Pérez-Ventana: 228; Prince Concepts: 87; GAP Photos/Hanneke Reijbroek – Location: The Gardens of Appeltern. Design: De Wilde Weelde: 303; Abigail Rex/GAP Photos: 27; Brian Reyes: 125; Richard Murphy Photography: 37; Photo: Beto Riginik: 126; Royal Botanic Gardens Victoria: 162; Photo: Prue Ruscoe: 75; Photo: Agustin Saguier: 251; Mariia Savoskula: 176, 323; © Stephen Schauer: 287; Jane Sebire: 295; © Seungmin Woo: 139; Photo: Erica Shank: 161; Shigeo Ogawa: 16; Photo: Scott Shigley. Courtesy Hoerr Schaudt Studio: 134; Photo: Scott Shigley: 187; Daniel Shipp: 93; Photo: Shogo Oizumi: 142; Photo: Andy Stagg: 212; Tim Street-Porter: 316; © StudioAntonioPerazzi: 226; Photo: Edmund Sumner: 175; Tyler Survant: 115; Courtesy SWA, photo by Chill Shine: 282; TAA Design: 283; Gert Tabak: 168; Jochen Tack/Alamy Stock Photo: 164; Photography © Claire Takacs: 13, 15, 24–5, 28, 48–9, 51, 72, 89, 90–1, 101, 102, 104, 112, 113, 118, 127, 131, 135, 146, 148, 149, 150, 158–9, 167, 179, 180, 185, 189, 194, 199, 206, 207, 214–15, 220, 229, 234, 239, 241, 248, 249, 252, 258, 262, 266, 268, 269, 271, 301, 307, 315, 317, 319; Photo: Louise Tanguay: 69; The Alnwick Garden: 227; Courtesy The Edible Schoolyard Project. Photo: Kelly Sullivan: 310; The Gardens of Trauttmansdorff Castle/KarlHeinz Sollbauer: 22; The Landscape Studio: 288; Courtesy The Mihara Garden, Nagasaki, Japan: 141; Alister Thorpe: 143, 169, 181, 275; Tom-Kichi/iStock. © ARS, NY and DACS, London 2025: 140; TOPOPHYLA: 296; Courtesy Turenscape: 296; Ueno Farm: 299; Photo: Claire De Virieu – Copyright 2007, all rights reserved. With Camille Muller Paysagiste's sincere thanks to Claire De Virieu, who so beautifully captures the gardens in the light of the setting sun: 193; © Vitra: Photograph Marek Iwicki: 216; Photo: Rachel Warne: 177; Photo: Virginia Weiler: 152; © West 8: 313; Photo: Mario Wibowo: 235; Kim Wilkie: 318; Photographer: Yi Dong Hyup: 263.

Phaidon Press Limited
2 Cooperage Yard
London E15 2QR

Phaidon Press Inc.
111 Broadway
New York, NY 10006

Phaidon SARL
55, rue Traversière
75012 Paris

phaidon.com

First published 2025
© Phaidon Press Limited

ISBN 978 1 83866 823 5

A CIP catalogue record for this book is available from the British Library and the Library of Congress.

All rights reserved. No part of this publication may be reproduced, stored in a retrieval system, or transmitted, in any form or by any means, electronic, mechanical, photocopying, recording or otherwise, without the written permission of Phaidon Press Limited.

Commissioning Editor: Victoria Clarke
Project Editors: Sorrel Everton and Rosie Pickles
Production Controller: Gary Hayes
Design: Melanie Mues, Mues Design Ltd, London

Printed in China

Editorial Note: Plant names in the book have been checked against Plants of the World Online (POWO) as a primary source (followed by the RHS Plant Finder). Launched in 2017 by the Royal Botanic Gardens, Kew, POWO is an international collaborative programme making available digitized data of the world's flora from the past 250 years of botanical exploration and research. Given the international spread of this book, any plants of interest to gardeners should be checked for local suitability and availability.